Conte

background 4–23

Introduction	4
Land and People	6
History	16
Governance	18
Culture	20

first steps 24–9

what to see 30–145

getting away 146–51

directory 152–89

Shopping	152
Entertainment	156
Children	158
Sport and Leisure	160
Food and Drink	164
Hotels and Accommodation	172
On Business	176
Practical Guide	178

index 190–2

Maps

Locator	4
New Zealand	5
Auckland and Northland	30–31
Auckland Environs	36–7
Devonport Walk	42
Central North Island	52–3
Coromandel Tour	75
Wellington and Taranaki	77
Wellington	83
Nelson and Marlborough	90–91
Kaikoura Peninsula Walkway	100
Central South Island	102–3
Christchurch	104–5
Banks Peninsula Tour	120
Hooker Valley Walk	122
TranzAlpine Express Tour	124
The Deep South	126–7
Otago Peninsula Tour	138
Milford Sound Tour	140
The Routeburn Track Walk	144

Features

Hot Lakes and Volcanoes	8
Ecotourism	14
Maori Arts, Crafts and Dance	22
Historic Houses	38
Early Explorers	50
Maori Society	68
Whale and Dolphin Watching	97
Sheep	110

Walks and Tours

Walk: Devonport	42
Tour: Coromandel	74
Walk: Wellington	88
Walkway: Kaikoura Peninsula	100
Tour: Banks Peninsula	120
Walk: Hooker Valley	122
Tour: TranzAlpine Express	124
Tour: Otago Peninsula	138
Tour: Milford Sound	140
Walk: The Routeburn Track	144

Introduction

Although a little further flung than most other travel destinations, New Zealand abundantly repays the effort it takes to get there – as many people are discovering. This beautiful country is now placed firmly on the world tourism map.

Greeting in the traditional Maori way

Extending just 1,600km from north to south, New Zealand has everything you could possibly want for a refreshing and completely different kind of holiday.

One of the country's most obvious attractions is the great outdoors: this clean, unpolluted land has 14 national parks, which between them cover over 30 per cent of the nation. These parks encompass lakes and rivers swarming with trout, stunning fiords and glaciers, mighty volcanoes and bubbling geysers, golden beaches and bays, and mountains and hills with fern-filled, mossy gorges, and tumbling waterfalls. This splendid landscape is ideal for sailing, skiing, hiking, fishing, and hunting, while hot-air ballooning and bungee jumping are also favourites with both young and old.

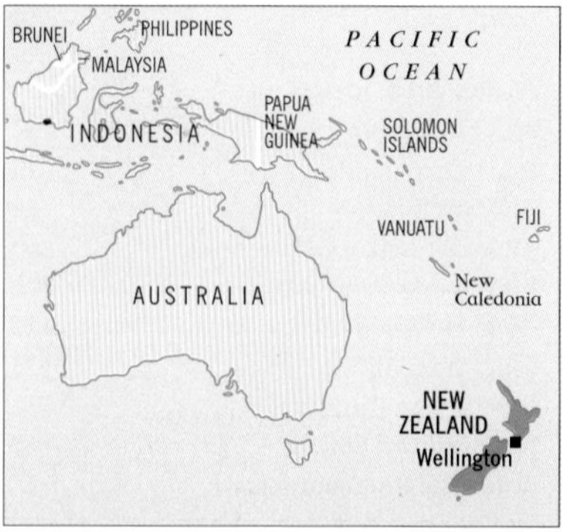

There are no native land mammals, but instead, New Zealand has a range of rare and extraordinary birds, making it a worthwhile destination for birdwatchers. Meanwhile, marine mammals such as whales, dolphins, and seals flourish in the surrounding seas.

This is the image of New Zealand we know, but less well publicised is a new-found intellectual and cultural confidence which is manifested in literature, film, painting and sculpture, handicrafts, performing arts, and even fashion design. Creativity has added a cosmopolitan air to many towns and cities, building on the unique blend of Maori and European cultures which is New Zealand's own.

Alongside this cultural outpouring, New Zealand cuisine has also shrugged off its boring image and developed a distinctive style which complements the nation's now famous wines. Once considered an unsophisticated backwater, New Zealand has developed excellent tourist infrastructure. The relaxed, welcoming attitude of the people of this un-crowded country, christened Aotearoa, or 'Land of the Long White Cloud', by Maoris, adds considerably to the enjoyment of visiting it.

New Zealand

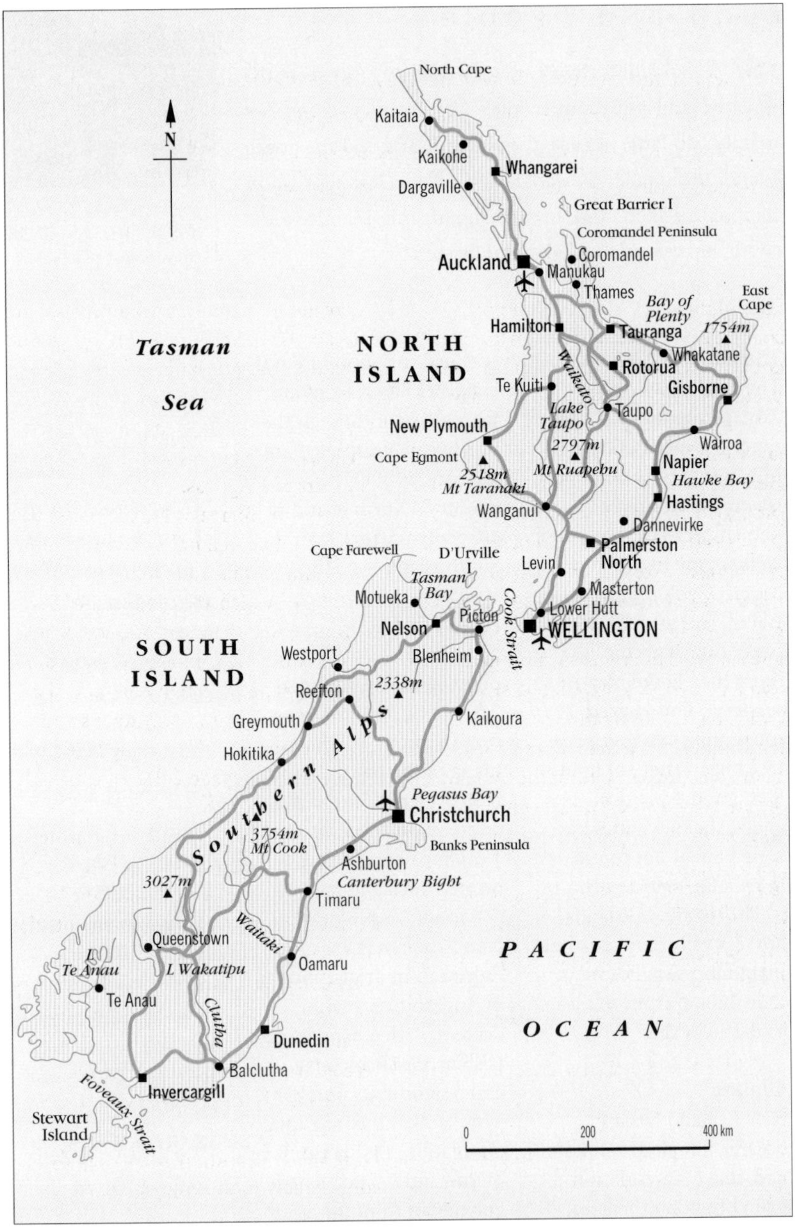
North Cape
Kaitaia
Kaikohe
Whangarei
Dargaville
Great Barrier I
Coromandel Peninsula
Coromandel
Auckland
Manukau
Thames
Bay of Plenty
East Cape
Hamilton
Tauranga
1754m
Tasman
Sea
NORTH ISLAND
Whakatane
Rotorua
Waikato
Te Kuiti
Gisborne
Lake Taupo
Taupo
New Plymouth
2797m
Wairoa
Cape Egmont
Napier
2518m
Mt Taranaki
Mt Ruapehu
Hawke Bay
Hastings
Wanganui
Dannevirke
Palmerston North
Cape Farewell
D'Urville I
Levin
Tasman Bay
Masterton
Motueka
Lower Hutt
Picton
Cook Strait
Nelson
WELLINGTON
SOUTH ISLAND
Westport
Blenheim
2338m
Reefton
Greymouth
Kaikoura
Southern Alps
Hokitika
Pegasus Bay
Christchurch
3754m
Mt Cook
Banks Peninsula
Ashburton
Canterbury Bight
3027m
Timaru
Waitaki
Queenstown
PACIFIC OCEAN
L Te Anau
L Wakatipu
Oamaru
Te Anau
Clutha
Dunedin
Balclutha
Invercargill
Foveaux Strait
Stewart Island
0
200
400 km

Land and People

This forest near Taupo is one of the country's numerous timber plantations

New Zealand lies almost exactly half-way between the Equator and the South Pole. The country comprises mainly two large islands, the North Island and the South Island, the smaller Stewart Island off the southern tip of the South Island, and a scattering of little islands to the south and east of the main land masses.

The Land

The landscapes of New Zealand are dominated by ranges of mountains and hills that run through both islands; there are 223 named peaks of more than 2,300m, the highest being Mount Cook in the South Island, and over 75 per cent of the country lies more than 200m above sea-level. This rugged topography has given rise to a huge variety of land forms and ecological zones, the only temperate-zone habitat not found here being true desert.

The two main islands are relatively narrow, so no inland location lies more than 110km from the sea as the crow flies.

Climate

New Zealand has an oceanic temperate climate and, due to its isolation from other land masses, seasonal variations are not extreme. The seasons are the reverse of those in the northern hemisphere (*see* Climate, *p180*). The country's North Island is generally warmer than the South Island.

Population

New Zealand's total population is just under 3.9 million, with 73 per cent (almost 3 million) living in the North Island. Nearly 28 per cent of the entire population (around 1 million) lives in the greater Auckland area.

Around 75 per cent of New Zealanders are European in origin, mostly of English or Scottish descent, with a handful of Irish or Welsh ancestry, and a significant number from Holland. Of the total population, 14.7 per cent is Maori, and 6.5 per cent is Polynesian from the South

THOMAS COOK'S NEW ZEALAND

Thomas Cook first included New Zealand in its Australasia tours in 1880, hailing it as 'the South Pacific Wonderland . . . undoubtedly the grandest country in the world for the tourist, being so remarkable for wild landscape beauty'. Recognising its potential for natural sites, the company offered excursions in 1881 from Auckland to the 'Hot Lakes' of the North Island ('ten days for Twelve Pounds, inclusive of all charges'), and the first Thomas Cook office opened in the capital in 1889.

Pacific islands (such as Samoa, Tonga, and the Cook Islands), who are mostly concentrated in Auckland. Recently, immigration has increased from Asian countries such as Vietnam, Laos, Cambodia, India, China, and Taiwan; the Asian population now accounts for 6.6 per cent of the population.

The Economy

Despite the lack of flat ground, agriculture and horticulture dominate the economy account for 58 per cent of export earnings (*see also* Sheep, *pp110–11*).

The country has some of the world's largest man-made forests, growing timber (mostly the versatile radiata pine, introduced from California) for use in pulp and paper mills, and for lumber. With a worldwide decrease in the amount of timber available, and the fact that much of New Zealand's 1.7 million hectares of planted forests is now reaching maturity, the country is expected to profit from this resource for many years to come.

Commercial fishing is also an important export earner, with an annual quota system ensuring the sustainable management of fish species within the country's 320km EEZ (Exclusive Economic Zone). Aquaculture (fish farming) is on the increase; there are hundreds of ideal sites in the bays and inlets around the country's 15,000km coastline. The increasing popularity of New Zealand's high-quality wines has also meant a boom in demand for the country's winemakers (*see p166*).

New Zealand tourism has experienced strong growth in the last decade of the 20th century, with international visitor numbers up by 85 per cent. Strategy 2010, launched in May 2001, maps a path for sustainable tourism growth, and conservatively suggests that by 2010 the country will welcome more than 3 million international visitors a year, spending over NZ$9 billion.

Cleared of forest in the last century, rolling farmlands now support millions of sheep

Hot Lakes and Volcanoes

The earth's crust is made up of moving plates up to 60km thick. New Zealand marks the boundary of two plates that are moving together. This area forms the southern extremity of the Pacific 'Ring of Fire'. On the North Island, one plate is constantly being forced under another (subducted), and the melting process produces the magma that is extruded through volcanoes. The underground water that meets this molten rock becomes superheated, returning to the surface as hot lakes or geysers. Under the South Island, meanwhile, the plates are forcing each other up, thus producing the mighty peaks of the Southern Alps.

Volcanic activity is largely responsible for shaping the surface of New Zealand, creating some of its most dramatic mountains and lakes. The city of Auckland stands on a series of 50 or more extinct volcanoes, while much of the central North Island was built up into a volcanic plateau by successive eruptions in the distant past.

A fault-line runs down the North Island; at its centre is Rotorua, the country's most famous thermal zone, and at its end is White Island, an active volcano 50 km offshore in the Bay of Plenty. To the south of Rotorua is the country's largest lake, Taupo, shaped by the violent explosions that began some 250,000 years ago; in the most recent eruption (AD 185) more than 150cu km of pumice and ash were ejected over vast areas of the North Island. But even this is dwarfed by an eruption that took place some 22,600 years ago (dubbed Kawakawa by geologists): new data shows that this was the largest eruption to have taken place in the world in the last 50,000 years.

Maori often used the region's geothermal power, siting their villages on active thermal fields which provided heating in winter and boiling pools for cooking. The energy is still being used: geothermal power stations such as Wairakei (near Lake Taupo) and nearby Ohaaki generate more than 17 per cent of the country's energy needs.

Volcanic activity *(facing page)* is harnessed to provide energy at Ohaaki and Wairakei geothermal power stations *(above and below)*.

This massive *kauri* in the North Island, Tane Mahuta, is thought to be 2,000 years old

FLORA

Many unique species of plants have evolved as a result of New Zealand's isolation from other land masses for millennia; many of them still survive, despite the effects of over 1,000 years of human settlement. No fewer than 3,400 plant species are endemic, including 1,450 of the 1,650 flowering plants found here.

Forest Types

Although only a quarter of the original forests (which once covered 80 per cent of the country) remain today, most of these are protected as national parks, forest parks, and reserves. The majority of indigenous trees are evergreens, with only a handful of deciduous species. In the North Island, the forests are mostly tropical or subtropical in nature, with a dense canopy and an understorey of almost impenetrable shrubs and tree ferns. Climbers and epiphytes (including orchids) flourish in these moisture-laden hothouses. The South Island forests show traces of their sub-Antarctic origin, with less undergrowth, and many species of beech.

Trees

Of particular note are the giant conifers such as the *kauri*, the king of the forests, magnificent trees which can reach heights of up to 60m, and take 1,500 years to reach full maturity. The first 20m or so of its massive, silvery-grey trunk soars upwards as a clean shaft, unblemished by branches. The fact that the *kauri* was perfect for ships' masts was soon recognised by early colonists; the straight-grained, unknotted wood was highly prized in the 19th century. Thus, most of the original 3 million hectares of *kauri* in the North Island were felled by 1860, leaving just 10,000 hectares standing today.

Other conifers include the *rimu*, which, like the *kauri*, has a straight, branchless trunk and was an important timber tree. Maori made considerable use of the *totara*, which is easily carved and handy for building canoes and houses; found all over New Zealand, this species can grow to a height of up to 30m. Man-made forest plantations are dominated by the *radiata* or Monterey pine, Douglas fir, and redwoods.

The most notable of the many

flowering trees in New Zealand is the beautiful *pohutukawa*, which grows largely around the North Island coast and flames into scarlet blossom in December – hence its nickname, the 'New Zealand Christmas tree'. Equally attractive are the rich red flowers of the *rata*, the golden-yellow *kowhai*, and the snowy-white ribbonwoods.

New Zealand has only one true palm, the *nikau* palm, which is the world's most southerly growing palm. The cabbage tree looks very much like a palm and adds a tropical air to landscapes everywhere, although in fact it belongs to the agave family.

There are also around 189 species of fern – as well as numerous hybrids – which range from tiny ferns which unfold only on rainy days, to giant tree ferns which grow to a height of more than 15m.

Alpine Plants

Above the forest line, scrub and tussock give way to rolling meadows which are ablaze with alpines during the summer. Gentians, eyebrights, forget-me-nots, giant edelweiss, and mountain daisies grow in profusion. Also found here are the world's largest buttercup, the Mount Cook lily, and forget-me-not, the Chatham Island lily.

Cushion Plants

One of the most curious plants in New Zealand is the vegetable sheep, which grows in low mounds and is covered in cream-coloured, woolly-looking leaves – hence the name, since from a distance it looks like a resting sheep! Another of the so-called cushion plants is the giant vegetable sheep, which only grows in the highlands around Nelson.

Crimson blossoms on the *pohutukawa* tree

FAUNA

It is clear that New Zealand must have split away from the ancient continent of Gondwanaland (present-day Australia, Antarctica, India, Africa, and South America) before the appearance of mammals, since none (apart from three species of bat) are endemic to the country. Instead, many unique flightless birds filled the ecological niches elsewhere occupied by mammals, the absence of predators making the country a paradise for them.

Extinct Species

But this paradise was not to last: the first Maori settlers brought rats and the Maori dog (now extinct), and Europeans introduced more than 50 species of animals. Captain Cook freed the first sheep, soon followed by pigs, cows, deer, rabbits, cats, and possums. Combined with the loss of forest habitat through clearance for agriculture, the effect on land-based birdlife was devastating: 43 species are now extinct, and 40 species remain threatened despite breeding and conservation programmes.

Among the more spectacular losses were the moas (of which there were once 11 different species, including the largest bird ever to walk on earth, the 4-m tall *Dinornis maximus*) and the New Zealand or Haast's eagle, the largest eagle ever known, with talons the size of a tiger's claws.

Flightless Birds

New Zealand's national bird, the kiwi, is the best-known flightless bird. There are three species of kiwi – brown, great spotted, and little spotted – all similar in appearance, with vestigial wings, strong legs, and nostrils on the end of a long, flexible beak. Kiwis are nocturnal, and may have evolved thus to avoid being preyed upon by the giant eagles; today, stoats, possums, and dogs are their greatest enemies. Population estimates are vague, but earlier optimism has been dispelled and kiwis are now classified as endangered.

The *tuatara* is one of the many reptiles native to New Zealand

More easily visible is the cheeky *weka*, a mischievous member of the rail family, which may often be seen strutting around campsites stealing food or shiny objects. You are unlikely to see the brilliant-hued *takahe* in the wild; once thought to be extinct, a small colony of these birds was discovered in Fiordland in 1948, but the total population still numbers only 250 nationally, with around 150 in Fiordland.

Other Birdlife

Other native species include the *kaka*, a forest parrot, and its cousin the *kea*, which is renowned for its destructive habits – hikers sometimes find their boots and even tents pecked to pieces by this fearless and intelligent bird. The unusual *kakapo* has long, hair-like feathers growing from the base of its bill, which it uses to find its way around at night; only 62 adult individuals of this highly endangered species are known to exist. The early 2002 breeding season saw the successful hatching of another 23 chicks, boosting numbers by nearly 40 per cent.

In rural areas you might hear a small native owl, the morepork, whose cry gave rise to its common name, and on forest walks the melodious songs of both the *tui* and the bellbird. The large and strikingly coloured native pigeon or *kereru* is found over most of the country; it feeds on shoots and berries.

New Zealand's black stilt, or *kaki*, is the world's rarest wading bird. These slender, red-legged birds were once widespread, but there are now only a few left in the wild near Twizel in Mackenzie Country. The white-bodied pied stilt is, however, common and can be found throughout wetland areas.

Reptiles

Among the range of small reptiles native to New Zealand is the extraordinary *tuatara*, which has the longest unbroken ancestry of any living animal and whose predecessors date back to the Triassic period, some 200 million years ago. It has a ridge of spines along its back, and can grow to be 24cm long. Often erroneously referred to as a lizard, the nocturnal *tuatara* lives on around 30 isolated, offshore islands, and is fully protected.

The kiwi is now an endangered species due to predation by stoats, possums, and dogs

Ecotourism

New Zealand's 'clean, green' image draws many thousands of visitors to the country, and yet the very presence of tourists may be threatening fragile areas as it has done in many other parts of the world. With a tourism strategy aiming to increase international visitor numbers to 3.2 million by the year 2010, can the environment withstand the impact?

Already some major natural attractions (such as the Waitomo Caves, Mount Cook National Park, and the Fox and Franz Josef glaciers) are close to capacity at peak times of the year, their facilities rapidly becoming inadequate in coping with visitor numbers. Many of the more popular three- to five-day walking tracks (The Great Walks) are also overcrowded, with insufficient space in overnight huts. Milford Sound is almost as busy as the Grand Canyon, with a constant procession of 'flightseeing' aeroplanes and helicopters drowning out the commentaries on the boats below.

Fortunately, many of these problems have been identified and strategies defined which will ensure that tourism develops on a sustainable basis. The tourism industry has produced its own

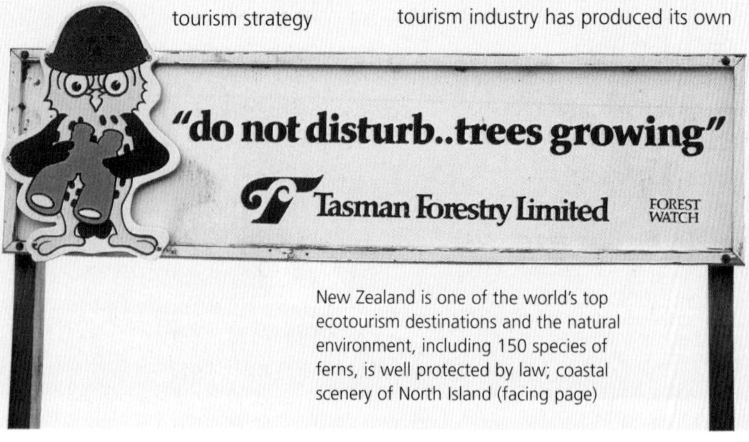

New Zealand is one of the world's top ecotourism destinations and the natural environment, including 150 species of ferns, is well protected by law; coastal scenery of North Island (facing page)

'Code of Environmental Principles', and most operators are aware that their resource base (nature itself) is their most important asset.

The tourism strategy is to 'Welcome Visitors', 'Protect our Environment', and 'Celebrate our Culture'. The Department of Conservation manages – more successfully than most such organisations in the world – more than 30 per cent of the country's land area in national parks, forests, and reserves.

Most important, New Zealand took a significant step in the right direction with the introduction in 1991 of the Resource Management Act, which enshrined in law the sustainable management of the environment (including the nation's cultural and historic heritage). This landmark legislation has been hailed as the leading edge of environmental planning, and other countries (including the USA) are now looking to New Zealand in an attempt to emulate its policies for tourism and nature conservation. It seems that here, at least, is one country where ecotourism may turn out to be more than just an empty buzzword.

History

Around AD 950	The Polynesian explorer Kupe discovers New Zealand, which he names Aotearoa ('Land of the Long White Cloud').
1350	Overpopulation forces many Polynesian islanders to set sail for Aotearoa in a fleet of large canoes.
1642	The Dutch explorer Abel Janszoon Tasman sights land at Hokitika on 13 December; he later anchors in Golden Bay.
1769	Captain James Cook arrives on board the *Endeavour* on 9 October at Gisborne. On this and subsequent voyages he plots the coastline.
1790	Sealers, whalers, and timber traders arrive. Maori exchange their traditional war clubs for firearms and inter-tribal wars take on a new, bloodier dimension.
1814	The Reverend Samuel Marsden of the Anglican Church Mission Society sets up the first mission station, gradually making converts and trying to halt cannibalism. The first settlers arrive.
1817	Britain extends New South Wales legislation to New Zealand.
1832	The first British Resident, James Busby, arrives from Australia, but his efforts to promote law and order and to protect the Maori are ineffective.
1839	Captain William Hobson is appointed Lieutenant Governor to persuade Maori chiefs to relinquish their sovereignty to the British Crown. Pressure mounts for the British to assume full authority.
1840	Hobson negotiates the controversial Treaty of Waitangi, which is signed by more than 45 chiefs on 6 February at Waitangi in the Bay of Islands. The treaty is later inked by another 500 chiefs.
1840–48	Numerous organised settlements are established, notably Wellington, Wanganui, Nelson, New Plymouth, Christchurch, and Dunedin.
1843	The first skirmishes of Land Wars between Maori and settlers.

1852	The first gold strikes are made in the Coromandel; gold rushes bring in thousands of prospectors in the next 15 years. The first large-scale sheep stations are established.
1860	The Land Wars escalate, lasting almost two decades in the North Island. The Maori, despite their impressive tactics, are overwhelmed by the better-equipped colonial armies. Vast areas of Maori land confiscated.
1865	Capital moved from Auckland to Wellington.
1867	Maori gain the vote; the first four Maori members are elected to Parliament.
1882	First cargo of frozen meat sails to Europe.
1893	New Zealand is the first sovereign state to give women the vote.
1907	New Zealand becomes an autonomous dominion within the British Empire.
1947	New Zealand becomes an independent member of the Commonwealth.
1973	Preferential trading links with Britain end with Britain joining the EEC (now European Union).
1975	The Waitangi Tribunal set up to hear Maori claims as specified under the Treaty of Waitangi.
1987	The Labour Party initiates a nuclear-free policy, and the USA excludes the country from the ANZUS defence pact. Free-market reforms are introduced.
1990	The National Party ousts Labour.
1993	In a referendum, New Zealanders endorse Mixed Member Proportional (MMP) representation.
1996	First MMP election held. New Zealand gets its first woman prime minister.
1999	Another woman prime minister takes over as head of Labour-led coalition.
2001	New Zealand government spends $885 million to rescue Air New Zealand.
2003	Auckland hosts America's Cup (yachting).

Governance

New Zealand is a sovereign state with a democratic government based on the British parliamentary system, except that there is no Upper House. The legislative body, the House of Representatives, currently comprising 120 members, is elected for a three-year term. The Queen is the titular head of state, represented in New Zealand by a Governor-General.

Dame Whina Cooper, an active campaigner for Maori rights

The Muldoon Muddle

Post-war politics in New Zealand was dominated by the National Party and, in particular, by its now-discredited leader, Sir Robert Muldoon. His interventionist regime controlled everything from subsidies to prices and pay, almost bankrupting an economy which was at the same time reeling from rising oil prices and the loss of protected markets when Britain joined the EEC.

Radical Reforms

In 1984 Muldoon was thrown out, and replaced by a Labour Party (led by the charismatic David Lange) whose sweeping reforms included privatisation, deregulation, and the removal of subsidies. This experiment in free-market economics, focused principally on agriculture and industry, reduced government deficit by the end of the 1980s, but the electorate balked at the high cost (principally an unemployment rate of over 9 per cent), and in 1990 Labour lost power to the National Party under the Right Honourable James Brendan (Jim) Bolger.

Stealing their rivals' ideological clothes, the National Party took the axe to the labour and financial markets and government spending – 'user pays' became a way of life. New Zealand is now reaping the benefits of these reforms, with falling inflation and a growth rate that continues to exceed predictions.

Constitutional Changes

In 1993, following a referendum on constitutional change, the electorate voted to adopt MMP (Mixed Member Proportional) representation, a system which gives smaller parties a say in Parliament. The first MMP elections were held in 1996; National and Labour shared the majority of the vote, but the balance of power was retained by the newly-formed New Zealand First, a Maori-dominated party. The Maori voice is now being heard in Parliament as never before.

Land Rights

The issue of land rights has dominated Maori politics since the Land Wars of the last century. The problem originated with the Treaty of Waitangi in 1840, which comprised two texts, in English and in Maori, each differing significantly in the translation. In the English text,

Maori ceded 'sovereignty', but in the Maori text they gave the British only the right of governance. The wordings also differ on the issue of land ownership.

A century and a half of frustration over the alienation of Maori from their land came to a head in 1975 when Maori civil rights campaigner Whina Cooper, then 80 years old, captured the public imagination with her 'great march' on Parliament, drawing 5,000 supporters along the 1,100km route. Later made a Dame, she was the most influential Maori woman of the 20th century, known as 'the Mother of the Nation'. She died in 1994.

The Waitangi Tribunal was set up in 1975 as the official forum for resolving grievances. The same year, the government proposed an all-embracing settlement encompassing all land seized, stolen, or taken by unfair means in the country. Potential cost to the Crown: NZ$1 billion over the next ten years.

The current view is that the Waitangi Tribunal is a permanent commission of enquiry – a forum to address contemporary issues affecting Maori. Since its inception up to June 2001, 956 claims were registered with the Treaty office, 73 of which were registered in the year ending June 2001.

Clearly, the disputes continue, although the current government's stated aim is to have all claims settled by the year 2012.

The 'Beehive' parliament building, Wellington

Culture

Whether they arrived by canoe, boat or aeroplane, all New Zealanders can trace their ancestry to immigrant stock, the legacy of which is a strongly pragmatic streak in the nation's character. Kiwi ingenuity and a 'let's fix it' attitude apply as much to topical political issues as to broken-down farm machinery. These traits – combined with an innate sense of fairness and a strong sense of principle – are an integral part of the national identity.

Dame Kiri Te Kanawa

Just Beer, Rugby, and Racing?

The popular image of New Zealanders is that their interests focus around just three things – beer, rugby, and racing. The first needs no explanation. As for the second, it might be more accurate to say simply that New Zealanders love sport, for although the country's national rugby team, the All Blacks, has a devoted following, so do many other sports, from aerobics to yachting. Horse-racing is a particular passion, and many towns and communities have a racetrack just outside town.

While there is a great deal of truth in this image, it also belies a cultural sophistication which is less well known. Despite the country's small population, music and live theatre flourish.

There is also a strong strand of talent in opera: New Zealand opera singers include the late Oscar Natzke and Inia Te Wiata (both basses), as well as Sir Donald McIntyre, Dame Malvina Major, and Dame Kiri Te Kanawa, to name only the best known.

New Zealand's artists embrace styles as diverse as those of Colin McCahon, a pioneer modernist, and Ralph Hotere, who draws on Maori and Pacific Island motifs for inspiration.

Contemporary Maori art – particularly carving – has become a significant movement.

Perhaps the best-known New Zealand writer was Katherine Mansfield, but a new generation has now risen to international prominence, starting with Keri Hulme (whose novel *The Bone People* marked a fresh strand in Maori writing), Patricia Grace, and Witi Ihimaera.

The film industry is also thriving, with Jane Campion's Oscar-winning *The Piano,* followed soon after by the release in 1995 of Lee Tamahori's *Once Were Warriors*, a raw, violent story about contemporary urban Maori life, based on Alan Duff's book. New Zealander Russell Crowe, who won the Oscar for Best Actor in 2000 for his performance in *Gladiator*, is now a famous Hollywood star.

Wellington is home to Peter Jackson and the production team of JRR Tolkien's saga, the *Lord of the Rings* trilogy. All three films were shot over a

15-month period at various 'Middle Earth' locations around the country. The first, *The Fellowship of the Ring*, was released in December 2001, winning Oscar awards (details on the locations used can be found at *www.jasons.co.nz/destinationlordoftherings*).

The Kiwis

As well as being the name for the national bird, the word kiwi is widely used to describe New Zealanders themselves.

In the money markets it is also a nickname for the New Zealand dollar, and Americans use it as an abbreviation for kiwifruit (although no Kiwi would use it in this way).

Pakeha is the Maori word for a Kiwi of European descent, and is widely used. Interestingly, Maori had no collective name for themselves before the coming of the Europeans, and it was only later on that they used the word *maori* to refer to themselves – in their language, it means 'usual' or 'normal'.

New Zealanders are often self-deprecating when it comes to their own achievements – except when they beat their nearest neighbours, Australia, on the rugby or cricket field.

'Oz' is generally regarded with friendly rivalry and derision, and in much the same way people in the South Island (to which they refer jokingly as 'the mainland') complain that North Islanders ignore them politically and – almost as bad – prefer to go overseas for their holidays rather than visit them.

Children playing rugby, the country's favourite sport

Weaving and Tattoos

The early Maori used seal and dog skins to stay warm in Aotearoa's relatively cool climate but, more important, they developed the use of flax as the main source of material for clothing. Flax fibres were twisted into patterns to create fabrics, a form of hand-weaving that produced exceptionally fine work; cloaks were also decorated with feathers, dyed strands, or fur.

Tattooing (*moko*) was an important part of an individual's identity and status, and warriors would often be tattooed not only all over their faces but on their thighs and buttocks as well. Women's tattoos extended only over the chin. The process was long and extremely painful, with designs actually cut into the flesh with a chisel before soot was rubbed into the pattern.

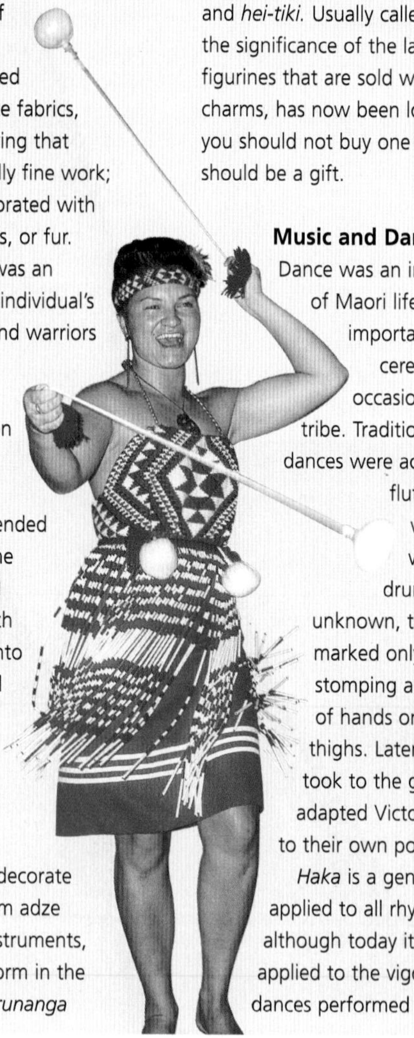

Carving

Carving was used to decorate almost everything from adze handles to musical instruments, reaching its highest form in the decoration of *whare runanga* (meeting-houses) and food storage houses. Master carvers enjoyed high status in the community.

The most common motifs are the *manaia* (a bird-like, half-human figure) and *hei-tiki*. Usually called simply *tiki*, the significance of the latter, small figurines that are sold widely today as charms, has now been lost. However, you should not buy one for yourself; it should be a gift.

Music and Dance

Dance was an integral feature of Maori life, signalling important events or ceremonial occasions within the tribe. Traditionally, songs and dances were accompanied by flutes (made from whalebone and wood), and, as drums were unknown, the rhythm was marked only by foot stomping and the slapping of hands on the chest and thighs. Later, Maori also took to the guitar and adapted Victorian melodies to their own poetic songs.

Haka is a generic term applied to all rhythmic dances, although today it is usually applied to the vigorous, shouted dances performed by men, such as the *haka taparahi* and the *peruperu* (war dance). *Peruperu* dancers use fearsome facial gestures (staring eyes and protruding tongue) to signal to potential enemies: 'You look good, and I am going to eat you!'

The national rugby football team, the All Blacks, uses *haka* choruses to great effect at the start of international matches. The intricate *poi* dance, in which flax balls attached to string are swirled in time to music, is performed only by women.

Maori cultural heritage includes superb carvings and animated song and dance

Impressions

New Zealand has such an incredible range of action-packed attractions that deciding where to go and what to see may be daunting. However, it is a fairly compact country, and you can do an enormous amount in a relatively short space of time if you set your mind to it. Since many activities are weather-dependent, you should not structure your trip too tightly: a flexible itinerary will help you make the most of the endless repertoire of things to do.

Floatplanes are just one option for aerial sightseeing

Planning your Itinerary

A hit list of the best New Zealand has to offer might includes the following:

Aerial sightseeing – ballooning (Christchurch), ski-plane landings (Mount Cook), helicopter flights (Mount Tarawera from Rotorua, Fox and Franz Josef glaciers, Mount Cook).
Beaches – Bay of Islands, Bay of Plenty, East Cape, Coromandel, Waiheke Island, Abel Tasman National Park.
Birdwatching – Cape Kidnappers, Farewell Spit, Hauraki Gulf, Mount Bruce National Wildlife Reserve, Paparoa National Park, Stewart Island, Taiaroa Head (Otago Peninsula).
Cruising – Hauraki Gulf, Bay of Islands, Marlborough Sounds, Fiordland.
Dramatic scenery – almost everywhere, but particularly the Mount Cook National Park, Fox and Franz Josef glaciers, and Fiordland.
Museums – the Auckland Museum, the National Maritime Museum, Kelly Tarlton's Underwater World, and the Antarctic Encounter (Auckland); the Museum of New Zealand, Katherine Mansfield Birthplace (Wellington); the International Antarctic Centre and the Canterbury Museum (Christchurch); the Otago and Settlers Museum (Dunedin).
Thrills and spills – black-water rafting (Waitomo), jet-boating and white-water rafting (almost everywhere), bungee-jumping (Queenstown, Lake Taupo, and Rangitikei).
Wildlife – swimming with dolphins (Bay of Islands and Whakatane), whale-watching (Kaikoura), seal- and penguin-watching (Otago Peninsula).
Volcanic activity – Rotorua, Tongariro National Park, White Island.

Getting Around

Despite the wild, rugged nature of much of New Zealand, the distances between places of interest or activities aren't overwhelming because the country has a well-developed transport system. Travelling around, by public transport or by car, is quick and easy.

By Air
Air New Zealand, Qantas, and Origin Pacific Airways provide scheduled services between major cities, towns and resorts.

By Rail
Tranzrail provides several different InterCity rail services. One of the most popular rail routes for visitors is the TranzAlpine Express *(see pp124–5)*.

By Coach
There is an extensive network of coach services linking most towns and cities. Several companies offer 'alternative' coach services, particularly popular with young travellers, which provide stops at places of interest and a casual, friendly atmosphere; this is a great way to meet people as well as get to know the country. Bus and coach services within towns and cities are also good.

By Car
The flexibility and independence which a rental car provides makes it by far the most attractive option for touring New Zealand. For short periods rental cars are fairly expensive, but generous discounts can often be negotiated for longer-term rentals of a month or more. A car and tent is a good combination; alternatively, consider hiring a campervan if you are travelling with your family.

New Zealand has an extensive network of sealed (tarmacked) roads, but some backcountry roads are still unsealed, and in some areas there may

Touring by coach is one way to appreciate the scenic splendours of New Zealand

be restrictions for rental cars. On the whole, driving is a pleasure, despite several Kiwi peculiarities – such as one-way, single-lane bridges on some main roads – of which you should be aware. (For more details on internal travel, *see pp182–3.)*

Information

One of the great things about travelling around New Zealand is the amount of detailed information available to help you make the most of your trip. Much of this is channelled through numerous information centres, co-ordinated by Tourism New Zealand, which forms the Visitor Information network (*see p189;* also *www.tourisminfo.govt.nz*). The friendly, helpful staff at the centres provide impartial, up-to-date information on everything, from bus travel to bungee-jumping.

A complementary service is offered by the Department of Conservation (DOC), which runs equally efficient and helpful visitor centres in national parks and at major natural attractions. The DOC visitor centres often incorporate high-quality displays on the local environment.

The network of AA offices is also a source of information for visiting members and offers them reciprocal services.

Meeting Kiwis

New Zealanders are renowned for their friendliness and hospitality, and have an outgoing, relaxed attitude towards visitors. Apart from the usual courtesies, there are no particular pitfalls to beware of – with the possible exception of comparing them unfavourably with Australians!

One of the best ways of meeting people and finding out more about the Kiwi way of life is to spend a few days in a homestay or farmstay *(see p174).* These range from the cheap and cheerful to the highly sophisticated.

A network of information centres provides friendly, helpful advice

The *hongi*, a Maori form of greeting

Maori Etiquette

All Maori tribes, many sub-tribes and community groups, and even universities and schools still have their *marae* (courtyard/square/plaza – *see p68*). The protocol governing *marae* is highly formalised, and it is very important that you seek permission before entering the *whare runanga* (meeting-house) on any *marae*, and walk around the *marae* rather than across it; footwear must be removed before going inside a *whare runanga*. It is more than likely, however, that your visit to a *marae* will be part of an organised tour, in which case you will be told what to do.

The Maori greeting *kia ora*, which means both 'good health' and 'welcome', accompanied by rubbing noses, is answered with the same words.

Smoke-free Zones

New Zealand is a health-conscious nation and smoking is on the decline (it has the lowest rate of tobacco consumption of any First World country). Smoking is banned on all public transport and in most public places (such as government offices). Many restaurants are also completely non-smoking, although you can still light up in bars and clubs.

What to Bring

Almost any item you may require, from camera film to contraceptives, is easily obtainable in New Zealand, and despite the relatively small market base and a Goods and Service Tax (GST) of 12.5 per cent, many goods are priced similar to those in the United Kingdom.

With the depletion of the ozone layer, covering up in the sun is increasingly important

It is also worth noting that the weather can be highly variable from one area to the next: one day you might be comfortable in a T-shirt and shorts, the next you might be better off in a sou'wester! The best advice is to come prepared for highly changeable conditions.

In a country which is so geared towards the outdoors, dress is casual, but if you plan to sample any of the more up-market restaurants in the cities it is a good idea to pack some smart clothes, as many establishments set minimum dress codes.

Sandflies and Sunburn

New Zealand has neither dangerous animals nor snakes, but, as if to make up for this total lack of hazards, it does have the ubiquitous sandfly. These vicious insects were noted even by Captain Cook, who wrote in his journal on 11 May 1773, at Dusky Sound: 'The most mischievous animal here is the small black sandfly which are exceeding numerous and are so troublesome that they exceed everything of the kind I have ever met with, wherever they light they cause a swelling and such an intolerable itching that it is not possible to refrain from scratching and at last ends in ulcers like the small pox.'

A Maori legend has it that the gods who created Fiordland were so pleased with their work that they sat back to relax and admire it; seeing this, the goddess of life and death, Hinenui te pou, created *te namu*, the sandfly, to goad them back to work. Apply insect repellent, and if you are bitten, try to refrain from scratching for 30 minutes – the itching will go away.

The other vital precaution to take is against sunburn. The clarity of the air in New Zealand allows more harmful ultraviolet rays to reach ground level than elsewhere, a situation that has intensified with the growing hole in the ozone layer over the Antarctic. Outside, wear sunglasses and/or a hat, as well as plenty of sunblock, even on overcast days. Travellers arriving from winter in the Northern Hemisphere are particularly susceptible to sunburn unless adequately protected.

Young travellers and students can benefit from a wide range of discounts

Auckland and Northland

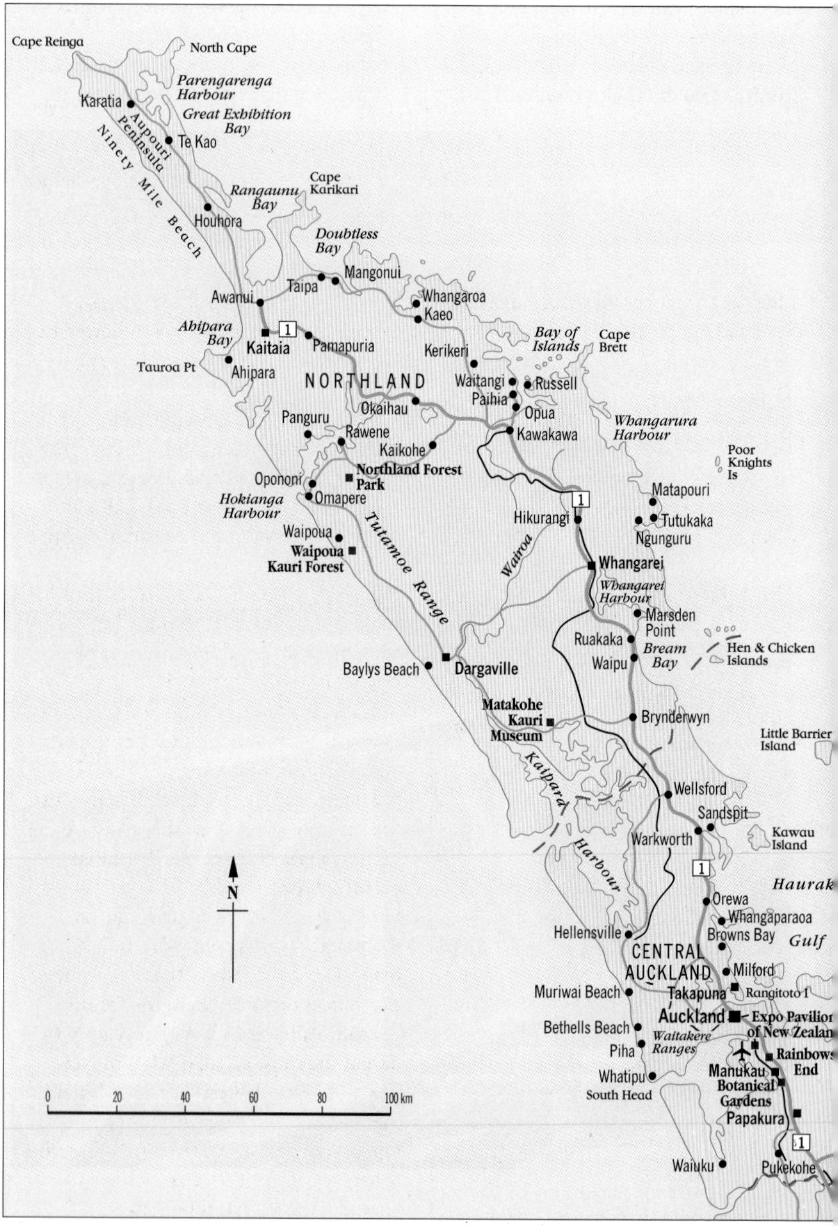

The historic home of Alberton in Auckland

Auckland and Northland

The majority of visitors to New Zealand arrive in Auckland, the country's largest and most dynamic city. You should plan to spend at least a few days here, orientating yourself and exploring the city's many attractions before setting off further afield.

A logical starting point from Auckland is to head up towards Northland, the irregularly shaped, 240-km long peninsula that juts out at an odd angle from the North Island's top corner. Stretching out towards the Equator and bisecting the 35th parallel – Northland revels in a mild sub-tropical climate which has earned it the nickname of the 'winterless North'.

Northland has a rich historical legacy.

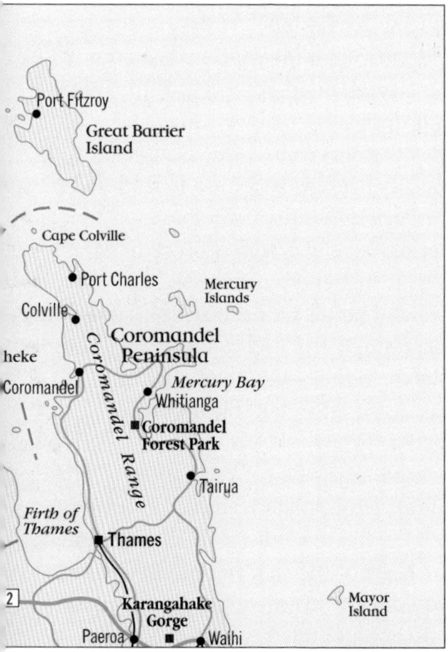

It was here that the first Polynesian explorers settled, later to be followed by the Europeans on their whaling ships. Ancient legends, tribal battles, and warfare between the Maori and European colonists are all woven into the fabric of Northland. The main resort area in Northland is the scenic Bay of Islands, with 800km of coastline facing 150 or so offshore islands.

There are no resorts on the islands themselves; most accommodation surrounds the bustling town of Paihia, that copes with its annual summer influx of over 70,000 visitors. Alongside Paihia is Waitangi, the site of the 1840 treaty signing which forms such a pivotal role in the country's history. Just to the north of the Bay of Islands are the orchards of citrus and kiwifruit that surround the township of Kerikeri. On the west side of the peninsula at Waipoua, nature's own work is magnificently visible in the form of the magnificent *kauri* trees in the forests.

From Paihia it's a long journey up to one of the most isolated spots in New Zealand, Cape Reinga. In Maori legend, this was the starting point for an even longer journey: it was from here that the spirits set off for the ocean voyage to Hawaiki, the ancestral homeland.

Auckland

The country's largest city is sprawled across the narrowest point of North Island. Auckland is almost completely surrounded by water: to the south and west, Manukau Harbour opens out into the Tasman Sea; to the north and east, Waitemata Harbour gives on to the Hauraki Gulf and, eventually, the Pacific.

In the Maori section of the Auckland Museum

The second most noticeable feature about Auckland are the volcanic cones which randomly dot the city. At one time there were more than 50 volcanoes here, and when the district was most heavily populated by Maori tribes in the mid-18th century nearly every single one of them was home to a fortified settlement, or *pa*. Inter-tribal warfare brought this prosperous period to a close at the end of that century, and by the time Auckland was chosen as the new capital after the Treaty of Waitangi in 1840, the region was almost deserted.

Eventually, 49 of these volcanic cones were used for landfill; the most prominent of those that remain, including Mount Eden and One Tree Hill, provide spectacular viewpoints over the city. If you are visiting on a weekend, the panorama will reveal a flotilla of yachts cruising the harbour waters. Not for nothing is Auckland known as the 'City of Sails' – reputedly, there are more boats per person here than in any other city in the world.

Despite Auckland's urban sprawl, the proximity of vast stretches of coastline mean that deserted coves and surfing beaches are never more than a short drive (or sail) away; with the added bonus of an agreeable climate, many people feel that the Auckland lifestyle is one to be envied.

The city can justifiably claim to be the most sophisticated and cosmopolitan in the country, with a wide range of cultural activities, world-class museums, hundreds of busy boutiques and shops, and scores of excellent restaurants and chic bars. The high-rise Sky Tower houses the the country's second casino, the Skycity Casino.

As the main international gateway for New Zealand, Auckland is the initial entry point for many visitors, and a major export centre. In recent years the city has also become a focal point for Pacific Islanders, who have flocked here in search of work or to pursue higher education. As New Zealand builds on historic links and increasingly ties itself to other far-flung islands in the South Seas, Auckland has cast itself in the role of 'hub of the Pacific'.

With nearly 28 per cent of the country's population (just over a million people) living within a 40km radius of the heart of the city, you might think it would seem crowded, but Aucklanders have always preferred low-density housing, and even the humblest home has its own garden – hence the sprawling suburbs. For the visitor, this has its drawbacks as, with the exception of the downtown area, it is not an easy city to get around without transport. Unless you have hired a car, the best options are either to buy a 'Busabout' pass (daily or weekly rates include unlimited rides) or use the Link, which travels a circular route between major attractions on a regular basis, or the Explorer Bus which departs from the Ferry Building to 14 of Auckland's attractions. (*For information, call toll-free 0800 439 756.*)

Auckland Domain and War Memorial Museum

The Domain is Auckland's biggest public park, 80 hectares of rolling lawns, gardens, and the splendid subtropical conservatory called the Wintergardens. At the centre is the Auckland War Memorial Museum.

Originally opened in 1929, the Greek Revival-style building has undergone an ambitious five-year restoration and exhibition renewal programme. With its extensive collections, amassed since 1852, the three-storey museum provides an excellent introduction to the peoples of the Pacific and New Zealand, and the remarkable flora, fauna, and geography of the area.

It also houses some of the world's finest, most important collections of Maori Treasures (*taonga*).

The museum covers 9,000m, with two vibrant 'Discovery Centres' for children, a cafeteria, a 'must visit' museum store and two interactive information centres. A Maori cultural group performs three times daily, at 11am, noon, and 1.30pm, and tickets can be purchased in advance. Entrance to the museum is free, though a donation (*koha*) is suggested.
The Domain. Tel: (09) 309 0443.
Buses: 63, 64, 65, & The Link from downtown (alight at Domain Drive).
Wintergardens open: daily 10am–4pm.
Free admission. www.akmuseum.org.nz

Yachts, launches, and ferries continually criss-cross Auckland's busy harbour

Auckland Zoo

Linked to MOTAT 1 (*see p37*) by a tramway, the zoo houses the usual exotic creatures as well as native species such as the kiwi in a nocturnal house, and indigenous birds in a forest aviary. A Sealion Penguin Shores development has recently been opened. On weekends and holidays the keepers give regular talks at various enclosures.

Motions Rd, Western Springs. Tel: (09) 360 3819. Open: daily (except Christmas) 9.30am–5.30pm. Admission charge.

City Art Gallery

The gallery is divided between two buildings. The Heritage Gallery, on the corner of Wellesley and Kitcher streets, houses traditional works of art, including those of the country's best known artists, C.F. Goldie (1870–1947), who specialised in Maori portraits. The New Gallery contains modern pieces with particular Maori influence and use of bright colours.

Tel: (09) 379 1349. Open: daily (except Christmas & Good Friday) 10am–5pm. Guided tours. Admission free, but charge for special shows. New Gallery. Cnr Wellesley & Lorne sts. Admission charge.

National Maritime Museum

Housed inside old warehouses surrounding a small marina, this museum is an evocative celebration of the country's maritime heritage, and the seagoing traditions of the South Pacific. It seems almost a shame to label this dynamic enterprise with the dusty tag of 'museum', so skilfully have traditional-style displays been woven together with workshops (including one which runs boat-building and restoration courses, as well as others housing sailmakers, riggers, and wood-carvers). There is also the marina itself (where canoes and veteran craft, including a brigantine and a scow, bob on the waves), sailing trips aboard an old steam launch, and historic exhibits, such as the reconstruction of a steerage cabin on an early immigrant ship which sways and creaks convincingly as you explore its interior.

In addition, there is an outstanding collection of Pacific canoes, historic yachts, and coastal vessels, and an intriguing passenger-shipping database where descendants of early immigrants can look up the names and dates of the ships their ancestors arrived on – the computer contains the details of nearly 100,000 arrivals. Another innovative feature is an 'oral history cabin' where shipwrecked sailors, whalers, and lighthouse-keepers recount their experiences on tape.

What's new is a 12-minute film reconstructing Te Waka, the last great migratory voyage which brought the Maori to Aotearoa, showing how they survived, and how they navigated using sun, stars and birds.

Cnr Quay & Hobson sts.
Tel: (09) 373 0800. Open: daily (except Christmas) 9am–5pm. Admission charge.

Kelly Tarlton's Antarctic Encounter and Underwater World

Kelly Tarlton was a famous underwater explorer; his vision led to the building of the Underwater World. He died in 1985, seven weeks after seeing his dream come true, but his legacy has turned out to be one of the country's most popular tourist attractions. The main feature of this underground aquarium is a circular acrylic tunnel with a moving walkway which carries you through large tanks teeming with fish, stingrays, and several species of shark.

Underwater World has been extended to include the Antarctic Encounter, which opened in 1993. Inside, there is a brilliant replica of the hut used by Sir Robert Scott on his last, ill-fated expedition in 1910–12. The musty, gloomy interior (which even smells authentic) vividly recreates the working lives and day-to-day activities of Scott's team in this harsh environment. Then you board a snow cat to 'experience' the Antarctic; this includes a simulated (and disorientating) white-out, a mock Orca whale which rises from the depths to devour a seal, and a real penguin colony.
23 Tamaki Drive, Orakei Wharf, Orakei, approximately 6km from the city centre. Tel: toll-free 0800 805 050. Open: daily, summer 9am–9pm – last admission 8pm; winter 9am–6pm. Buses: 74, 75, & 76 from Downtown. Admission charge.

Mount Eden and One Tree Hill

The top of Mount Eden (at 196m, Auckland's highest volcanic peak) presents a fabulous panorama of the city and its surrounding bays and harbours. This strategic point was once an important *pa* (fortified settlement), occupied soon after the landing by Polynesians in 1350; ancient terracing is visible around the summit.

One Tree Hill offers another (less spectacular) viewpoint. One Tree Hill was an even bigger *pa* than Mount Eden, and terracing is also evident here. Sadly, the tree was removed in 2000 and a replacement is still awaited.
Mount Eden lies off Mount Eden Rd. Buses: 274 & 275 from downtown. One Tree Hill lies off Manukau Rd. Buses: prefixed 30–31; from Queen & Victoria sts.

Mount Eden is the highest volcanic peak in Auckland, and offers spectacular views over the city

Auckland Environs

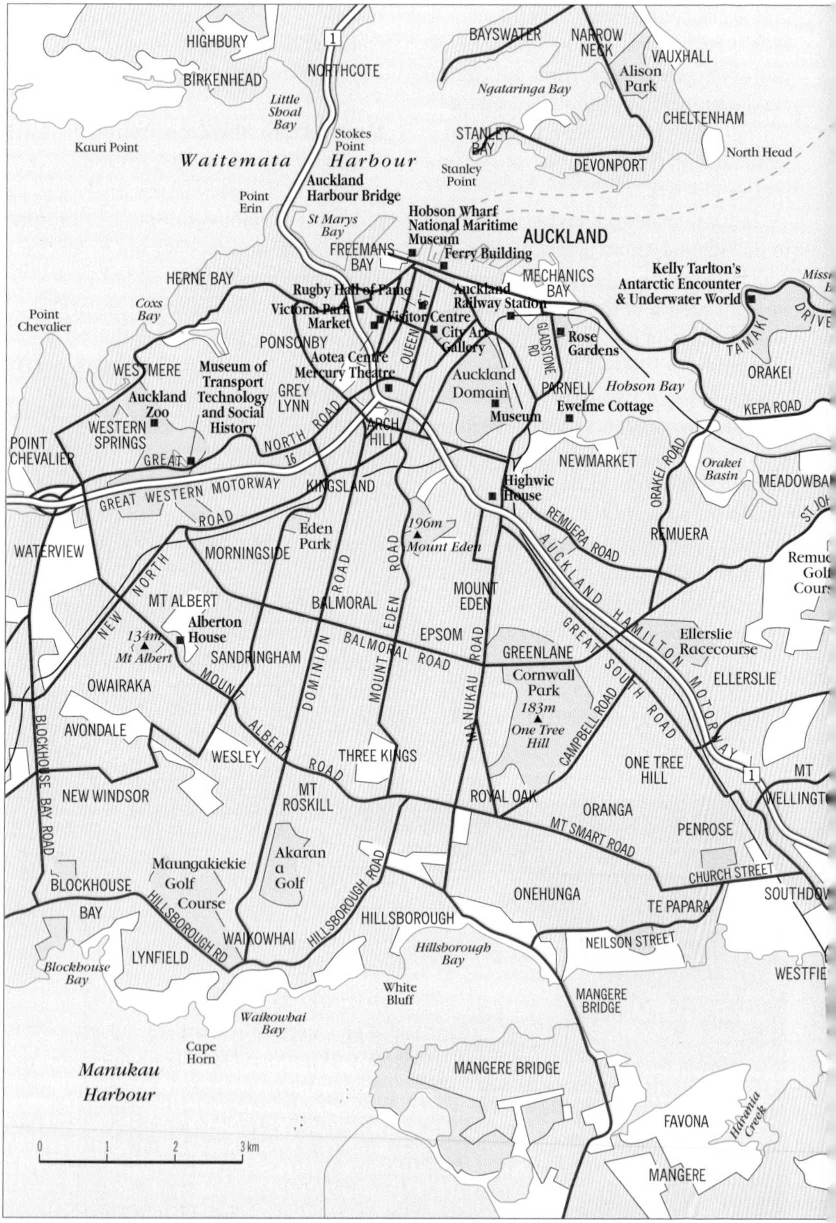

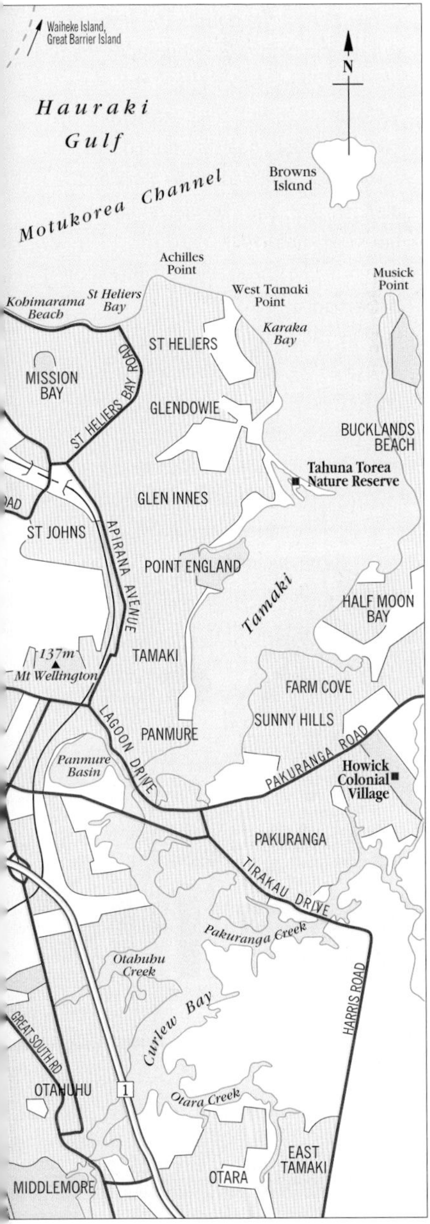

Museum of Transport Technology and Social History

The Museum of Transport Technology and Social History is spread over two separate sites alongside the Auckland Zoo. The main site, MOTAT 1, contains exhibits ranging from vintage machinery and equipment to a historic beam engine. Of particular interest are the remains of the plane flown by Richard Pearce, the pioneering South Island aviator.

MOTAT 2 (1km away) has a fascinating collection of aircraft, including the only Solent Mark IV flying boat left in the world.

805 Great North Rd, Western Springs. A tramway links MOTAT 1 with the zoo. Tel: (09) 846 7020. Open: daily 10am–5pm. Bus: 045 from Downtown. Admission charge.

Parnell

Parnell is a trendy, gentrified suburb, one of Auckland's oldest, full of art galleries, craft shops, bookshops, fashion boutiques, cafés, restaurants, wine bars, and pubs. At its heart is Parnell Village, a Victorian-style arcade of shopping enclaves and restored houses connected by boardwalks and wooden bridges.

30-minute walk from downtown, or take bus 63, 64, or 65, or the Link.

Victoria Park Market

The present-day market is a large rambling complex with a wide range of market stalls, cafés, bars, and outdoor eating areas. It is very lively at weekends.

Cnr Victoria St West & Wellesley St. Tel: (09) 309 6911. Open: daily 9am–6pm. On the Link circular route.

New Zealand has a wealth of historic buildings ranging from the earliest surviving building, Kemp House in Kerikeri *(see p47)*, to old lighthouses and pioneer cottages. Auckland itself has several historic houses which can be visited conveniently in a single day.

Highwic

This is one of New Zealand's finest houses in the timber Gothic style. Built by Alfred Buckland in 1862, it was designed in the early English style with steep slate roofs, vertical boarding, dormers, and latticed casement windows. The house was expanded several times to accommodate Buckland's family (twice married, he fathered 20 children) and servants. The earlier part of the house is far less ornate and of simpler proportions than later additions, which reflect the High Victorian style with their excessive ornamentation, heavily embroidered furnishings, and dark walls. Buckland died in 1903, and Highwic remained in the family until 1978.

Alberton

Built in 1863, Alberton was the home of Allan Kerr Taylor (1832–90), who made his fortune in farming and gold-mining. This grandiose mansion is unusual because of its fairy-tale towers and decorative verandas. The interior is furnished in typical Victorian style.

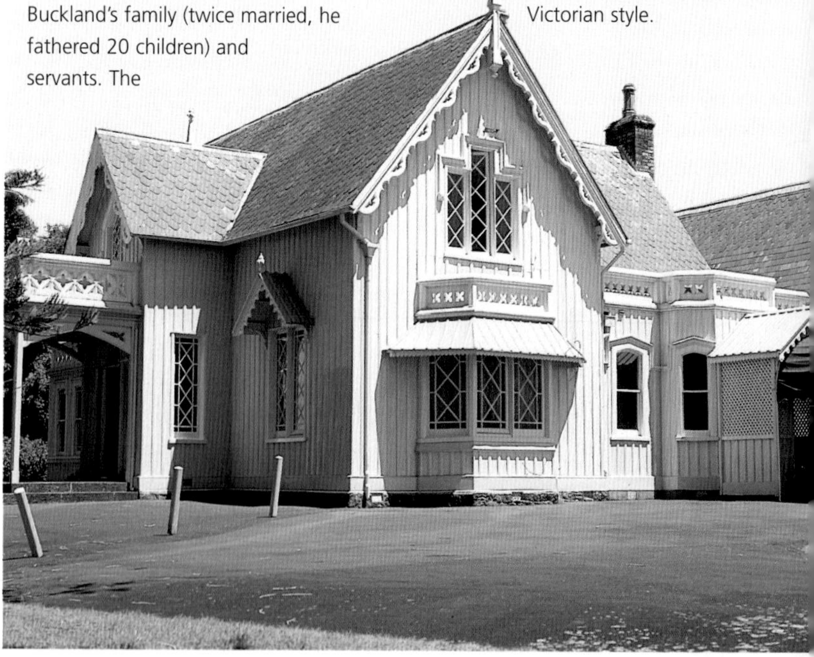

Ewelme Cottage

When Ewelme Cottage was built in 1863–4, the district of Parnell consisted mostly of open fields. Today, the house stands surrounded by others in what is now a busy inner-city suburb, but it still embodies the feel of the pioneer lifestyle. Designed by a clergyman and his wife, Vicesimus and Blanche Lush, Ewelme was built using local *kauri* wood and is shingle-roofed. It was lived in by the Lush's descendants until 1968; nearly all the furniture and personal effects are original. Several rooms in Ewelme were used as sets for the Oscar winning film *The Piano.*

Several historic homes survive in Auckland such as the Highwic House, Mortimer Pass (facing page) and the Ewelme House, Ayr Street (above)

Highwic 40 Gillies Ave, Epsom.
Tel: (09) 524 5729.
Alberton 100 Mt Albert Rd, Mt Albert.
Tel: (09) 846 7367.
Ewelme Cottage 14 Ayr St, Parnell.
Tel: (09) 379 0202.
Highwic and Alberton open: Wed–Sun 10.30am–noon, & 1–4.30pm.
Ewelme Cottage open: 10.30am–noon, 1–4.30pm. All are closed on Christmas Day & Good Friday. Admission charge.
These houses are just three of the many properties in the country owned or administered by the Historic Places Trust (*Pouhere Taonga* in Maori), which also helps with the protection of Maori heritage sites. UK National Trust members enjoy reciprocal rights. For more details, contact: New Zealand Historic Places Trust, PO Box 2629, Wellington. *www.historic.org.nz*

Auckland Environs

Beaches

There is a good selection of beaches along the coastline near Auckland and around the harbour. Travelling eastwards, Tamaki Drive runs along the shoreline, past several fine beaches such as **Mission Bay**, Kohimarama, and St Heliers. On the North Shore, there are many good beaches between Devonport and Long Bay, some of the more popular of these being Takapuna, Milford, and Browns Bay, with Orewa further north. The West Coast is dominated by rolling surf off the Tasman Sea; some of the better-known surf beaches are Bethells, Whatipu, Piha, and Muriwai. (Care must be taken at all times on this coast.)

Hauraki Gulf

Nestling between the mainland and the Coromandel Peninsula to the east, the Hauraki Gulf is a popular yachting area. Most of it lies within the **Hauraki Gulf Maritime Park**, which encompasses more than 50 islands. Some of these islands can be reached on day-trips, while others are more remote, and require additional time and energy to explore. Most of them are, however, serviced by regular ferries or light aircraft. A selection of the more popular islands includes the following:

The Mansion House on Kawau is surrounded by lovely gardens

Great Barrier Island

The largest of the Gulf islands, the Great Barrier has a population of slightly more than 1,000 people spread over 110sq km, with wilderness areas and beautiful beaches to explore. The wildest areas are in the northern section, which has many rare bird and plant species. Excellent hiking trails and campsites make this a walker's paradise, while fishing, diving, and kayaking are all possible around the extensive coastline. The island has a handful of guest houses and hostels in addition to the DOC campsites.

Fullers Ferries. Tel: (09) 367 9111.
A fast ferry can take you to the islands. Great Barrier Airlines flies several times daily from Auckland. Tel: toll-free 0800 222 123. DOC Information Centre: Port Fitzroy. Tel: (09) 429 0033.
Book accommodation and activities in Auckland through the New Zealand Adventure Travel Services, PO Box 7011, Wellesley St, Auckland.

Kawau Island

Tucked into the coastline above Auckland, Kawau's main attraction is the historic **Mansion House**; originally built by a mine manager, it was restored by Sir George Grey (one of the country's early governors) in the 1860s. The house

Waiheke is just one of several islands in the Hauraki Gulf which can easily be visited from Auckland

and gardens are open to the public. Elsewhere on Kawau there are old copper mines, walking tracks, and secluded beaches and picnic spots.
Kawau Cat departs several times daily (journey time 45 minutes) from Sandspit, near Warkworth, one hour's drive north of Auckland. Or join the Royal Mail Run (departs daily, 10.30am), which stops at all the bays and inlets to drop off mail. Mansion House tel: toll-free 0800 888 006. Open: daily 10am–3.30pm. Admission charge.

Rangitoto Island

Rangitoto emerged from the sea around 600 years ago, and is one of Auckland's youngest volcanoes. There are walking tracks across the intriguing volcanic landscape, and lava caves and fern groves to discover.

The island has the country's largest remaining forest of *pohutukawa* trees *(see p11)*, and more than 200 species of native trees and flowering plants. There are terrific views from the 259-m summit (allow an hour each way).
The DOC visitor information kiosk has walking maps. Fullers Ferries run the Rangitoto Volcanic Explorer.
For information: Tel: (09) 366 2166.

Waiheke Island

Waiheke is one of the closest islands to Auckland. Its many attractions – fine beaches, bush-walking tracks, vineyard trails, good restaurants, and a thriving arts and crafts community – make it a popular weekend getaway. Another reason for the island's popularity may be that it is reputed to be an average 5°C warmer than the mainland! It also offers mountain biking, horse-riding, and kayaking around the coast.
Visitor Centre: 2 Korara Rd, Oneroa.
Tel: (09) 372 9999.
Fullers Ferries ply regularly up to 15 times a day (journey time 35 minutes); fewer runs at weekends. Buses connect with ferry arrivals and departures.

Walk: Devonport

This is an easy walk which takes you through the historic settlement of Devonport, and then a short ferry ride takes you across the harbour from central Auckland. The walk takes in fine views of the Hauraki Gulf and its islands.
Allow 2 to 3 hours.

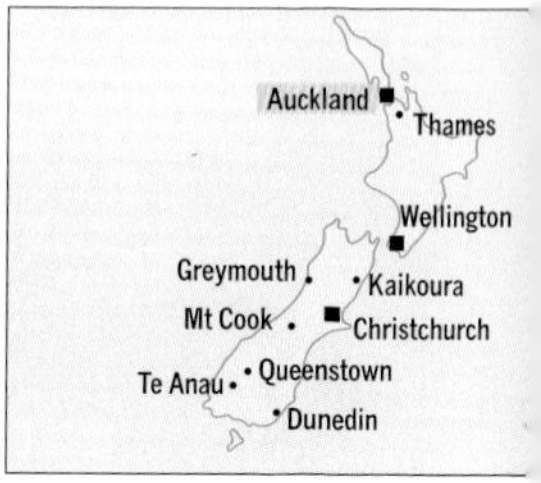

Take a Fullers Ferry from the Downtown Ferry Terminal. (For a timetable call (09) 367 3118.) On leaving the Devonport Wharf building, turn left along Queen's Parade. Turn right at the end, down Spring St, to the Navy Museum.

1 The Royal New Zealand Navy Museum

This small museum has a rich collection of items relating to New Zealand's naval heritage, with a huge array of medals, models, and memorabilia from various campaigns. There are also ships in bottles, a cat-o'-nine-tails, figureheads, and armaments.
Retrace your steps and turn left up Victoria Rd. Notice the elegant shop façades that have stood for over a hundred years.

2 Victoria Road

This main thoroughfare is lined with bookshops, craft galleries, outdoor cafés, and antique and souvenir shops. On the corner, commanding the seafront, is the Esplanade Hotel. Built in 1902, it was modelled on the popular English seaside hotels of the era.
At the end of Victoria Rd, on the corner with Kerr St, keep going up the path which leads to the top of Mount Victoria, an extinct volcanic cone with the outline of ancient Maori fortifications clearly visible around the summit.

3 Mount Victoria

From Mount Victoria, which is 196m high, there are 360-degree views over Hauraki Gulf and its islands and back

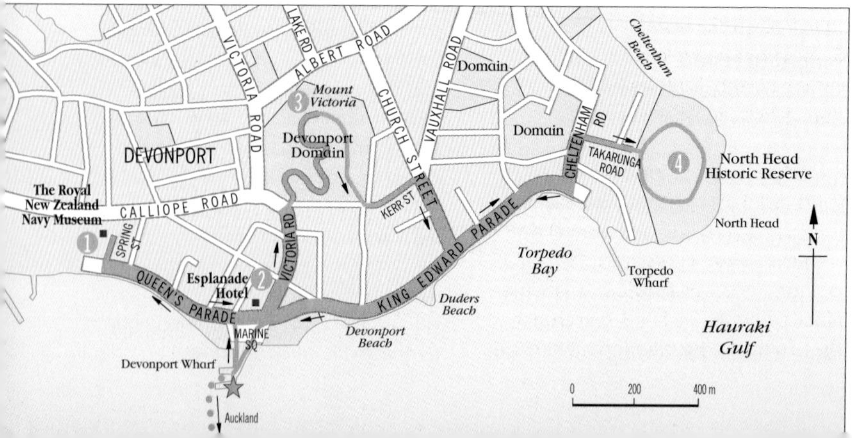

Mount Victoria rises up behind historic Devonport, a short ferry ride from the city centre

across the city and its harbour. An orientation table at the summit enables you to identify the surrounding local landmarks; on a clear day the views extend as far as the Great Barrier Island and out to the Coromandel Peninsula.

The outlines of terraces and pits can be distinguished on the hill top, principally on the northern and eastern elevations. *Follow the path back down the east side of the hill. Turn right on to Kerr St to enter Church St. At the seafront, turn left on to Kings Parade and follow the road round past the playing fields up Cheltenham Rd, turning right up Takarunga Rd.*

4 North Head Historic Reserve

North Head, like Mount Victoria, was a strategic *pa* (fortified settlement) due to its commanding views across any potential routes of attack. It became a military post in the late 19th century, when fears of a Russian invasion in 1885 prompted the building of gun batteries; one of these housed an unusual 'disappearing gun' which recoiled underground after firing – it is just one of the defences that can still be seen today.

The whole hillside is riddled with ancient guns, searchlights, a network of old tunnels, and other fortifications, most of which can be explored with the aid of a torch.

Follow the road back along the seafront to return to Victoria Rd and the ferry terminal.

The Royal New Zealand Navy Museum
Tel: (09) 445 5080. Open: daily 10am–4.30pm. One hour guided tours at 1pm & 2.30pm. Free admission.
North Head Historic Reserve. Open: daily 6am–10pm. Free admission.
Fullers Ferries run at 20-minute intervals, 6am–11pm.
Devonport Visitor Centre Victoria Rd. *Tel: (09) 446 0677.* Open: daily 10am–4pm.

Bay of Islands

This is one of New Zealand's most historic regions, and it is also one of the most popular resort areas of the North Island. Paihia, Waitangi, and Russell are the three most important towns on the bay.

Ninety Mile Beach sweeps down Northland's west coast from Cape Reinga

Paihia and Waitangi

Paihia, the main hub for excursions and accommodation in the Bay of Islands, is a busy resort with many opportunities for boat trips, diving, swimming, and yachting. Excursions to swim with dolphins are also popular, and Paihia is a major centre for deep-sea fishing.

Just over 2km from Paihia on the north side of the Waitangi River is the 506-hectare **Waitangi National Reserve**, at the centre of which is the historic Waitangi Treaty House. The Treaty House was the setting for the first signing of the Treaty of Waitangi (1840). The house itself, one of the country's oldest surviving buildings, was completed in 1834 and was the home of James Busby, the first British Resident. The interior has been partially restored. Outside the house, overlooking the Bay of Islands, a huge flagpole stands on the site where the treaty was signed. To one side is an unusual *whare runanga* (meeting-house), each of its 28 carved interior wall slabs representing a different group of tribes. A short walk away, on Hobson's Beach, is an impressive *waka* (war canoe); the 37-m long *Ngatokimatawhaorua* was built for the 1940 Centennial celebrations of the signing of the treaty. At the entrance to Waitangi National Reserve is a well-equipped visitor centre with half-hourly audio-visual presentations on the Treaty.

Half-way between Paihia and Waitangi is the **Museum of Shipwrecks**, housed on board the *Tui*, an old sailing ship built entirely of *kauri* wood. The museum houses artefacts dredged from the deep by Kelly Tarlton, the famous underwater explorer who died in 1985. His collection covers treasures brought up from more than 70 wrecks.

Waitangi National Reserve. Tel: (09) 402 7437. Open: daily, summer 10am–6pm; winter 10am–5pm. Admission charge.
Kelly Tarlton's Museum of Shipwrecks, Waitangi. Tel: (09) 4027 018. Open: daily 10am–6pm. Admission charge.

Russell

Russell's first outside settlers were ex-convicts and sailors who deserted from the whaling ships which stopped here in the early 19th century. By 1840, it was the largest European settlement in the country and a notorious frontier town, with no less than 40 'grog shops' and brothels. The missionaries called it the 'hell-hole of the Pacific'.

Today, Russell is a tranquil township where life revolves around big-game fishing, messing about in boats, and a handful of historic attractions. Prime among the latter is **Christ Church**, the oldest surviving church in the country. The church still bears the marks of musket balls from an attack in 1845, and the churchyard contains many historic graves.

Just across from the church is the **Russell Museum**, containing a wide range of memorabilia relating to maritime history and the early settlers, as well as a remarkable one-fifth scale reproduction of the *Endeavour.*

A key feature of the town is an unusual building known as **Pompallier House** (named after the first Catholic bishop of the South Pacific), an elegant two-storey house built by French missionaries for their printing presses. It is New Zealand's oldest surviving industrial building and has been restored to its former role as a printing and book-binding works. You can buy the beautiful volumes made here at a small shop here.

A short walk or drive up the hill above town brings you to Flagstaff Hill, with panoramic views of the Bay. Hone Heke, a Maori leader, chopped down the flagstaff – a symbol of the hated settlers – four times in the 1840s.

Christ Church is on the corner of Church & Robertson sts.
Russell Museum: York St. Open: daily 10am–4pm. Admission charge.
Pompallier House: The Strand.
Tel: (09) 403 7861. Open: daily (except Christmas) 10am–5pm.
Admission charge.
Ferries depart at regular intervals throughout the day from Paihia wharf (crossing time 10 minutes).

The sheltered harbour at Russell has been a haven for seafarers since whaling days

Cape Reinga

Cape Reinga is the most northerly point in New Zealand which can be reached by road. (From Cape Reinga you can see North Cape, to which there is no public access and which lies, in fact, 5km further north.) From the Cape Reinga promontory you get spectacular sea views, especially of waves sometimes 10m high crashing over Colombus Reef, just offshore where the Pacific Ocean and Tasman Sea meet.

An integral part of all Cape Reinga tours is a trip back down the west side of the peninsula along the **Ninety Mile Beach**. In fact, the beach is 90km long (the misunderstanding is attributed to a French explorer who merely marked '90' on his chart, subsequently interpreted as miles by the English).

On the east side of the peninsula, most tours also stop off at Houhora, where there is an extensive and well-displayed old collection of Victoriana, stuffed birds, shells, and Maori exhibits at the **Wagener Museum**, as well as an early pioneer house, the **Subritzky Homestead**, next door.

Cape Reinga is 115km northwest of Kaitaia. Day-trips operate from Kaitaia and Paihia. It is better to go from Kaitaia, since the round-trip tour from Paihia is 500km. Wagener Museum and Subritzky Homestead, Houhora tel: (09) 409 8850. Open: daily 8.30am–4pm. Admission charge.

Doubtless Bay

The first landing here was by the legendary Polynesian explorer, Kupe, in AD 950. In 1769, the *Endeavour* arrived here and the lookout boy shouted 'Land on three sides, Sir'. Cook replied 'Doubtless, a bay', and the name stuck. It has beautiful beaches (at **Cable Bay**, **Cooper's Beach**, and **Taipa**) and is fast becoming a holiday-home centre. At the eastern end of Doubtless Bay is the laid-back waterfront community of Mangonui, a former *kauri* export depot.

Approximately 30km from Kaitaia.

Hokianga Harbour

The deep inlet of Hokianga Harbour on the western coastline of Northland presents one of those strange contrasts in landscape which are typical of New Zealand: on the southern spur of the harbour is deep forest, while the northern head consists of a single enormous sand dune rising up above the water. The harbour was in use in the early 19th century, but later developments passed it by, and it is now a peaceful area where the main activities are fishing, boating, and lazing on the beach. The two main settlements are **Omapere** and **Opononi**.

70km north of Dargaville & 80km northwest of Whangarei.

Kaitaia

Northland's second-largest town after Whangarei, Kaitaia has no special attractions, but it is a useful base for visiting Cape Reinga to the north.

155km northwest of Whangarei.

Kerikeri

Thanks to its fertile volcanic topsoil, the Kerikeri district is one of the richest agricultural areas in Northland and produces quantities of citrus fruit in the orchards that lie hidden behind the tall hedges lining the roadside. This small community has developed into a centre for pottery and handicrafts.

Kerikeri was the site of the country's second mission station, established here by the Reverend Samuel Marsden in 1819. The wooden **Kemp House**, built in 1822, stands above the picturesque Kerikeri inlet alongside the **Stone Store**, the oldest stone building in New Zealand (completed in 1836); the latter is still in use as a shop today, and has a small museum on its first floor. Just across the bridge over the inlet is **Rewa's Maori Village**, a full-scale replica of an old Maori fishing village.

Kerikeri is 22km north of Paihia.
Kemp House open: daily, summer 10am–5pm; winter 10am–4pm.
Stone Store Museum open: daily, summer 10am–5pm; winter Sat–Wed.
Rewa's Maori Village open: daily 10am–4pm.
Admission charge for all three.

The Kerikeri Basin, with two of New Zealand's oldest houses

Matakohe Kauri Museum

Kauri logging was one of the most important industries in Northland at the turn of the century, reaching its peak between 1870 and 1910. This excellent museum traces the history of *kauri* logging, and displays include old milling equipment, a bushman's shanty, and some gigantic *kauri* planks, the size of which (up to 8m long and over 2m wide) brings home exactly why this timber was so valuable.

Adjoining rooms show the end result in the form of a recreated settler's house with *kauri* panelling and some fine pieces of *kauri* furniture. The museum also houses a huge collection of *kauri* gum in raw and worked form; this amber-coloured resin was once hugely popular as a craft medium.

In the adjoining shop you can pick up small souvenirs made from swamp *kauri* (preserved tree trunks excavated from the swamps) which has been carbon-dated at around 44,000 years old.
26km from the Brynderwyn junction on Highway 1 (signposted).
Tel: (09) 431 7417. Open: daily 9am–5pm. Admission charge.

Waipoua Kauri Forest

In the Maori creation myth, Tane Mahuta, Lord of the Forest, brought light to the world by thrusting his feet upwards to separate Rangi (the Sky Father) from Papa (the Earth Mother). It is easy to imagine how this cosmology originated when you stand beside the awesome trunk of New Zealand's largest tree, named after Tane Mahuta, in the Waipoua Forest. Its height is impressive (over 50m) but it is really the girth

The Whangarei Falls, a picturesque spot outside the city

(nearly 14m around) that gives such a powerful impression of strength and longevity.

Tane Mahuta is just one of several massive *kauris* in the forest, all easily accessible by boardwalk from the main road (Highway 12) which runs through the forest. Nearby are Te Matua Ngahere (Father of the Forest – the oldest *kauri* in the forest, about 2,000 years old), the Four Sisters (a grove of four graceful *kauris* growing close together), and the Yakas Kauri (a 30-minute walk from the road).

Waipoua and the neighbouring forests of Mataraua and Waima together make up the largest remaining tract of native forest in Northland, and are home to threatened species such as native forest parrots (*kakariki* and *kaka*) and the North Island brown kiwi. There are a number of marked walking trails through the forest, ranging from one to six hours in duration; information and route maps are available from the DOC Visitor Centre.

Waipoua is 2km off Highway 12, around 50km northwest of Dargaville. Waipoua Forest Visitor Centre: Private Bag, Waipoua. Tel: (09) 439 3011. Open: daily. Free admission.

Whangarei

Northland's only city, Whangarei, faces an extensive, sheltered harbour – one of the deepest in New Zealand – and the country's only oil refinery. Points of interest include **Claphams Clock Museum**, with more than 1,000 clocks and watches, and the **Quarry Craft Co-operative**, which has a range of weaving, hand-dyed clothing, and ceramics.

The **Whangarei Falls**, 6km outside town on the Ngunguru road, is a popular picnic spot. The 25-m high cascade tumbles into a bush-fringed pool and there is a pretty walk down through native woodlands to the base, with another path continuing across a wooden bridge and up the other side again (a 20-minute circuit). You can swim in the pool above the falls.

Whangarei is 169km north of Auckland. Claphams Clock Museum, New Town Basin. Tel: (09) 438 3993. Open: daily, summer 9am–8pm; winter 10am–4pm. Admission charge.

Northland Craft Trust at the Quarry, Selwyn Ave. Open: daily 8am–5pm. Free admission.

An old log hauler outside the Kauri Museum in Matakohe

Early Explorers

In legends passed down from generation to generation, it was the great Polynesian voyager Kupe who discovered New Zealand, landing in the far north of the country around AD 950. He came from a homeland known to the Maori as 'Hawaiki', which is now thought to have been one of the Society Islands in East Polynesia. Kupe circled the islands, naming this new country Aotearoa, 'Land of the Long White Cloud'. He saw no inhabitants, and eventually returned to Hawaiki with the sailing instructions which would enable others to follow.

Around 200 years later, Chief Toi and his grandson, Whatonga, landed in Aotearoa after a series of mishaps. Strangely, they found the land inhabited (a fact for which we have no explanation), and stayed to intermarry with the peoples already there.

In the 14th century, a number of other canoes set off to look for Aotearoa, to ease over-population in the Society Islands. At least 12 named canoes are known to have arrived, and even today many Maori tribes are known by the name of the canoe from which they claim descent.

Europeans had long speculated on the existence of an undiscovered land mass in the southern hemisphere, and in 1642, the Dutch East India Company ordered Abel Janszoon Tasman to look for this missing continent.

On 13 December he became the first European to set eyes on the country when he spied land near Hokitika. He sailed north and reached Golden Bay, but after a brief skirmish with the Maori he put back to sea.

In 1768, Captain James Cook sailed in the *Endeavour* to Tahiti, where he opened the 'secret instructions' which ordered him to proceed to New Zealand. The *Endeavour* arrived in Gisborne on 7 October 1769, but after a hostile encounter with the Maori two days later, he was forced to sail away again.

Apart from the initial misunderstanding at Gisborne, Cook found the Maori friendly and helpful, and his accounts of this rich, fertile land and its hospitable people created a great deal of interest in Europe.

Maori seafarers discovered New Zealand some 800 years before Captain Cook

Central North Island

The central North Island has a variety of landscapes and destinations. Lying across the Hauraki Gulf from Auckland, the Coromandel Peninsula was more popular with city-dwellers than tourists, but that's changing now that its superb beaches, laidback lifestyle, and rugged scenery are becoming better known.

Coromandel's east coast merges into the Bay of Plenty. Here, too, the beaches are a major attraction (particularly for 'surfies'), and the seas offshore are renowned for big-game fishing. Beyond the Bay of Plenty's coastal resorts are the wild and sparsely populated coastlines of the East Cape, leading round into Poverty Bay and Gisborne, the most easterly city in the country. Hawke's Bay, south of Gisborne, is well known for its wines and sunshine. The seaside city Napier and the neighbouring Hastings are famous for their Art Deco architecture.

Volcanic activity is never far away in the North Island, and Lake Taupo was created by massive eruptions in the past. The main geothermal area lies slightly to the north of Taupo, focused on the city and the lake of Rotorua.

To the south of Lake Taupo, the volcanic belt reaches its southernmost point beneath the peaks of the Tongariro National Park. No tour of central North Island is complete without a visit to the Waitomo Caves.

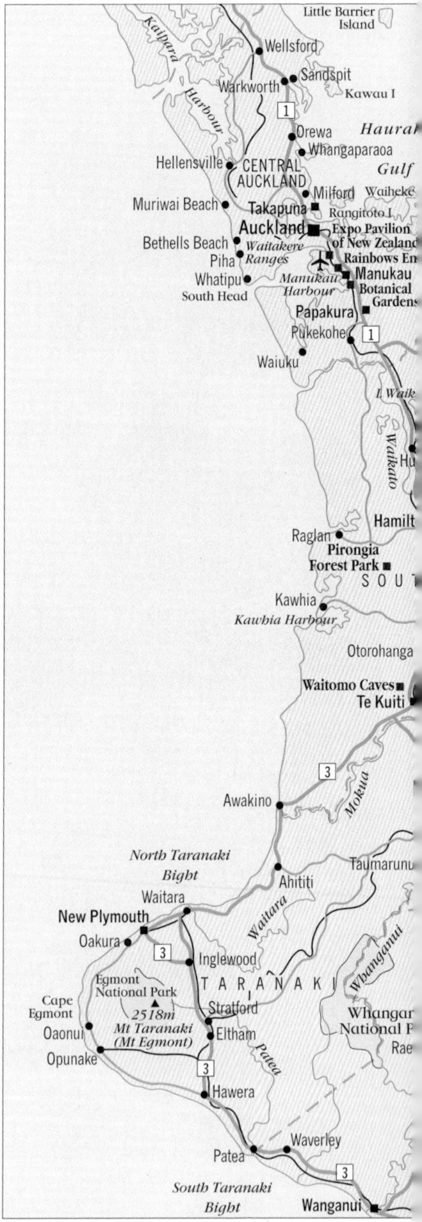

Central North Island

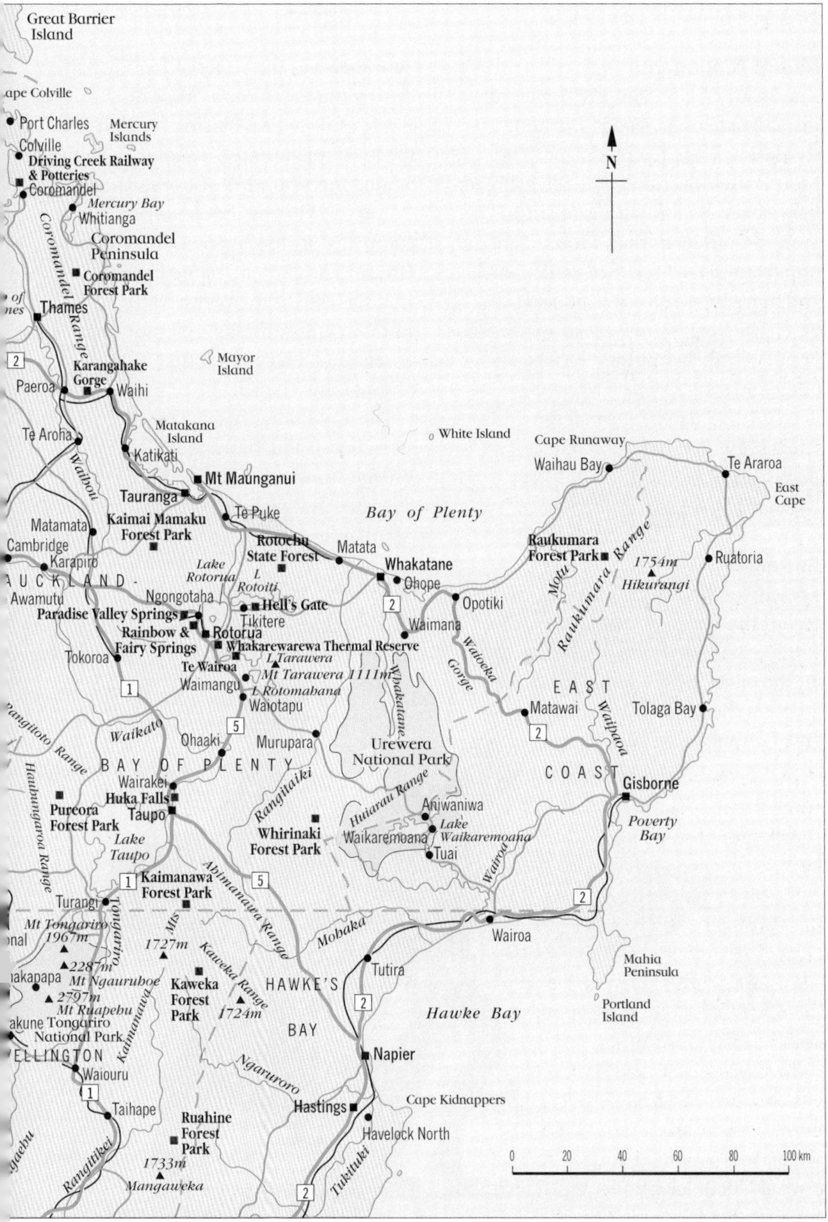

Bay of Plenty

Mount Maunganui

The Mount Maunganui resort lies on the east side of Tauranga Harbour, straddling a narrow peninsula. The Mount itself overlooks the township and its beaches. Walking trails take you around the 232-m high Mount (once an important *pa*, or fortified settlement), and to the hot salt-water pools at its base. The long, sandy, oceanside beach is popular with swimmers, surfers, and body-surfers.

Tel: (07) 575 0868. Open: daily 6am–10pm (on Sun, from 8am). Accessible by bus or car across the harbour bridge from Tauranga.

Tauranga

The city of Tauranga lies at the western end of the Bay of Plenty, and is a busy commercial centre, its prosperity based on the citrus trees and kiwifruit that grow on the fertile areas inland, and Tauranga Harbour, the largest port in the country for exports.

Tauranga was the scene of bloody battles during the Land Wars (most notably, the Battle of Gate Pa). During the fighting the local missionary, Archdeacon Brown, tended the wounded of both sides.

You can visit the house which Brown completed in 1847, called **Elms Mission House**. The garden, planted in the 1830s, is one of the oldest in the country, and contains a picturesque library and a reconstruction of the original tiny chapel.

The city's other main historical attraction is the **Tauranga Historic Village/Museum**, with its many relocated and restored old buildings. Among the exhibits are a recreation of the 'Main Street' of yesteryear, displays of ancient radios, a Maori village, and a steam train.

Young surfers on the popular ocean beach at Mount Maunganui, across the harbour from Tauranga

A giant kiwifruit near Te Puke

Back in the city centre, don't miss the Te Awanui war canoe resting in its shelter at the top end of the Strand. Built entirely from *kauri* wood, this replica is often paddled out into the harbour during ceremonial occasions.
Tauranga is 88km north of Rotorua.
Elms Mission House: Mission St. Tel: (07) 577 9772.
Gardens open: Mon–Sat 9am–6pm. Guided tours: 2pm. Free admission.
Tauranga Historic Village/Museum: 155 17th Ave West. Tel: (07) 578 1302. Open: daily 9am–6pm. Admission charge.

Te Puke

Te Puke is dubbed the 'kiwifruit capital of the world'; the first kiwifruit vines were planted here in 1937. Learn all about this fuzzy fruit at **Kiwifruit Country**, a horticultural theme park with rides through the orchards, visits to the packing sheds, tastings of kiwifruit wines, and other activities.
Te Puke is 31km southeast of Tauranga.
Kiwifruit Country: Box 541, Te Puke, on the main Rotorua-Tauranga Rd (Highway 2), 6km south of Te Puke. Tel: (07) 573 6340. Open: daily 9am–6pm; 8 tours. Admission charge.

Whakatane

At the opposite end of the Bay of Plenty to Tauranga is Whakatane, another popular holiday base with a long, sweeping beach over the headland at Ohope. In the town itself is the diminutive **Whakatane District Museum and Gallery**, displaying Maori tools, cloaks, flaxwork, weapons, and ornaments that belonged to the descendants of the Polynesians who landed here in the Mataatua canoe around AD 1350. Whakatane is noted for its deep-sea fishing, and is the main access point for White Island (*see below*), just offshore.
Whakatane is 100km southeast of Tauranga.
Whakatane District Museum and Gallery: Boon St. Tel: (07) 307 9805. Open: weekdays 10am–4.30pm, Sat 11am–1.30pm, Sun & public holidays 2–4.30pm. Admission charge.

White Island

Visible on a clear day from Whakatane, White Island is an active volcano that smoulders 50km off shore. Sulphur deposits were mined here from the 1870s until 1934. You can see the abandoned workings alongside the active craters, sulphur vents, boiling pools, and huge gannet colonies.
Scenic flights to White Island are operated by Vulcan Helicopters, PO Box 10, Waimana. Tel: toll-free 0800 804 354. All-day cruises are operated by the Pee Jay. Tel: (07) 308 9588.

Coromandel Peninsula

Colville

This is the last settlement in the northern Coromandel on the scenic Cape route *(see p75)*.

Coromandel

This delightful township at the base of the Coromandel Range is a magnet for craftspeople and those seeking 'alternative' lifestyles, as well as the focus of anti-mining campaigns in the peninsula. The town and peninsula were named after HMS *Coromandel*, which called in for *kauri* spars in 1820. In 1852 New Zealand's first gold finds were made here, and 300 prospective miners flooded in from Auckland. However, the boom proved premature, and it wasn't until the late 1860s that viable gold reefs were discovered. Those first gold strikes were made at Driving Creek, now the site of the **Driving Creek Railway and Potteries**. The narrow-gauge railway, built by potter Barry Brickell to bring clay down from the hills to his kilns, now serves a dual purpose as a tourist attraction with the 'station' lying in the middle of his potteries yard.

Just near Driving Creek, the methods used to separate gold from quartz are demonstrated at the restored **Coromandel Stamper Battery**, one of the first such works to be built in New Zealand. Early mining tools, rock samples, and various colonial artefacts are on display in the **Coromandel Mining and Historical Museum**, in the original School of Mines building. Most of the craft workshops around Coromandel welcome visitors; their locations are listed in the 'Coromandel Craft Trail' leaflet, available from the information centre. There is also a garden trail around five beautiful gardens just outside the Township.

There is an impressive grove of *kauri* trees on Highway 309, some 15km from Coromandel.

Coromandel is 55km north of Thames.
Driving Creek Railway and Potteries: 3km north of town. Tel: (07) 866 8703.
Trains run daily at 10am & 2pm all year; in summer, also at noon & 4pm.
Admission charge.
Coromandel Stamper Battery: 2km north of town. Tel: (07) 866 7933.
Open: summer 10am–5pm; weekends only in winter. Admission charge.
Coromandel Mining and Historical Museum: Rings Rd. Tel: (07) 866 8598.
Open: summer 10am–3pm; weekends, only in winter. Admission charge.
Information Centre: 355 Kapanga Rd. Tel: (07) 866 8598. Open: weekdays 9am–5pm, Sat 10am–noon, until later in summer.

Thames

Thames was built on the exploitation of gold and *kauri* in the late 19th century, and used to be one of the largest towns in New Zealand, with a population of 18,000 and over 70 working gold mines in the vicinity. It is now the principal gateway and shopping centre for the Coromandel Peninsula. The gold bonanza days are recalled in the **Historical Museum**, while the nearby **Mineralogical Museum** has one of the largest collections of minerals and fossils

in the country. The Hauraki Prospectors Association runs tours through the **Gold Mine and Stamper Battery** just outside Thames. Alternatively, details of a walk along Rocky's Goldmine Trail are available from the town's information centre.
Thames is 119km southeast of Auckland.
Historical Museum: corner of Pollen & Cochrane sts. Tel: (07) 868 8509.
Open: daily 1–4pm. Admission charge.
Mineralogical Museum: corner of Brown and Cochrane sts. Tel: (07) 868 6227.
Open: Tue–Sun 11am–4pm.
Admission charge.
Thames Gold Mine Tours: corner of SH25 & Moanataiari Creek Rd.
Tel: (07) 868 8514.
Underground tours: daily 10am–4pm.
Thames Visitor Centre: 206 Pollen St.
Tel: (07) 868 7284. Admission charge.

Whitianga

Whitianga is a busy summer resort town in Mercury Bay on the peninsula's east coast. The resort is renowned for its fishing (particularly game fishing, which peaks during February and March), watersports, and beaches. There are numerous good swimming beaches nearby, plus the novelty of **Hot Water Beach** at the mouth of the Tauwaiwe River to the south, where you can dig your own spa pool in the sand.

From Whitianga's wharf, ferries ply back and forth to **Ferry Landing**, site of the original settlement on the other side of the Narrows, from where you can walk or cycle to a number of lovely beaches and lookout points over Mercury Bay.
Whitianga is 95km north of Thames.

Cattle graze the lowland slopes of the Coromandel Ranges

East Cape

The East Cape coastline encompasses some of the most dramatic and unspoiled scenery in the North Island. For many years the rugged **Raukumara Range** – which runs down the centre of the cape – made transport difficult, and the Maori who lived here were left in peace. Even though a 334-km coastal road from Opotiki to Gisborne has since been built, the region remains quiet and laid-back, with small Maori communities dotted along the coast between a succession of beautiful coves and beaches.

Gisborne

This is the first city in New Zealand to see the sun rise every day; its other claim to fame is as the site of Captain Cook's first landfall on 9 October 1769. Cook's men unfortunately mistook the Maoris' *haka* (challenge) as an attack, and promptly shot them; further misunderstandings led to several more Maori deaths before the *Endeavour* sailed away. Cook named the spot Poverty Bay 'because it afforded us not one thing we wanted'.

Poverty Bay was, in fact, a complete misnomer, since the fertile plains around Gisborne are dotted with market

The MV *Waipa Delta* cruises the Waikato River from the city of Hamilton

gardens, maize fields, and vineyards (*see p166*). Cook's landing site is marked by an obelisk on the north side of the Turanganui River, and his statue gazes landwards from the top of Titirangi Hill above the port.

Near the town centre on the riverbank is the **Museum and Arts Centre**, which includes a number of interesting *taonga* (treasures) in its changing displays of Maori culture and colonial history.

Behind the main museum is the **Maritime Museum**, housed inside the bridgehouse of *The Star of Canada,* wrecked on the beach here in 1912.

Gisbourne is 216km northeast of Napier.
Museum and Arts Centre and Maritime Museum, 18–20 Stout St. Tel: (06) 867 3832. Open: weekdays 10am–4pm; weekends & public holidays 1.30–4pm. Admission charge.

Hamilton

This prosperous city, a centre for the rich farmlands of the Waikato district, sits on New Zealand's longest river, the Waikato. Behind Hamilton's gleaming new buildings lie several scenic riverside parks. You can also cruise along the Waikato on the old paddle-steamer, the MV *Waipa Delta.*

The **Waikato Museum of Art and History** houses an extensive collection of artefacts from the local Tainui people, including the war canoe *Te Winika*, built in 1836, and contemporary Tainui carvings, a large collection of historic photographs, and excellent displays of modern art.

Hamilton is 126km south of Auckland.
The MV Waipa Delta *cruises for lunch, tea, & dinner. For information & booking, tel: toll-free 0800 472 335.*
Waikato Museum: corner of Grantham & Victoria sts. Tel: (07) 838 6533.
Open: daily 10am–4.30pm.
Admission charge.

Hastings

Hastings, sister town to Napier (*see p60*) in Hawke's Bay, has few of the latter's charms and far fewer Art Deco buildings to see in its tawdry town centre. The main attraction lies just outside town at the family-oriented **Splash Planet**, a 23-hectare park with castles, pirate ships, train rides, and other amusements.

Beyond Hastings at the southernmost extremity of Hawke's Bay is **Cape Kidnappers**, one of the few mainland nesting sites for the striking Australian gannet, which congregates here in large numbers between late October and late April. You can visit the gannet colonies from mid-October to April (closed from July to mid-October to prevent disturbance).

Hastings is 236km south of Gisborne.
Splash Planet: Grove Rd.
Tel: (06) 876 9856. Open: weekdays 9am–4.30pm, weekends 9am–5am.
Admission charge for adults.
Charge for cinema & some rides.

For information on the gannet colony, contact:
DOC Centre, 59 Marine Parade, Napier.
Tel: (06) 835 0415. Open: daily 9am–4.15pm.
Gannet-viewing tours operated by:
Gannet Beach Adventures tel: toll-free 0800 426 638.
Gannet Safaris tel: toll-free 0800 427 232.
Open: daily. Admission charge.

An Art Deco window in Napier

Napier

Lying at the southern end of Hawke's Bay, Napier would have remained a humdrum seaside resort had it not been for the events of 3 February 1931, when a massive earthquake measuring 7.9 on the Richter scale levelled most of the township, killing 258 people. The survivors set about rebuilding with unprecedented vigour, and within two years a completely new town had risen from the rubble. The architects adopted Art Deco or Spanish Mission styles (in vogue in America at the time), and the result is a town with a wealth of classic, 1930s style features which have been carefully preserved to this day. The best way to explore Napier's Art Deco heritage is on a guided walking tour or, alternatively, by taking a stroll through the streets using the detailed leaflet, 'Take an Art Deco Walk'.

The story of the earthquake is related in an audio-visual exhibit at **Hawke's Bay Museum**, which also has a good selection of decorative arts from the 1930s, and a well-designed exhibition of carvings from the Ngati Kahungunu peoples of the east coast.

Napier's seafront esplanade, Marine Parade, is a broad avenue lined with Norfolk pines; it has several attractions including **Kiwi House**, **Marineland**, the **Napier Aquarium**, and various gardens. The earthquake story is also retold (with 14 seconds of simulated earthquake) at the **Stables Complex**, which includes a waxworks museum.

Napier is 216km southwest of Gisborne. The following attractions along Marine Parade are within a few minutes' walk of each other. All have an admission charge.

Hawke's Bay Museum: Tel: (06) 835 7781.
Open: daily 9am–6pm.
Kiwi House: Tel: (06) 834 1336.
Open: daily 11am–3pm.
Marineland: Tel: (06) 835 7553.
Open: daily 9am–4.30pm.
Napier Aquarium: Tel: (06) 834 1404.
Open: daily 9am–5pm.
Stables Complex: Tel: (06) 835 1937.
Open: daily 9am–5pm.
Guided walking tours: From the Art Deco Shop, 163 Tennyson St.
Tel: (06) 835 0022. Oct–Jun, daily 2pm; Jul–Sep, Wed, Sat & Sun.
'Take an Art Deco Walk', with a self-guide walk map, costs NZ$1.50 from the Art Deco Shop, Hawke's Bay Museum, or the Visitor Centre.

Otorohanga

This small town on the way to the Waitomo Caves (*see pp72–3*) is worth a stop for the **Kiwi House** and **Native Bird Park** (just off the main road). Here there is a nocturnal house with brown kiwis, a water-bird section, and a huge, walk-in aviary with native forest birds such as the *kea*, *tui*, and *kaka*.

Otorohanga is 60km south of Hamilton on Highway 3.
Kiwi House and Native Bird Park: Alex Tefler Drive. Tel: (07) 873 7391.
Open: daily 10am–5pm, up to 4pm in winter. Admission charge.

Urewera National Park

This is the third-largest national park in New Zealand, covering just under 213,000 hectares of untamed forests in the Urewera Range, and is the largest untouched stretch of native forest in the North Island, with more than 650 types of native flora. Urewera shelters many notable species, including *kaka* and *kakariki,* plus the New Zealand robin, New Zealand falcon, and rifleman. Deer, possums, and pigs are actively hunted. At the centre of the park is the magnificent **Lake Waikaremoana** ('Lake of Rippling Waters'), almost entirely surrounded by bush, except on the south side, which is dominated by the dramatic **Panekiri Bluff**. Following the shoreline for most of its 51km length, the Lake Waikaremoana Track takes three to four days to walk, and is one of the most popular in the North Island. Information on short walks is available from the visitor centre at Aniwaniwa.

Waikaremoana and Aniwaniwa are accessible via SH38, which runs from Wairoa on Hawke's Bay through to Murupara (to join the SH5 near Rotorua). InterCity buses operate from Rotorua to Wairoa on Mon, Wed, & Fri.
Aniwaniwa Visitor Centre: Private Bag 2213, Wairoa. Tel: (06) 837 3900.
Open: daily 8am–5pm.

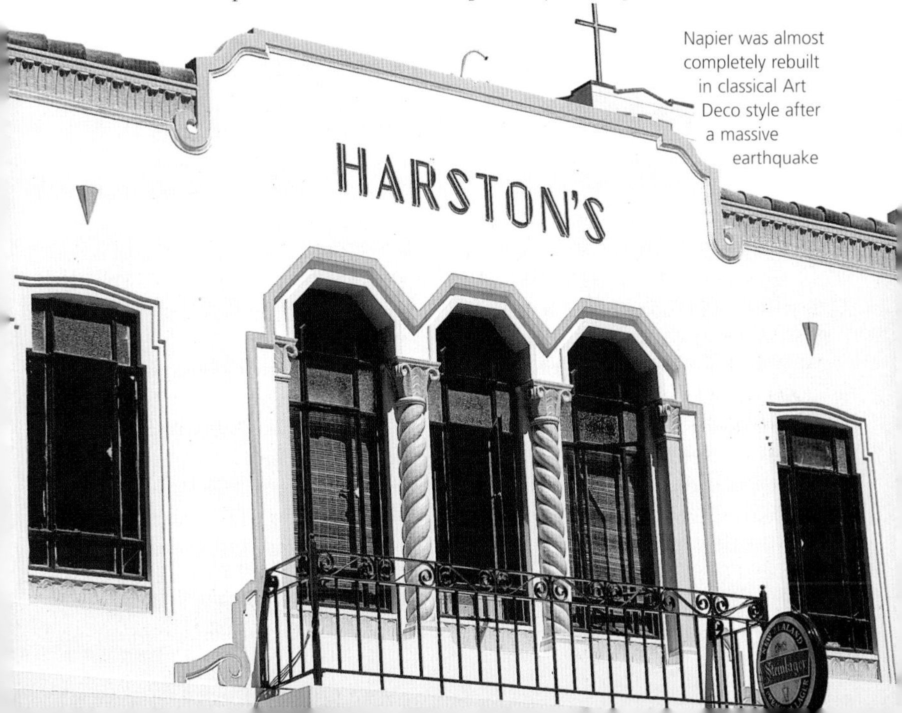

Napier was almost completely rebuilt in classical Art Deco style after a massive earthquake

Rotorua

Rotorua is at the centre of what is known as the Taupo Volcanic Belt, which runs from the Tongariro National Park in the south to the White Island in the Bay of Plenty. Volcanic activity is, however, most evident in Rotorua: even if you don't notice the steam escaping from back gardens, road drains, or rocky patches, your nose will certainly warn you of the ever-present hydrogen sulphide – it smells like rotten eggs – which wafts over the city.

Thermal pools are one way of relaxing in Rotorua

The area was first inhabited by the Te Arawa tribe in the 14th century after they had made their way inland from the point at which their canoe beached in the Bay of Plenty. They used the boiling volcanic pools for cooking and heated their houses *(whare)* naturally by building them on warm soil. During the 19th century the Arawa were usually at war with neighbouring tribes. Once the local feuds ceased in the 1870s, tourists came in for cures in the thermal waters, and Rotorua took off as a spa town.

The first building in the resort was the Tudor-style **Bath House**, built in 1908 at the centre of Government Gardens on the shores of the lake. It houses the **Rotorua Art and History Museum**, and features several interesting permanent exhibitions. The two most important exhibitions are: *In the Shadow of the Volcano*, which tells the story of Tarawera Mountain and the fatal eruption on 10 June 1886 (*see* Te Wairoa Buried Village, *p66*), and *Nga Taonga o Te Arawa* (The Treasures of the Arawa People), which includes superb, unusual carvings and important artefacts.

Nearby is the **Polynesian Spa**, with 30 pools (including eight hot mineral springs) in the garden, helpful for rheumatism and arthritis as they have a high acidic content. There are several private spa pools and a large mineral pool (with high alkalinity) for families and children.

Renovated to celebrate the Millennium, the **Blue Baths,** in a magnificent Spanish Mission style building, have been meticulously restored, re-opening 68 years to the date they were first opened. Bathe in the thermally heated waters, then take tea in the elegant Tea Rooms upstairs. The old changing rooms house an exhibition on the history of the building and the Baths. **Tikitere Springs Spa and Resort** is a new spa coming up 6km from the city centre on Lake Rotokawau Road.

From a quay further along, on the lakeside, explore Lake Rotorua and the Mokoia Island by paddle-steamer, cruise boat, jet hydrofoil, float plane, or helicopter. A short walk past the quay is **Ohinemutu Marae**, a Maori village which was once the main settlement on the lake before the spa town developed. The main attractions are a Tudor-style Anglican church, **St Faith's** – its graveyard contains many important tombs – and a richly carved meeting-house, Tamatekapua, opposite the church, named after the captain of the *Arawa* canoe.

For other attractions in the area (*see pp64–7*), you need your own transport, or hop on and off the Sightseeing Shuttle, which takes in city centre sights, and several on the outskirts. Get off the bus at any stop and board whichever bus comes along after you have finished sightseeing. Also view Rotorua from the 900-m summit of Mount Ngongotaha; to get there, take the **Skyline Gondola,** a five-minute ride from Fairy Springs Road (*tel: (07) 347 0027*).

Rotorua is 221km southeast of Auckland.
Art and History Museum: Government Gardens. Tel: (07) 349 4350. Open: daily, winter 9.30am–5pm; summer till 6pm. Admission charge.
Blue Baths complex: Open: daily from 10am. Closing time: varies with the season and day of the week.
www.rotoruamuseum.co.nz
Polynesian Spa: Hinemoa St. Tel: (07) 348 1328. Open: daily 6.30am–11pm. Admission charge.
Super Shuttle tel: toll-free 0800 748 8853.

The Bath House in Rotorua's Government Gardens now houses the city's Art and History Museum

Rotorua Environs

Sheep are the stars in entertaining farm shows around Rotorua

Agrodome and Rainbow Farm

Both of these locations offer a similar type of experience – essentially a one-hour show about sheep. If you thought sheep were too boring to merit such coverage, then think again! The shows are highly entertaining, and as well as explaining the differences between up to 19 different varieties of sheep on display, there is a sheep-shearing demonstration, a mock sheep auction, lamb-feeding, and plenty of audience participation. Both offer farm tours and horse treks; the Agrodome also has a model railway display.

Agrodome, Western Rd, Ngongotaha, is 7km northwest of Rotorua city centre on Highway 5. Tel: (07) 357 1050. Shows: daily 9.30am, 11am, & 2.30pm. Admission charge.

Rainbow Farm, Fairy Springs Rd, Ngongotaha, is 5km north from the Rotorua city centre on Highway 5. Shows: daily 10.30am, 11.45am, 1pm, 2.30pm, & 4pm. Admission charge.

Hell's Gate

In 1934, the English playwright George Bernard Shaw visited Hell's Gate and is reputed to have said: 'Hell's Gate, I think, is the most damnable place I have ever visited, and I'd willingly have paid ten pounds not to have seen it.' Quite why this sensitive soul was so upset by a few boiling sulphur cauldrons is perhaps a matter for theologians, but children (and probably adults too) will love the walk through Hell's Gate, where they can wonder at the bubbling pools, sulphurous jets of steam, boiling whirlpools, mud volcanoes, and 'plopping liquids' in this 10-hectare reserve. Notices warn of the dire consequences of stepping off the path – temperatures in some pools reach 115°C.

Tikitere, Rotorua, 16km from the city centre on Highway 30. Tel: (07) 345 3151. Open: daily 9am–5pm. Admission charge.

Paradise Valley Springs

Similar in concept to the Rainbow and Fairy Springs but less crowded, Paradise Valley Springs also has trout pools, native flora and fauna, including a wetlands area for New Zealand water-birds, and other animals on display, including a pride of lions, and cubs (under 6 months old) which can be

patted and photographed. Lions are fed at 2.30pm daily.
Paradise Valley Rd, 11km from the city centre, signposted off Highway 5.
Tel: (07) 348 9667. Open: daily 8am–5pm. Admission charge.

Rainbow and Fairy Springs

Fairy Springs first opened to the public in 1898 and is one of the most powerful natural springs in the region, gushing forth at the rate of around 23 million litres of water a day. The smaller Rainbow Springs flows at the rate of around 4.5 million litres per day; both are now part of a massive tourist complex which includes trout pools, native flora and fauna, and a nocturnal kiwi house. Hundreds of rainbow trout swim upstream from Lake Rotorua to spawn in the Rainbow Spring pools, and these are supplemented by juveniles reared in hatchery pools here. The pools are shaded by the deep green fronds of ferns and tree ferns.

The complex includes displays of animals introduced to New Zealand (such as deer, Himalayan thar, and the massive 'Captain Cooker', a pig species brought here by Cook over 200 years ago), and native birds (like the *kea* and the *kaka* parrots), New Zealand wood pigeons (*kereru*), the mellifluous *tui*, and the Paradise duck. It also serves as a conservation and breeding centre for protected species such as kiwis and the endangered *kokako*. A souvenir shop, a restaurant, and the adjoining Rainbow Farm complete the facilities.
Rainbow Springs, Fairy Springs Rd, Auckland Highway, is 5km north from the city centre on Highway 5.
Tel: toll-free 0800 724 626. Open: daily 8am–5pm. Admission charge.

Rainbow trout swim upstream to spawn in the clear waters of the Rainbow Springs

Te Wairoa Buried Village

In the mid-19th century, Rotorua was famous not only as a spa centre but also for its fabulous Pink and White Terraces, a celebrated attraction of fan-like silica formations on the shores of Lake Rotomahana, usually visited by canoe from the Maori village of Te Wairoa.

However, on the morning of 10 June, 1886, Mount Tarawera (previously thought to be dormant) exploded, burying the villages of Te Wairoa, Moura, and Te Ariki in nearly 3m of ash, lava, and mud. More than 150 people died, and the famous Pink and White Terraces were obliterated forever.

Parts of Te Wairoa have since been excavated, including the hut of the local *tohunga* (priest), who predicted the disaster and remained buried alive here for four days. Other remnants include the old Rotomahana Hotel, and an unusual stone storehouse with carvings on the lintel – very rare in New Zealand, since Maori seldom carved in stone. There is a new museum complex which contains fascinating displays, as well as a waterfall trail.

15km east of the city centre, on the Tarawera Rd. Tel: (07) 362 8287.
Open: daily from 9am. Admission charge.

Waimangu Volcanic Valley

This is another impressive volcanic area, with all the different attractions visible on a pleasant, downhill walk to Lake Rotomahana (around an hour one way; a free bus carries you back up again).

The main sights include the **Frying Pan Lake**, which is the world's largest hot spring, the former site of the Waimangu Geyser, and the **Inferno Crater**, which contains a steaming, pale-blue lake.

14km south of Rotorua on Highway 5, signposted off the main road, then a further 6km. Tel: (07) 366 6137.
Open: daily 8.30am–5pm.
Admission charge.

The brilliant colours of the Champagne Pool at the Waiotapu Thermal Wonderland

Waiotapu Thermal Wonderland

Billed as the country's 'most colourful thermal area', Waiotapu ('Sacred Waters') is worth the journey out from Rotorua city if only to see how natural chemicals have rendered an incredible range of tints and hues in thermal zones such as the **Champagne Pool** and the **Artist's Palette**.

Nearby is the Lady Knox Geyser which is 'soaped' every day at 10.15am (the soap acts to disperse the upper layers of water, thus allowing the super-heated steam to burst through from the reservoir below); even so, the perform-ance of the geyser is unpredictable. If there is enough water in the reservoir, Lady Knox can reach heights of around 20m and play for an hour; if not, it

might only fizzle briefly to a height of around 5m.
27km south of Rotorua on Highway 5, signposted off the main road. Tel: (07) 366 6333. Open: daily 8.30am–4.30pm. Admission charge.

Whakarewarewa Thermal Village
'Whaka' (as most people call it) is the closest of the major thermal reserves to Rotorua city centre, best known for its twin geysers which spout at regular intervals. The first (and smallest) of these is the Prince of Wales Feathers, which reaches a height of around 12m and always precedes the eruption of its neighbour, **Pohutu** (Maori for 'splashing'), which can reach 20–30m, playing sometimes for 20 minutes or more. Nearby are silica formations, boiling pools, and a Maori village.

Within the reserve is the **New Zealand Maori Arts and Crafts Institute**, set up in the 1960s to revive the dying art of Maori woodcarving. One of the first tasks of the artisans was to produce the carvings in the Te Aronui a Rua meeting-house, where afternoon concerts are now held daily at 12.15pm. You can see Maori carvers at work inside the institute, and finished pieces are placed in the institute gallery.
Hemo Rd, Rotorua, 3km from the city centre. Tel: (07) 349 3463. Open: daily, winter 8am–5pm, summer till 6pm. Tours: on the hour 10am–4pm. Admission charge.
Maori Arts and Crafts Institute tel: toll-free 0800 494 252. Open: daily 8am–5pm. Admission charge.

The Tarawera Legend Tour combines a visit to Rotorua Museum, Te Wairoa, and the Thermal Village at Whakerewarewa. For reservations, *tel: (07) 349 3463*.

Volcanic activity is the main attraction at the unpronounceable Whakarewarewa Thermal Reserve

Maori Society

Traditional Maori society was organised into the *whanau* (extended family groups), the *hapu* (sub-tribes, made up of several *whanau*), and the *iwi* (tribes). The *whanau* were ruled over by *kaumatua* and *kuia*, the male and female elders, who were in turn subject to the *ariki* (chiefs) of the *hapu* and the word of the *tohunga*, the priests who were entrusted with the secrets of tribal lore.

Every facet of Maori life was regulated by the dual concepts of *tapu* ('sacred', from which we derive 'taboo') and *mana* (which relates to prestige, pride, and dignity). Any slight to one's *mana* had to be met with *utu* (retribution), a social code that gave rise to incessant inter-tribal conflict – although this was only seasonal, and war didn't take place when the *kumara* (sweet potato) crops needed attention.

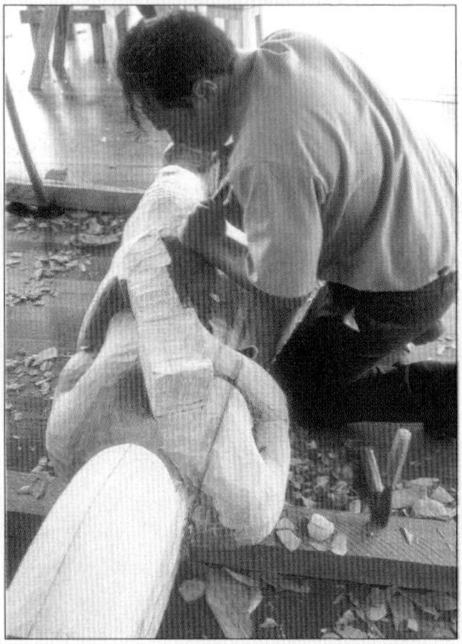

The constant fighting meant that principal villages were often located on hill tops and were fortified; many hills still bear the distinctive terracing which marks the ramparts and ditches surrounding *pa* (hill forts).

At the centre of all villages was the *marae*, an open courtyard which served as a focal point for community life. Facing the *marae* was the *whare runanga* (meeting-house), which was often elaborately carved to represent the spirit of famous ancestors and contained tribal artefacts revered as treasures.

Religion and Legends

An important part of Maori cultural heritage is their vast store of imaginative and colourful legends, which were passed down from generation to generation. Maori mythology reveals a depth of thought and religious feeling which is closely tied in with their animist beliefs and reverence for nature. Traditionally, Maori worshipped many gods and goddesses, although, unlike other Pacific peoples, they also believed in a 'supreme being', Io. This concept made it much easier for them to adapt to Christianity in the 19th century, which many did.

Language

Spoken fluently, the Maori language is highly allegorical and riven with ancestral and spiritual references, but usage has fallen away in recent years. A campaign is on for greater use of Maori in everyday life. Te Reo Maori is now being taught in language classes in schools.

Many aspects of traditional Maori culture, such as carving, survive today
Above: fearsome facial expressions are made during the *peruperu* (war dance)

Taupo and Lake Taupo

The resort town of Taupo enjoys a spectacular setting on the shores of Lake Taupo, New Zealand's largest lake (600sq km) which lies at the geographical heart of the North Island. From Taupo town, looking across the lake, you can see the distant peaks of the Tongariro National Park. This busy tourist centre has a wide range of attractions, from fishing trips to lake cruises, bungee-jumping, and visits to geothermal areas.

The shores of Lake Taupo, New Zealand's largest lake

This enormous, water-filled crater was formed by a series of massive eruptions which began around 250,000 years ago. Taupo's violent past is, however, masked by the tranquil lake waters which draw thousands of fishermen each year to what is claimed to be one of the best trout fisheries in the world.

Taupo's geothermal heritage is more evident in the thermal pools, such as **AC Baths**, just outside of town, which has several mineral pools and private spas. Similar facilities are available at the **Taupo Hot Springs**, hidden in a wooded valley off the Taupo-Napier highway.

Lounging around in hot pools is one way of using up geothermal heat, but at the **Wairakei Geothermal Power Station** it generates up to 1,550GWh (Giga watt hours) of power for the national grid. Completed in 1958, this was the second geothermal power station in the world, and you can see how 1,200 tonnes of steam per hour are captured at the **Wairakei Steamfield** just outside Taupo. There is a visitor centre at the entrance to the steamfield.

Other geothermal phenomena in the vicinity include the **Craters of the Moon** area, with its bubbling mud pools – run by DOC free of charge – and the **Wairakei Thermal Valley**, just past the steamfield.

Hot water is also put to good use at the **Wairakei Prawn Farm**, where you can round off a tour of the prawn ponds with a meal in the grillhouse afterwards (reservations recommended, *tel (07) 374 8474*). From the nearby landing stage a vintage riverboat, the *African Queen*, cruises up the Waikato to the spectacular Huka Falls. A speedier way of getting there is on the *Huka Jet*, or you can walk there along the Huka Falls Road.

Elsewhere along the river you can go rafting or jump off a 45-m high cantilever platform above the water at **Taupo Bungy**. There are many options for lake cruises, most of which visit contemporary Maori rock-carvings on the lake's shore; the most popular ships are the *Barbary* (a 1920s wooden racing yacht once owned by Errol Flynn) and the *Ernest Kemp*, a replica steam ferry. If you prefer modern transport, enjoy a

cruise on the *Cruise Cat* catamaran, which offers daily sailings and can be privately chartered.
Taupo is 84km southwest of Rotorua.
AC Baths: Spa Rd. Tel: (07) 378 3600. Open: daily 8am–9pm. Admission charge.
Taupo Hot Springs and Health Spa is 1km along the Taupo-Napier highway. Tel: (07) 377 6502. Open: daily 7.30am–9.30pm. Admission charge.
Wairakei Steamfield: Open: 24 hours.
Visitor Centre. Wairakei Rd. Tel: (07) 374 8216. Open: daily 9am–4.30pm. Free admission.
Craters of the Moon: 5km north of Taupo. Open: dawn–dusk. Free admission.
Wairakei Natural Thermal Valley: Wairakei Park. Tel: (07) 374 8004. Open: daily 8am–5pm. Admission charge.
Wairakei Prawn Farm: Wairakei Park. Tel: (07) 374 8474. Tours: daily, on the hour from 11am–4pm (summer), noon, 2pm, & 4pm (winter). Admission charge.
The African Queen *tel: toll-free 0800 278 336; departs daily 11am, 3pm, 6pm; also 9pm in summer.*
The Huka Jet *tel: (07) 374 8572 or toll-free 0800 4852 538; departs daily every half-hour.*

An attractive park on the shores of Lake Taupo

Taupo Bungy: 202 Spa Rd. Tel: (07) 377 1135 or toll-free 0800 888 408.
The Barbary *tel: (07) 378 3444; departs daily 10am & 2pm.*
The Ernest Kemp *tel: (07) 378 3444; departs daily, summer 10.30am & 2pm; winter 2pm only.*
Cruise Cat Lake Taupo Cruising Company: PO Box 1020. Tel: (07) 378 0623 or toll-free 0800 825 825.

Tongariro National Park

Created in 1887, Tongariro was New Zealand's first national park. The three main peaks in Tongariro are **Ruapehu** (2,797m), the highest peak on the North Island), **Ngauruhoe** (2,291m), the most active of the three, with a symmetrical cone, and **Tongariro** (1,967m), the oldest volcano. The first tourists began arriving in 1901. The famous Chateau Tongariro, one of New Zealand's best known hotels, was completed in 1929. Skiing began in the 1930s. All three volcanoes have erupted during the last century; an early warning system and evacuation plans posted on hotel walls are a constant reminder of the unpredictability of this dramatic area.

The main access points to the park are Ohakune, Turangi, and Whakapapa Village (leading from the settlement of National Park). Ohakune has the best selection of motels, restaurants, and other amenities, while Turangi is handy for walking tracks in the northern section of the park. Chateau Tongariro and the main DOC visitor centre (with audio-visual displays on volcanic activity and the Maori heritage) are at Whakapapa Village.

The National Park is primarily a service centre and stop on the main trunk railway line. There is excellent walking throughout the park, from short 30-minute rambles over volcanic features to the more demanding Round the Mountain Track; details available from the DOC centre.
Whakapapa is 354km from Auckland, 341km from Wellington.
DOC Visitor Centre: Whakapapa. Tel: (07) 892 3729. Open: daily 8am–5pm.

Waitomo Caves

The Waitomo Caves are ranked as one of the great natural wonders of New Zealand, primarily thanks to the presence of a particular type of glow-worm (*Arachnocampa luminosa*).

The larvae of the glow-worm cling to cave roofs, spinning a delicate thread which they use to ensnare insects that are attracted to their light. The glow-worms are found in the main cave, **Waitomo.** Here, after the usual tour, you board a boat for a short trip down the underground river to the Glowworm Grotto. The effect is magical: thousands of glow-worms suspended on the cave roof above appearing like twinkling stars on a clear night. In peak season 1,500 people descend daily into the Waitomo Cave, so try to come either early in the morning or late in the afternoon if you don't want to find yourself on a tourist conveyor belt. The second main cave is the **Aranui**. It doesn't have glow-worms, but it is still worth visiting for its delicate limestone formations.

The only way to see the third cave, **Ruakuri**, is by black-water rafting: you descend into the cave system and float along on your back, propelled by the current and supported by a rubber tyre. Ruakuri also has glow-worms, and there are plans to open it up to more general access to ease overcrowding in the main caves. Just near the Waitomo Cave is the **Museum of Caves**, with audio-visual shows and displays about the glow-worms.

On the road out to Waitomo, it is worth stopping at the **Ohaki Maori Village**, a replica Maori village complete with *wharetohutohu* (nursery/learning houses), *wharepunis* (sleeping houses), and *pataka* (food-storage houses).
Waitomo Caves are 150km from Rotorua, signposted off the main Highway 3 on SH37.

Guided tours for Waitomo Cave on the hour 9am–4.30pm, until later in summer; Aranui Cave, five times daily 10am–3pm, more frequently in busy times. Tickets for both available at Waitomo Cave, Te Anga Rd. Tel: (07) 878 8227.
Museum of Caves: Waitomo Cave Village. Tel: (07) 878 7640. Open: daily 8.30am–5pm, Jan–Feb till 8pm. Admission charge.
Ohaki Maori Village: Tel: (07) 878 6610. Open: daily 10am–8pm.
Admission charge.
Black-water Rafting: 585 Caves Rd, SH37, Waitomo Cave. Tel: (07) 878 6219 or toll-free 0800 228 464. Waitomo Adventures Ltd: Waitomo Caves Rd. Tel: (07) 878 7788 or toll-free 0800 924 866.

Mount Ngauruhoe, one of the three major volcanic peaks in Tongariro National Park

Tour: Coromandel

This route follows the beautiful west coast of the Coromandel Peninsula up to remote Fletcher Bay, where the road ends. It passes deserted beaches – where you can stop for a swim – then runs alongside the peninsula's rugged, forested hills. The last section of the journey (north of Colville) is along gravel roads, so if you have a hired car you may need to check insurance restrictions.
Allow a whole day, one way.

From Thames, follow the coast road (SH25) north to Tapu. Just past Tapu is Te Mata Beach.

1 Te Mata Beach
The Coromandel has yielded a wider variety of gemstones than anywhere else in the country, and Te Mata Beach is a particularly good place to look for large specimens of carnelian agate. Elsewhere, you might come across jasper, amethyst, chalcedony, and petrified wood on the peninsula's beaches.
Continue until the road climbs a bluff to the Mount Moehau lookout.

2 Mount Moehau
Beneath you is the wide sweep of Coromandel Harbour, with the Moehau Range rising up ahead towards the middle of the peninsula. The highest point is Mount Moehau (892m); the

A focal point for the community, the General Store is the only shop in Colville

mountain is a sacred Maori site and the burial place of Chief Tamatekapua, captain of the *Arawa*, one of the early canoes carrying immigrants from Hawaiki which arrived here around 1350 AD. The range is also home to a rare native frog, *Leiopeima archeyi*, although you may well have to trek part of the way up Mount Moehau for a chance to spot this small, primeval creature.
Descend into Coromandel (see p56) and follow the signs for Colville.

3 Beaches and Bays

The road winds up over a hill before descending into Oamaru Bay (where there is a campsite), and then continues on to the Papa Aroha Scenic Reserve, a small area of native bush on the headland. A 20-minute amble through the reserve's typical coastal forest of *pohutukawa*, *puriri*, and *kohekohe* takes you to a quiet little beach.
Colville lies a further 12km from Papa Aroha.

4 Colville

Once a major centre for *kauri* milling, this small community on Colville Bay is now surrounded by farmland and arts and crafts communities. This is your last chance to stock up on picnic supplies or stop for refreshments before tackling the Cape road.
A short distance further on, the road divides – take the left fork which is signposted to Port Jackson.

5 The Cape Road

The road hugs the shoreline most of the way up the coast from here, passing between the gnarled trunks of ancient *pohutukawa* trees; in summer their bright red blossoms hang from boughs over the beaches and rocks. Passing the campsite at **Fantail Bay**, the road becomes more and more tricky – which is why this is known as one of the most hair-raising roads in North Island – but the views become increasingly spectacular until, just after the big beach at Port Jackson, you finally arrive at Fletcher Bay. This cove has a campsite, good fishing, and, if you are feeling energetic, the option of a short hike over the headland to the 150-m high Needles.
Return to Coromandel along the same road.

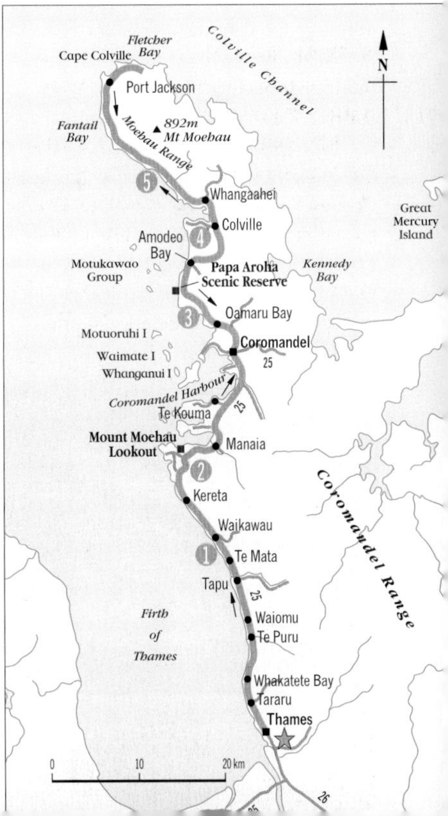

Wellington and Taranaki

The Taranaki region, on the west coast of the North Island, is dominated by snow-capped Mount Taranaki/Egmont. The eruptions of this now-dormant volcano have covered the surrounding lands with fertile ash. This, and the high rainfall on Taranaki's slopes, have created lush pastures, which have been put to good use by the numerous local dairy herds which produce some of the country's finest cheeses.

The lighthouse at Cape Egmont

This region has not always been so peaceful, for it was here that the Land Wars of the 1860s between *pakeha* and Maori erupted, and some of the bloodiest engagements took place in these surroundings.

From Taranaki's upper slopes there are sweeping panoramas across to the fuming cones of the Tongariro National Park and out along the coastline. On the mountain's north side, the city of New Plymouth spreads along the coast, its vast offshore reserves of natural gas creating energy for the national grid. The city is also renowned for its extensive displays of rhododendrons and azaleas, and surfies and board-sailers are drawn to the rolling breakers that crash in off the Tasman Sea on to the beaches nearby.

Martinborough is well known for its vineyards

Heading south from Taranaki you soon come to the mighty Wanganui River, the longest navigable river in the country. Steamers, jet-boats, and other assorted craft offer rides upstream from the riverside city of Wanganui, which also has a good museum and art galleries. Inland lies **Palmerston North**, a thriving agricultural centre forming the crossroads between Taranaki, Wellington, and central North Island.

If you cross the Tararua Range eastwards from Palmerston North, you reach the rolling plains which descend to the Pacific Ocean. These form the dairy and sheep pastures of the Wairarapa, with the regional centre, Masterton, playing host to the annual 'Golden Shears' international sheep-shearing competition. In contrast to the untold numbers of sheep surrounding them, just a handful of some of the rarest and most endangered bird species

Wellington and Taranaki

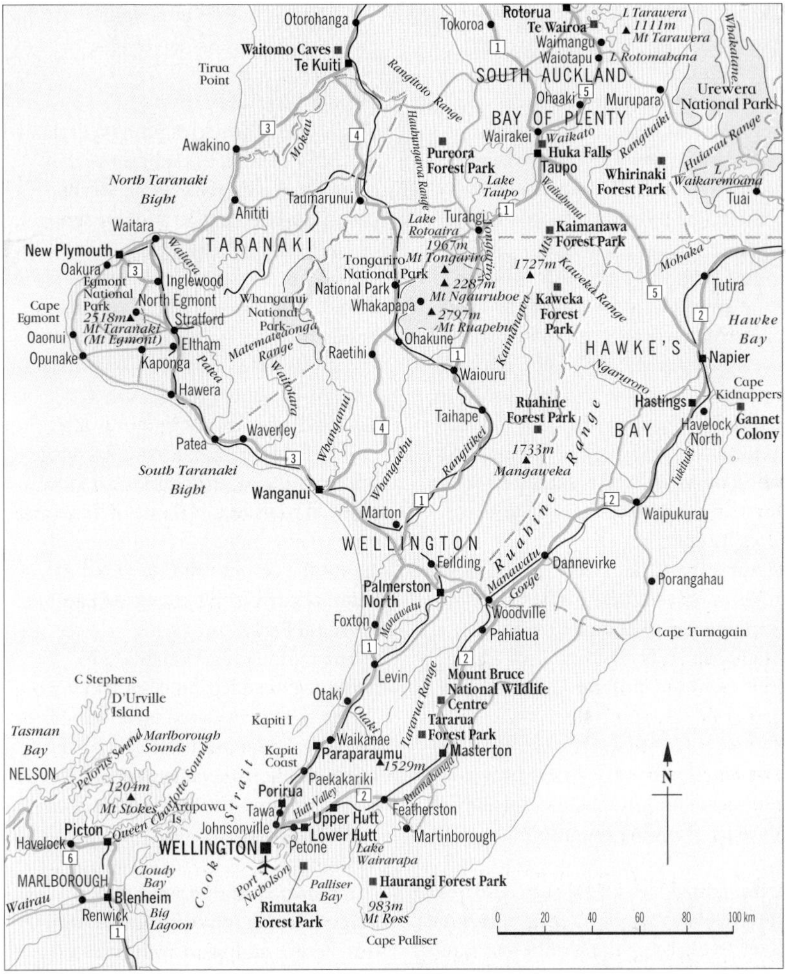

in the country are nurtured and protected at the Mount Bruce National Wildlife Centre, just north of Masterton, a must for wildlife enthusiasts.

South of Masterton, the vineyards of Martinborough are fast gaining a reputation for their fine wines, while eastwards the sea beats mercilessly on the rugged, inhospitable Wairarapa coastline. Heading south again across the Rimutaka Range, you reach the dormitory cities of Upper Hutt and Lower Hutt. These eventually merge into the outskirts of Wellington, the nation's capital, set amidst steep hills overlooking the vast harbour.

Mount Bruce National Wildlife Centre

The National Wildlife Centre consists of numerous aviaries which have been built around native bush on the slopes of Mount Bruce. The centre plays a crucial role in ensuring the survival of some of the most threatened and endangered species in New Zealand.

The centre was established in 1958 in an attempt to captive-breed the *takahe,* a bird which was thought to be extinct until the dramatic discovery of a small colony in Fiordland in 1948. Today, the centre offers the opportunity for visitors to see some of the rarest species in the world, many of which cannot be seen anywhere else since they only live on offshore islands.

Apart from the *takahe* (of which there are now only around 250 left), you may see the *kokako*, saddlebacks, and stitchbirds from the bush, rare black stilts from wetland areas, and the nocturnal morepork forest owl.

The centre has the largest nocturnal house in the country, where brown kiwis have been bred successfully for the last 30 years. Breeding programmes have now started for the great spotted and little spotted kiwis. The heated burrows with one-way windows maximise your chances of seeing the elusive and rare lizard-like *tuatara* (*see p13*).

Currently, the centre focuses on six priority species: the Campbell and Auckland Islands' teals, the shore plover, the stitchbird, the *kaka*, and the *kokako.* The latter is one of the most endangered species in the world, with only eight known breeding females alive today.
30km north of Masterton on SH2. Tel: (06) 375 8004. Open: daily 9am–4.30pm. Admission charge.

Mount Taranaki/Egmont

Dominating the surrounding dairyland for miles around, the solitary peak of Mount Taranaki rises up on North Island's west coast like a lonely sentinel. Because it adjoins the sea, it even has its own weather system and is often shrouded in cloud – Abel Tasman, sailing by in 1642, missed it altogether and it was left to Captain Cook to name it when he sighted the peak in 1770. Cook called it Mount Egmont (after the Earl of Egmont, then First Lord of the Admiralty) and, although it has since reverted to its Maori name of Taranaki, it now goes under the joint name Mt Taranaki/Egmont. The surrounding national park is still known as **Egmont National Park**.

The mountain is rich in Maori mythology and legend. Taranaki has always been considered *tapu* (sacred) by the Maori, who used to travel up the surrounding river valleys to collect red ochre and bury the bones of their chiefs and *tohungas* (priests) in secret caves on its slopes.

Taranaki is an unpredictable mountain, sunny and clear one minute, treacherous and windswept the next. Many climbers have lost their lives here, but this is still one of the country's most frequently climbed peaks – largely thanks to the local alpine club's open invitation climbs which allow up to 600 people to reach the summit in a day.

On a clear day there are magnificent views from the Taranaki summit across to Tongariro and out over the Tasman

Sea. The peak can be climbed in a single day. Always consult park staff as to conditions.

The main visitor centre is at North Egmont, where there is a comprehensive exhibition centre, and details on routes and mountain huts.

Even if you are not tempted to take on a major climb, it is worth the effort driving out here on a fine day and taking one of the marked trails which leads through the surrounding *kamihi* and *totara* forest.

North Egmont Visitor Centre: Egmont Rd, 26km from New Plymouth, signposted off Highway 3 from Inglewood.
Tel: (06) 756 0990.
Open: daily 8.30am–4.30pm in summer.
Closed: Mon & Tue in winter.

New Plymouth

Midway between Auckland and Wellington on the west coast is New Plymouth, an energy-production centre. Oil drilling began here in 1865, but was eclipsed by the discovery of vast natural gas reserves in the offshore Kapuni field in 1962 and the Maui field in 1969.

Among the parks in the city centre, the best known is **Pukekura Park**, with

Mount Taranaki/Egmont

lakes, streams, rolling lawns, native and exotic trees, fern gullies, and flowers. Neighbouring **Brooklands** has formal European-style gardens, such as the 3.6-hectare **Tupare Gardens**. A half-hour drive out of the city takes you to the **Pukeiti Rhododendron Trust** (ablaze with rhododendrons and azaleas in Sep–Nov). On the way, visit **Hurworth**, a pioneer cottage built in 1885 by Harry Atkinson, an immigrant, and prime minister of New Zealand for four terms of office.

The city's **Govett-Brewster Art Gallery** is home to the Len Lye Collection. Len Lye, a New Zealander (died 1980), was an acclaimed writer-painter, but in Taranaki he's known for his kinetic sculptures, particularly 'wind wands' which have achieved cult status.

The biggest Taranaki cultural project, **Puke Ariki**, is located in the city centre on the foreshore, the site of an ancient Maori *pa*. The museum showcases the history and culture of the region's peoples.

New Plymouth is a convenient base for visiting Mount Egmont/Taranaki (*see pp78–9*). It has excellent surfing and windsurfing beaches, and a seal colony in the **Sugar Loaf Marine Park**, just past the power station.

New Plymouth is 180km southwest of Waitomo, 160km northwest of Wanganui. The main entrance to Pukekura Park and Brooklands is on Liardet St, a 10-minute walk from the city centre. Open: daily 9am–5pm. Free admission.
Tupare Gardens: Mangorei Rd. Open: Sep–Mar, daily 9am–5pm; Apr–Aug open by arrangement. Admission charge.

A bust of Sir Harry Atkinson at Hurworth Cottage, outside New Plymouth

Pukeiti Rhododendron Trust: Carrington Rd. Open: daily 9am–5pm. Admission charge.
Hurworth Cottage: 906 Carrington Rd. Tel: (06) 753 6545. Open: Wed–Sun 10am–4pm. Admission charge.
Govett-Brewster Art Gallery: Queen St. Tel: (06) 758 5149; Infoline: (06) 759 0850; www.govettbrewster.org.nz Open: daily 10.30am–5pm.
Seal colony trips are organised by Chaddy'ies Charters. Tel: (06) 758 9133.

Wanganui

This bustling city, at the mouth of New Zealand's longest navigable river, has been an important supply route to the interior since the first Maori settlement. Now, jet-boats and paddle-steamers, not canoes, carry passengers upstream on scenic trips. Sail upriver on the PS *Waimarie*, an original coal-fired riverboat, restored as a Millennium project for the people of Wanganui.

Cruises depart from the old Hattrick wharf just outside the Riverboat centre in the centre of the city at 1pm daily (*tel: (06) 347 1836*).

Running through the heart of Wanganui down to the river is Victoria Avenue; most of the city's attractions lie within a few minutes' walk of this busy shopping thoroughfare. Just off Victoria Avenue is the **Wanganui Regional Museum**, the largest regional museum, with an excellent collection in its Maori Court; the centrepiece is the historic war canoe *Te Mata-O-Hoturoa* of the 1870s (bullets are embedded in its hull). The museum also has the skeleton of a giant moa and colonial artefacts.

The nearby **Sarjeant Art Gallery** houses New Zealand and British works as well as contemporary art.

Wanganui has numerous parks (including a deer park, the Virginia Lake Scenic Reserve, and the Riverland Family Park), St Paul's, a church with Maori carvings at Putiki, and a hideous tower on Durie Hill (opposite side of the riverbank), with sweeping views.

Wanganui is 192km north of Wellington and 160km southeast of New Plymouth. Regional Museum: Wall St. Tel: (06) 345 7443. Open: Mon–Sat 10am–4.30pm, Sun 1–4.30pm. Admission charge. Sarjeant Art Gallery: Queen's Park. Tel: (06) 349 050. Open: weekdays 10.30am–4.30pm, weekends 1–4.30pm. Contact Wanganui Information Centre at 101 Guyton St for details on attractions and river trips. Tel: (06) 349 0508. Open: weekdays 8.30am–5pm, weekends 10am–2pm.

Pukekura Park is one of many beautiful gardens in the city of New Plymouth

Wellington

High-rise blocks crowd the waterfront in New Zealand's capital

According to Maori legend, the explorer Kupe was the first to discover Wellington's harbour. When the first Europeans arrived in 1840 the local Maoris welcomed them, hoping that they would provide protection against hostile neighbouring tribes. Wellington was the first of the several settlements set up by the London-based New Zealand Company, and it quickly became a successful trading post. Although Governor Hobson initially chose Auckland as his capital, it was too far away from the rapidly increasing population of the South Island, and a commission eventually chose Wellington as the new capital in 1865.

As the administrative capital and a rapidly growing business centre, the city's main disadvantage was the lack of flat land for building, so land reclamation (helped along by a huge earthquake which partially raised the sea bed in 1855) began in the harbour, a process that continues today. Squeezed in by the hills that surround it, Wellington is thus a very compact city and, unlike Auckland, easy to get around on foot. The lack of space means that many workers commute in from outlying suburbs and cities, such as Porirua and Lower and Upper Hutt to the north.

Dubbed the 'windy city', Wellington is noted for the winds that can whistle through the Cook Strait. These can reach speeds of over 100kph and are funnelled by the high-rise blocks into a fearsome maelstrom in the city centre. Blowing mostly in the spring and autumn, these enervating winds are, on the positive side, credited with blowing away smog and putting backbone into the Wellingtonian character!

While Wellington remains at heart a city of government bureaucrats, diplomats, and international business, it is also striving to create a role for itself as the events and cultural capital of the country. The city is home to the Museum of New Zealand, four professional theatre companies, the New Zealand Symphony Orchestra, and the Royal New Zealand Ballet. It hosts the biennial New Zealand International Festival of the Arts, just one of numerous festivals that take place here. An ever-expanding range of nightspots, cafés, and restaurants has also added to the vibrancy of the capital in recent years.

At the heart of Wellington's renaissance are the massive improvements to Lambton Harbour, just a few steps from the core business and shopping area along Lambton Quay. Old wharf buildings and sheds have been imaginatively renovated, and the star attraction of the development is the Museum of New Zealand (Te Papa Tongarewa) which opened early 1998. Housed in a huge purpose-built building, the museum covers every aspect of New Zealand's land, life, and loves, and will take at least a morning to browse around.

The country's capital also offers Frank Kitt's Park, Lagoon Beach (featuring water sculptures and boardwalks), dockside restaurants, apartments and shops, and a new marina.

Wellington

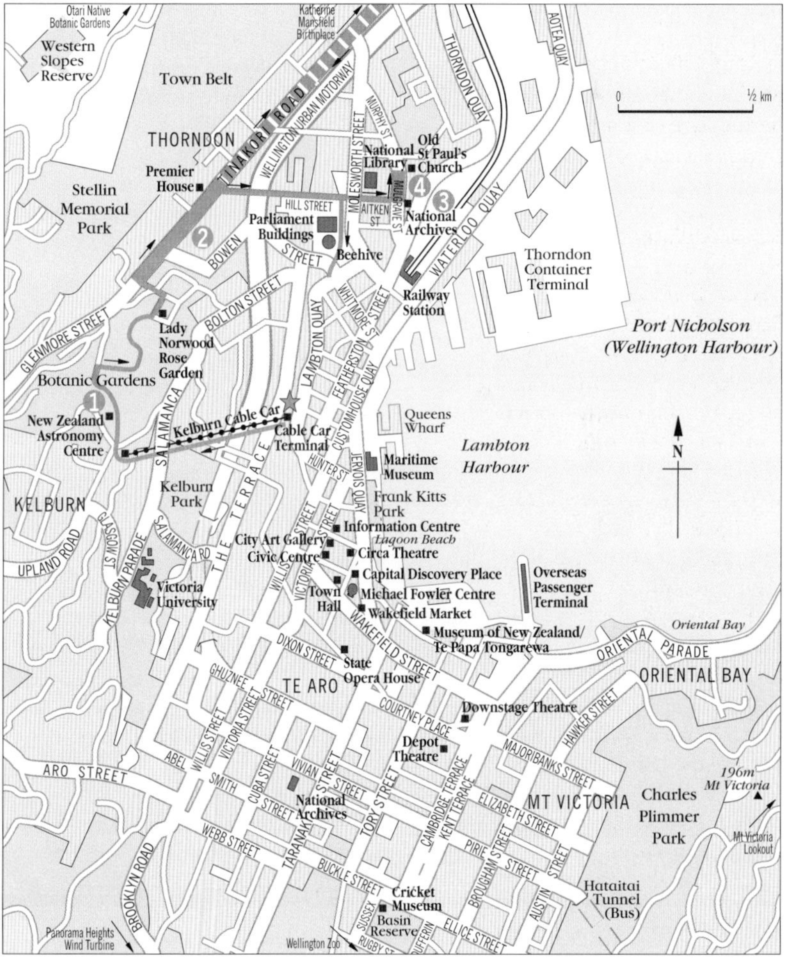

Botanic Gardens
See p88.

Capital Discovery Place
In the Civic Square under the 'city to sea' bridge is a unique hands-on exhibition and performance centre for children and families: there are performances by professional visiting theatre companies for children, or by children themselves. Creativity is encouraged in a fully-equipped television studio where Children ONTV is produced; and in the SoundHouse New Zealand, a video and sound engineering suite.
Civic Square. Tel: (04) 384 8502; www.capitale.org.nz Open: daily Tue–Sun 10am–5pm. Admission charge.

City Art Gallery
Since 1993 the City Art Gallery has been housed in the former Public Library overlooking Civic Square, a cavernous building with ample space for the many stimulating exhibitions put up each year. The extensive programme covers art, architecture, design, photography, and the moving image, and exhibitions are usually of a very high standard. With at least three or four main exhibitions running at any one time, it is always worth looking in to see what's on.
Civic Square. Tel: (04) 801 3952.
Open: daily 10am–5pm.
Guided tours: noon Sat & Sun.
Admission charge for visiting exhibitions.

Colonial Cottage Museum
This is central Wellington's oldest

A trip on Wellington's cable-car is a good way to gain an overview of the city

remaining building, built, by a carpenter, William Wallis, for his family in 1858. The house is furnished in Period style and displays give an indication of the difficulties in settling in the colonial days.

The garden occupies the remaining portion of the original 1840 New Zealand Company town acre on which the cottage was built.
68 Nairn St. Tel: (04) 384 9122; www.colonialcottagemuseum.co.nz
Open: Boxing Day–30 Apr, daily noon–4pm; 1 May–24 Dec, Wed–Sun noon–4pm.

Katherine Mansfield's Birthplace

Born in an unassuming two-storey wooden house in 1888, Katherine Mansfield became one of the world's best-known short-story writers and New Zealand's most famous author.

Mansfield left the country when she was 19, but many of her best stories (such as *Prelude, The Aloe,* and *A Birthday*) were based on her childhood memories of this house.

The house has been carefully restored and furnished with period antiques – even the wallpaper has been recreated from fragments found here. Photographs, videos, and tapes evoke Mansfield's short but eventful life.

The notes which you will be given on entry link the different rooms and settings to events in her stories.

The garden has also been replanted in its original Victorian design.
25 Tinakori Rd, Thorndon, a 10-minute walk from the railway station. Tel: (04) 473 7268. Open: daily 10am–4pm. Admission charge.

Kelburn Cable Car

Built in 1902, the cable car (now with modern Swiss cars) glides upwards past Victoria University of Wellington for a five-minute ride to Kelburn suburb and the Botanic Gardens (*see p88*).

Also check out the newly opened Cable Car Museum in the winding house at the Kelburn end.
Cable Car Lane, off 280 Lambton Quay. Open: weekdays 7am–10pm, weekends 9am–10pm. Single or return fares.
Cable Car Museum: Old Winding House at Kelburn End. Open: Mon–Fri 9.30am–5pm, weekends 10am–4.30pm.

Museum of Wellington City and Sea

Now located in the wonderfully restored **Bond Store** dating from 1892 within the old harbour board area of the city. Traditional museum techniques combine with holographic special effects, recreations, interactive exhibits, and a giant cinema screen take visitors on a journey through Wellington's past, present, and future.

The Wellington Gallery within the museum is a record of the social history of the area since Maori settlement.

Maori legends are told with holographic special effects, and in 'A Century Ago', experience life as it was for Wellingtonians at the beginning of the 20th century.
The Bond Store: Queens Wharf alongside Jervois Quay. Tel: (04) 472 8904; www.museumofwellington.co.nz
Open: weekdays 10am–5pm, weekends until 5.30pm, in summer until 6pm. Tours available.

Mount Victoria Lookout

The Maori name for this hill on the southeastern edge of the harbour basin was Matai-rangi, which means 'To Watch the Sky', indicating that it was probably once used as a lookout point. The panorama of the city and harbour from here has been somewhat overshadowed by the Brooklyn Wind Turbine *(see opposite).*

Mount Victoria is signposted from Oriental Bay and Courtenay Place and can also be reached via Constable St and Alexandra Rd. Otherwise, take bus 20 (Mon–Fri only) from the railway station.

Museum of New Zealand/ Te Papa Tongarewa

Magnificently situated in its new, purpose-built home on the stunning Wellington waterfront, Te Papa is a gateway for visitors to discover and understand the rich history of New Zealand. This exciting museum allows visitors to travel through time to visit New Zealand in the past and future, using a combination of displays and leading-edge technology. See how earthquakes, cyclones, and volcanoes have shaped the landscape. Experience the eruptions of Mount Ruapehu. Discover how New Zealand's native plants and animals, many of them unique, have adapted to their environments. Uncover a 'dinosaur' and explore some of the oldest rock formations in the country.

Within the building, high above the harbour is Te Marae, a fully functioning *marae,* and its focal point, Te Hono ki Hawaiki, a *wharenui* (meeting house).

Cable St. Tel: (04) 381 7000.

Open: daily 10am–6pm, Thu until 9pm. Free admission.

Te Papa Tongarewa

National Archives

See p89.

Old St Paul's Church

See p89.

Otari Native Botanic Gardens

This 90-hectare park is a sanctuary entirely devoted to the cultivation and preservation of indigenous plants, and contains the largest such collection in the country. There are picnic areas, rock gardens, more than 10km of walking tracks, and an information centre. The gardens are rich in native bird life; you may see *tuis*, fantails, grey warblers, and kingfishers flitting from tree to tree.

Wilton Rd, Wadestown. A 20-minute bus ride from the city centre (No. 14).

Tel: (04) 473 3245. Open: daily dawn–dusk. Information Centre open: weekdays only 8am–4pm. Free admission.

Brooklyn Wind Turbine

Opened in 1993, this massive 31-m high wind turbine generator is part of an experiment to see whether the 'windy city' really is windy enough to generate its own electricity. The graceful, Danish-designed turbine can generate up to 225KW – enough to power around 80 homes – on a blustery day.

Information boards (with a digital read-out of the energy being generated) are next to the car park at the top. There are fabulous views from the top – even Mount Victoria looks like a mere molehill way below in the distance.
Signposted off Brooklyn Rd, begins at the end of Willis St, about a 20-minute drive from downtown. Access road open: summer, daily 8am–8pm; winter 8am–5pm. Free admission.

Parliament Buildings

The old Parliament building, which once laid claim to being the largest all-wood building in the world, burned down in 1907. The building was replaced with the current Italianate-style building which houses the two debating chambers; it has recently undergone extensive renovation to make it earthquake-proof.

Next door is the unmistakable Beehive (which houses the executive wing of government), designed by Sir Basil Spence and completed in 1981. You can tour the Parliament building and visit the Public Gallery in the debating chamber.

The 'windy city' generates power from this experimental turbine above Brooklyn

Lambton Quay. Tel: (04) 471 9999. Free guided tours on the hour Mon–Sat 10am–3pm, noon–3pm on Sun.

Wellington Zoo

See native flora and fauna, as well as more exotic wildlife, on display at the zoo. For kiwis, visit the Nocturnal House.
*Manchester St, Newton, 4km from the city centre. Tel: (04) 381 6755.
Open: daily 9.30am–5pm.
Admission charge.
Nocturnal House open: daily 10am–4pm.
Bus: 10 from the railway station.*

Walk: Wellington

This walk encompasses several of the more interesting historic sights in Wellington's centre, as well as the extensive Botanic Gardens. It is an easy walk, largely because the cable car takes you to the top of the hill – after that it is a continuous descent. *For route, see map on p83. Allow around 2 hours (plus time to visit Katherine Mansfield's birthplace).*

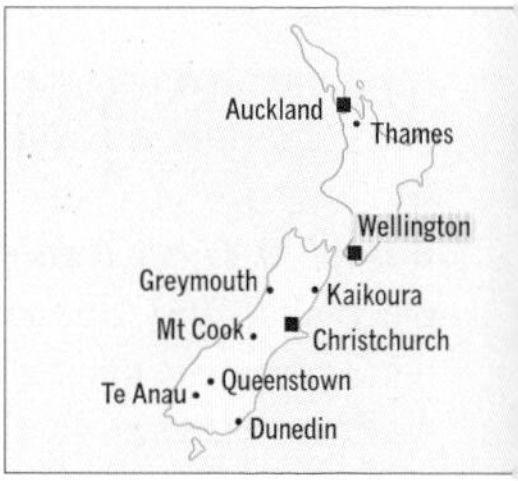

Start at Kelburn Cable Car terminal on Lambton Quay (see p85). Turn right immediately into the Botanic Gardens.

Old St Paul's is a delightful wooden building in the heart of modern Wellington

1 Botanic Gardens

The 25-hectare gardens have more than the usual variety of plantings, ranging from native bush to herb gardens, exotic fern gardens, and a circular rose garden. At the summit of the hill is the **Carter Observatory**, the Astronomy Centre of New Zealand, which has a planetarium, astronomy displays, and hands-on computer programmes. Wander down the hill, passing the Education and Environment Centre, ending up at the Lady Norwood Rose Garden at the bottom, and leaving via the Centennial Entrance on the north side.
Turn right and walk down Tinakori Rd.

2 Thorndon

Tinakori Road is the main artery of Thorndon, a suburb where the first Europeans settled in the 1840s. There are some charming old wooden houses on either side, many now converted into up-market shops, bistros, and cafés. Just past the junction with Upton Terrace is Premier House, which served as the prime minister's residence from 1875 until 1937 and is once again the official residence of the prime minister.

Continue to the bottom of Tinakori Rd to visit Katherine Mansfield's birthplace (see p85); allow an extra 40 minutes to see the house, then return to the Hill St turn-off. Turn right down Hill St, and continue to the junction with Mulgrave St. Directly opposite is the National Archives building.

3 National Archives

Inside the National Archives, turn right for the air-conditioned vault where the Treaty of Waitingi and several dozen other important historical documents are stored. The Treaty itself looks rather torn and battered (it travelled around the country for several months until the 213 signatures necessary for its implementation were collected), but it is the genuine article.

Turn right out of the National Archives to Old St Paul's Church.

4 Old St Paul's Church

Designed by parish vicar and architect Rev Frederick Thatcher in 1866, this all-wood church was built entirely using native timbers and is a marvellous example of the Gothic Revival style adapted to wood.

The soft lighting and dark timber of the panelling, pews, and soaring arches exude a sense of warmth and serenity alongside numerous brass plaques in honour of local parishioners.

This lovely church was scheduled for demolition to make way for a new cathedral, but in 1966 it was handed over to the Historic Places Trust. Now it is used for music and drama events and special services.

Go back down Aitken St (opposite the National Archives) and through the courtyard in front of Parliament Buildings and the Beehive (see p87), crossing Bowen St back to Lambton Quay.

Wellington's Botanic Gardens offer a respite from the bustle of the city

Botanic Gardens *Tel: (04) 801 3071.* Open: daily dawn–dusk. Free admission.
Carter Observatory *Tel: (04) 472 8167.* Open: weekdays 10am–5pm, weekends noon–5pm. Continuous shows on weekends 12.15–4.15pm. Admission charge.
Telescope Viewing Tue, Thu, & Sat evenings (weather permitting). Booking essential.
National Archives 10 Mulgrave St. *Tel: (04) 499 5595.* Open: weekdays 9am–5pm, Sat 9am–1pm. Free admission.
Old St Paul's 34 Mulgrave St. *Tel: (04) 473 6722.* Open: daily 10am–5pm.

Nelson and Marlborough

It doesn't take long to cross the often turbulent Cook Strait on the inter-island services from Wellington to the South Island, but once you pass the first headland there is still an hour's journey ahead before you reach the port of Picton. This massive inlet is part of the Marlborough Sounds, and a popular holiday area. There are plenty of boats to ferry you to isolated spots within the Marlborough Sounds Maritime Park to birdwatch or go camping.

Queen Charlotte Sound

At the head of Queen Charlotte Sound is Picton, the gateway to the South Island for ferry passengers. If you have plenty of time, the surrounding scenery is best appreciated by hiking along the Queen Charlotte Walkway; alternatively, an hour's drive or so along the coastline, on the Queen Charlotte Drive to Havelock, provides wonderful views of this beautiful area.

South of Picton lies Blenheim, the administrative centre of the Marlborough region and centre of a flourishing wine industry. Marlborough's benevolent climate is partly due to the protection offered by the Kaikoura Mountains to the south and east. The coastal town of Kaikoura, on the other side of this range, is a magnet for ecotourism thanks to the year-round presence of mighty sperm whales and other marine life.

Protecting Marlborough on its western flank, the Richmond Range marks the boundary with the neighbouring region of Nelson, known for its thriving horticulture and fruit-growing, its glacial valleys, forest parks, and

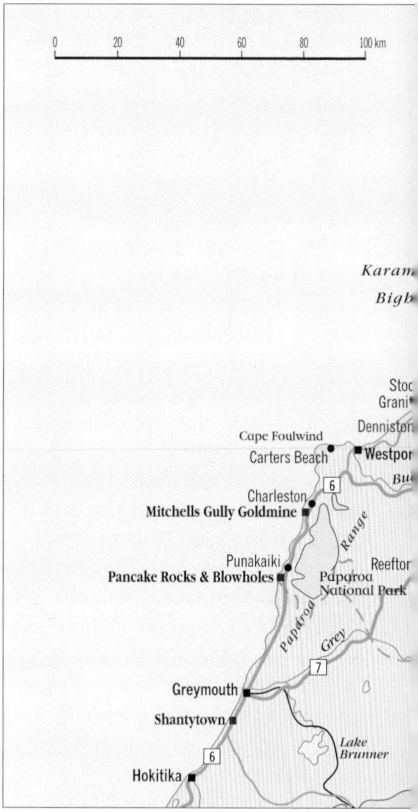

rushing rivers. Nelson city is the focal point of the region; the many sheltered bays and beaches nearby are popular for family camping holidays. To the south, the twin lakes of Rotorua and Rotoiti sit high up in the Nelson Lakes National Park, surrounded by forests which are criss-crossed with walking and hiking tracks. Hunting and fishing opportunities abound.

West of Nelson, the highway skirts Tasman Bay, before climbing steeply over Takaka Hill to descend into Golden Bay. The last sleepy outposts in this remote corner of the South Island come alive in the summer months as people flock to the beaches, or set off from here on famous trails such as the Heaphy Track and the Abel Tasman Coastal Walk. Curving round the top of Golden Bay, Farewell Spit is a 30-km long sand bar (mostly accessed on 4WD tours) where thousands of wading and wetland birds nest in the summer months.

Nelson and Marlborough

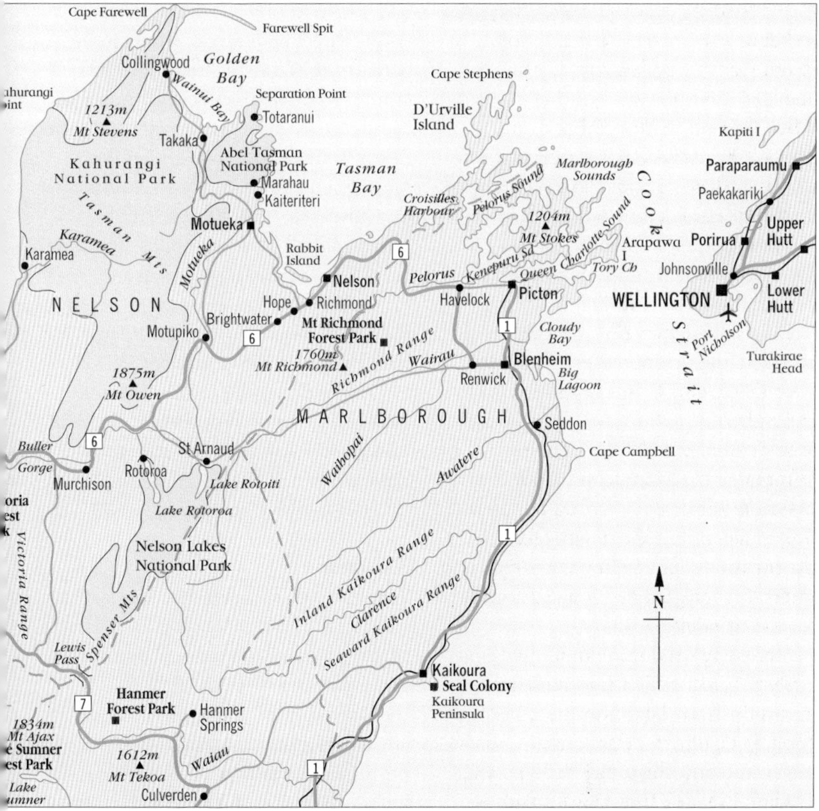

A blaze of colour in one of Blenheim's many gardens

Abel Tasman National Park

This is one of the smallest national parks in New Zealand; it covers just 22,350 hectares, and was named in honour of Abel Tasman on 19 December 1942, the 300th anniversary of his visit. In fact, Tasman's landfall here wasn't a happy one: his canoes were attacked by the local Maori; four men were killed, and he left quickly. French explorer Dumont d'Urville had better luck in January 1827, and, having befriended the locals, charted the coastline here.

Permanent European settlers arrived during the 1850s, logging the forests and quarrying for granite. Shipwrights also moved in, taking advantage of the protected bay and fine timber. Logging came to a halt after a vigorous campaign spearheaded by a local woman, Perrine Moncrieff, who persuaded the government to create the park in 1942. Despite its small size, Abel Tasman is one of the most popular national parks in the country with hikers. The coastal track follows a succession of beautiful clean beaches and shimmering bays backed by rolling hillsides of rainforest thick with *nikau* palms, vines, perching plants and tree ferns. An alternative inland route passes through magnificent beech forests. An added bonus is that the tracks are easy and accessible: there are no mountainous gradients on the coastal section, and scheduled boat services even hop between the bays to drop off and pick up day-trippers and backpackers.

The three main access points to the park are at Marahau, Totaranui, and Wainui Bay. Marahau lies just north of Motueka (*see p98*), while Wainui Bay lies 21km from Takaka (*see* Golden Bay, *pp94–5*) and Totaranui lies 12km further on (this last section is on a narrow, unsealed road). For day walks, Totaranui and Marahau are the best bets (*see p148* for more details on the track).

For details on day trips, contact local DOC offices at Motueka (tel: (03) 528 9117) or Takaka (tel: (03) 525 9061). For details on travelling around the Park, contact Abel Tasman National Park Enterprises, 234 High St Motueka (tel: toll-free 0800 223 582).

Blenheim

This busy provincial centre, the largest town in the Marlborough region, is situated at the confluence of the Taylor and Opawa rivers in the flatlands of the Wairau Plain. The region has an enviable sunshine record, which prompted the setting up of the Montana vineyards here in the late 1960s.

Blenheim is now the centre of a flourishing wine industry.

This neatly laid-out town is renowned for its gardens such as Pollard Park (just off Parker Street), which covers 25 hectares around the spring-fed Fulton Creek. There are rock gardens and herbaceous borders to admire; there is a fitness trail too, as well as a children's playground. Seymour Square, in the town centre, is an attractive mix of lawns, specimen trees, and floral displays.

The town's main historical interest lies in the **Brayshaw Historic Museum Park**, which has an extensive collection of vintage farm machinery, relocated colonial buildings that create a turn of the century streetscape, and a miniature railway.

Blenheim is 28km south of Picton, 132km north of Kaikoura.
Both gardens open during daylight hours.
Brayshaw Historic Museum Park: New Renwick Rd. Tel: (03) 578 1712.
Open: Tue–Sun 1–4pm. The timings could vary since the museum is fairly casual about opening times. Besides, it might close earlier or stay open longer depending on the number of visitors on any particular day.
Admission charge.

The mild climate in the Wairau Plain has led to the growth of numerous vineyards around Blenheim

The waters of Golden Bay are good for sailing

Golden Bay

Golden Bay lies at the mouth of the Takaka river valley and is reached by a tortuous mountain road over Takaka Hill from Motueka. Like the Coromandel, Golden Bay became something of an 'alternative lifestyle' centre in the 1970s because of the availability of cheap smallholdings; today it is known mostly for its safe swimming beaches (with good windsurfing) and for the intensive dairy farming in the valley. Golden Bay is also one of the main access points for the coastal track through the Abel Tasman National Park (*see p92*).

The main centre for Golden Bay is the small township of **Takaka**. On the main street are the information centre, the DOC office, and the **Takaka Museum**. The museum documents Tasman's arrival in the bay, and has the usual collection of early settlers' mementoes, as well as shells, minerals, and a few Maori artefacts.

Just outside Takaka, **Pupu Springs** (abbreviation of the Maori name, Waikoropupu) are the largest freshwater springs in New Zealand. Water from the upper river valley disappears down into a huge underground cave system and emerges here at the rate of around 21cu m per second. There are at least 16 springs in the vicinity; the two main springs can be seen from a platform located a short walk from the car park.

North of Takaka is the even smaller community of **Collingwood**, first settled during the 1850s' gold boom. Visitors to Collingwood today (with its one general store, hotel, garage, and café) will find it hard to believe that at one time there was even a proposal to make it the capital of the country.

Beyond Collingwood is **Farewell Spit**, a 24-km long sand bar which acts as a breakwater for Golden Bay. The 20-m high sand dunes form an internationally renowned bird sanctuary, with over 90 species having been recorded here. Hundreds of thousands of migratory waders spend the summer here, including large flocks of bar-tailed godwits (up to 20,000) and knots (up to 30,000), and turnstones, long-billed curlews, and many others. There are also large numbers of gulls, gannets, cormorants, and other sea birds. Access to this area is strictly controlled.

Takaka is 57km from Motueka on SH60. The Information Centre, at Takaka's southern entrance tel: (03) 525 9136.

Takaka Museum and Gallery. Commercial St. Open: daily 10am–4pm. Admission charge.
Pupu Springs are 5km north of town, signposted off the SH60.
Collingwood is 28km from Takaka on the SH60.
Farewell Spit: You can visit only the small area which is at the base of Farewell Spit, unless you go along with licensed operators, such as Farewell Spit Safaris (tel: toll-free 0800 808 257), or Farewell Spit Nature Tours (tel: toll-free 0800 250 500).

Havelock

Havelock lies halfway between Picton and Nelson, and stands at the head of Pelorus Sound, the largest of the Marlborough Sounds. The town is the main landing point for the tasty green-lipped mussels which are grown on ropes suspended in Marlborough Sounds and brought here for processing and export. Scallops are another local delicacy, and if you want to catch your own fish there are plenty of small boats for hire at the wharf.
70km west of Picton, 76km east of Nelson.

An aerial view of Havelock

The seaside town of Kaikoura on the South Island's east coast

Kaikoura

The small seaside town of Kaikoura curves around an attractive bay, with the snow-capped peaks of the Kaikoura Mountains rising up behind it. This former whaling port is now enjoying a huge boom in ecotourism as people flock here to watch the sperm whales, seals, and dolphins that abound in the offshore waters and around the rocky coastline of the peninsula.

Kaikoura has always been known for its sea life: the Maori came here for the same reason and christened the spot *kai* (meaning 'food' or 'to eat') *koura* (meaning 'crayfish').

Whaling began here in 1842. The only building still standing from this era is **Fyffe House** (1860), the residence of George Fyffe, one of the original whaling masters. The piles of his weatherboard cottage are giant whale vertebrae; the house has been restored by the Historic Places Trust. Other reminders of whaling days are on show in the **Kaikoura Museum**, which also displays various local mementoes and a 1910 police lock-up (complete with padded cell).

Just outside the town is **Maori Leap Cave**. Discovered in 1958, the 90-m long sea cave is known for its delicate cave straws, tubular formations that grow at the rate of about 25mm every hundred years.

Other activities in and around Kaikoura include fishing, diving, swimming, and snorkelling with seals and dolphins, or exploring the scenic Kaikoura Peninsula Walkway (*see pp100–101*).

The **Kaikoura Visitor Centre** has an excellent audio-visual theatre which features spectacular multimedia presentations on the whales, dolphins, seals, and seabirds. Shows are held on the hour. There is an admission charge.

Kaikoura is 132km south of Blenheim.
Fyffe House. 62 Avoca St. Open: summer, daily 10am–5.30pm; winter Thu–Tue 10am–4pm. Admission charge.
Kaikoura Museum. 14 Ludstone Rd. Open: daily 2–4pm. Admission charge.
Maori Leap Cave, 3km south on the SH1, behind the Caves Restaurant. Tel: (03) 319 5023. Conducted tours six times daily. Admission charge.
Information Centre, West End Esplanade. Tel: (03) 319 5641. Open: daily 9am–5pm.

Whale and Dolphin Watching

Marine mammals abound in the waters around New Zealand, but there are few places in such a fortunate position as Kaikoura when it comes to close-up viewing. Kaikoura's abundant marine resources are due to two phenomenon. First, nutrient-rich sub-antarctic waters meet subtropical waters here, resulting in an abundance of microscopic phytoplankton, which form the basis of a complex food chain. Second, the sea-bed drops away nearly 1,000m into the Kaikoura Canyon, a mere 1km from the coast, which means that deep-water feeders such as sperm whales surface in these coastal waters alongside the dolphins and seals.

Although the sperm whales are the main attraction, you may also spot the tiny Hector's dolphin (the world's rarest dolphin), bottlenose and dusky dolphins, orcas and pilot whales, and sea birds including albatross, petrels, and shearwaters.

The whale-watching boats use hydrophones (underwater microphones) to locate the distinctive clicking of the sperm whale. A tell-tale plume from the whale's blowhole pinpoints the spot where it has surfaced, and where it will remain for 10–12 minutes while it replenishes its oxygen supply before diving again. At this point the whales raise their massive tail flukes above the surface before disappearing from sight.

It is rare to see a sperm whale 'breach' (leap into the air) in the way humpbacks do, and only a small proportion of the resting whale is visible on the surface until it starts to dive. For some, this is frustrating, but for others it is privilege enough to be so close to this once-threatened creature.

Whale Watch Kaikoura operates four boats with four tours daily, 6am–2pm (tour time 3½ hours). Advance reservations are advisable; allow more than one day in case ocean conditions force cancellations. **Whale Watch Kaikoura Ltd:** The Whaleway Station, PO Box 89, Kaikoura. *Tel: (03) 319 6767* or *toll-free 0800 65 51 21.*
Tours: adults NZ$99.50; children NZ$60.

Tourists watch a sperm whale dive down to the depths off Kaikoura

Motueka is a pleasant base from which to explore the Abel Tasman National Park

Motueka

Motueka is a busy base for trekkers and day-trippers setting off for the Abel Tasman National Park (*see p92*), and for seasonal fruit workers who arrive in the autumn. Motueka has a range of accommodation, plus shops for stocking up on supplies if you are tramping.
51km northwest of Nelson, reached via Highway 6 and then Highway 60.

Nelson

Nelson is a bright, breezy city humming with activity, particularly arts and crafts, as many potters have been drawn here by the availability of good local clay. You can explore Nelson's numerous galleries and workshops with the 'Arts Trail and Gallery Guide' leaflet (available at the Information Centre), or by taking an Arts Trail Guided Walk.

A good place to browse is at **Craft Habitat**, with its ceramics, stained glass, weaving, and jewellery workshops. Crafts are also often on display alongside a fine collection of early colonial oils and watercolours in the **Suter Art Gallery**.

Nelson's **Christ Church Cathedral** stands at the end of the main thoroughfare, Trafalgar Street. Colonial architecture is represented by an early cob house, **Broadgreen House** (1855), whose interior has been restored in period style. Another historic homestead, **Isel House**, is surrounded by century-old trees, rhododendrons, and azaleas in the superb setting of Isel Park. Both are in the neighbouring suburb of Stoke, a 10-minute drive from the city centre.
Visitor Information Centre at Trafalgar & Halifax sts. Tel: (03) 548 2304.
Open: daily 7.15am–5pm (closes later in summer).
Craft Habitat: Just outside Richmond on SH6. Tel: (03) 544 7481. Open: weekdays 9am–5pm, weekends 10am–5pm.
Suter Art Gallery: Queen's Gardens, Bridge St. Tel: (03) 548 4699. Open: daily 10.30am–4.30pm. Admission charge.
Broadgreen House: 276 Nayland Rd, Stoke. Tel: (03) 547 7887. Open: Tue–Fri 10.30–4.30pm, weekends 1.30–4.30pm in summer. Admission charge.
Nelson Museum: Isel House, Isel Park, The Ridgeway, Stoke. Open: Tue–Fri 10am–4pm; weekends 2–5pm. Admission charge.

The World of Wearable Art and Collectable Car Complex

Opened in October 2001, this centre is home to the spectacular World of Wearable Art collection. It has been

built up since the Montana Wearable Art awards – an alternative fashion show – started in Nelson in 1987. The WOW gallery showcases garments from this collection; it features moving mannequins, and an Illumination Experience. The second gallery features an array of collectable cars from around the world displayed alongside the theatrical show from the fashion world.
Annesbrook, Nelson. Tel: (03) 548 9299: www.worldofwearablearts.co.nz
Open: daily (except Christmas Day).

Nelson Lakes National Park

The Nelson Lakes National Park covers 102,000 hectares of forests, mountains, and river valleys, and is perhaps best known for its two beautiful lakes, Rotoiti and Rotorua, which nestle beneath scenic alpine peaks.

The main gateway to the park is the tiny hamlet of St Arnaud, on the shores of Lake Rotoiti, which is beautiful in summer as in winter when the ski fields of the Rainbow Valley and Mount Robert beckon.

The lake is fringed by beech forests, and there are opportunities for boating, fishing, short walks, and picnics. Water taxis ply the lake for short cruises or drop-offs to hiking tracks.

Lake Rotorua has fewer facilities – and more sandflies – but is popular with fishermen after rainbow trout.
Nelson Lakes Transport tel: (03) 521 1802. Operates daily buses.
DOC Visitor Centre: View Rd, St Arnaud. Tel: (03) 521 1806. Open: daily 8am–4.30pm (longer during summer).
St Arnaud lies 119km southwest of Nelson on Highway 6, then along Highway 63.

Picton

Lying at the southernmost point of Queen Charlotte Sound, Picton is the terminus for the Cook Strait services and the starting point for exploring the Marlborough Sounds. If you are waiting for a ferry (or a launch to whisk you off to a secluded beach) there are a couple of places to visit.

Next to the ferry terminal are the remnants of the last-surviving convict ship of the British East India Company, the *Edwin Fox*, gradually being restored at the **Edwin Fox Museum**. Built in 1853, the teak-hulled ship carried troops to the Crimean War and convicts to Australia before ending up as a storage hulk in Picton's harbour. Also on the waterfront, the **Picton Museum** is worth a visit for its whaling relics.
Edwin Fox Museum: Dunbar Wharf. Tel: (03) 573 6868. Open: daily 9am–5pm. Admission charge.
Picton Museum: Waterfront. Tel: (03) 573 8283. Open: daily 10am–4pm. Admission charge.

The small port of Picton is the gateway to the extensive Marlborough Sounds

Walkway: Kaikoura Peninsula

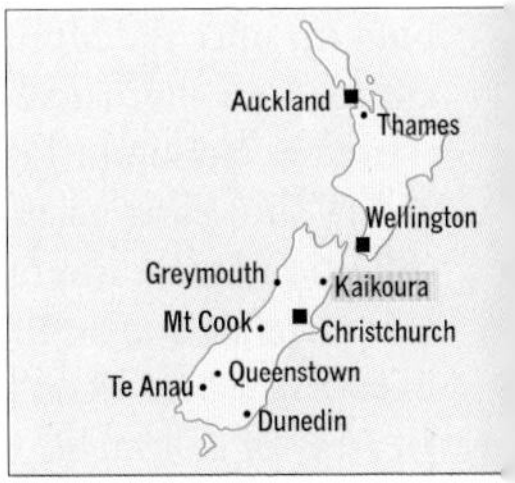

Kaikoura is renowned for its marine life (*see pp96–7*), and this walkway round the peninsula is a great way of getting close to New Zealand fur seals. The walkway also features ancient Maori stepped *pa* (fortified settlements), limestone caves, and wonderful views. This route follows the Clifftop Path (3.7km), returning along the Shoreline Path (4.5km). *Allow 2 hours each way, although the walk is easy and you can complete the circuit much faster if necessary.*

From Kaikoura, follow the Esplanade south for 5km until you arrive at Point Kean. Park here and take the path marked Clifftop Walk; the well-posted path is easy to follow.

1 Clifftop Walk

A short, steep climb up a zigzag path brings you to the grassy downlands on the cliff top, where the views stretch back inland to the Kaikoura Mountains and down the coast as far as the Banks Peninsula.

The grassy track is a good vantage point from which to observe the gull colonies below: around 10,000 adult red-billed gulls nest here, along with smaller colonies of black-backed gulls and white-fronted terns. This is a good place to spot waders such as turnstones, oystercatchers, and herons on the tidal platforms.

Continue on to Whalers Bay.

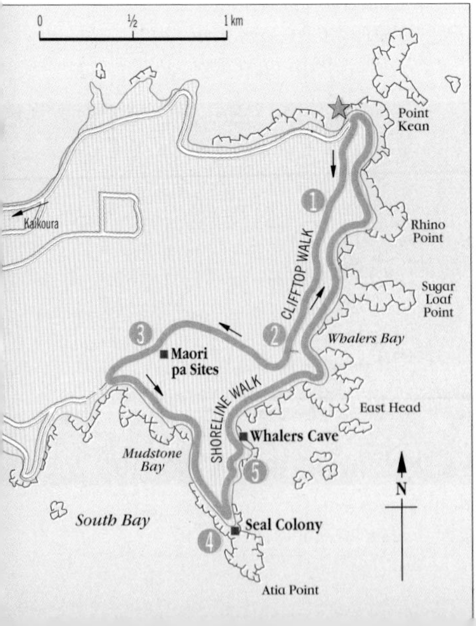

2 Whalers Bay

Whalers Bay once provided safe anchorage for whaling boats, and from the cliff top above the whalers watched and waited, looking for their quarry out to sea. The track used by the whalers to return to their boats descends the cliff face – you can use this as a short cut down to the Shoreline Walk if required.

Follow the signs for South Bay along the cliff top.

3 Maori Pa Sites

Taking advantage of the abundant seafood, the Ngati Toa occupied Kaikoura during the 16th century; they were driven south by the Ngai Tahu in the early 19th century, but during the intervening period they occupied at least 14 different *pa* sites on the peninsula. Some of these fortified settlements are clearly visible on this stretch of the track, the characteristic rounded hill tops edged with terracing.

Descend into South Bay, turning left where the tracks meet to follow the Shoreline Path.

4 Seal Colony

Skirting Mudstone Bay you come to Atia Point, which has one of the biggest seal colonies. Nearly 500 fur seals can be seen here during the winter months, but even in summer dozens of them bask on the rocks: they are so numerous you might have to scramble around the rocks to bypass them. Do not provoke the seals (especially large bulls or mothers with pups) as they may bite. Other seal colonies can be seen at **East Head** and **Point Kean**.

Continue around the base of the cliffs.

5 Hidden Caves and Limestone Outcrops

The peninsula is relatively young in geological terms, and the limestone base has been pounded by the sea into many weird and wonderful formations – particularly at **Atia Point**, which is best appreciated if you look back at it from the succeeding bays. This next section is also riddled with limestone caves, some of which connect one small bay to the next. One of the biggest caves is **Whalers Cave**, partially obscured by trees at the back of Whalers Bay.

Cross Whalers Bay, and continue past Sugar Loaf Point and Rhino Point to return to the car park via Point Kean.

Tread carefully – you might bump into a seal pup

Central South Island

Separated from one another by the Southern Alps, the western and eastern coasts of central South Island are as different as chalk and cheese. Hemmed in by the Alps on one side and the Tasman Sea on the other, the west coast is a rugged, wild strip of land where the one constant factor is the almost incessant rain, though between showers you will be rewarded with magnificent views of jagged Alpine peaks, tumbling waterfalls, tranquil lakes, and the spectacular glaciers descending into the rainforests at Fox and Franz Josef. The east coast is cultivated plains.

The Southern Alps aglow at sunset

In the heady gold-rush days of the 1860s, the west coast was one of the busiest, wealthiest areas in the country. Around Ross and Greymouth you can still try your hand at gold fossicking, or see how the experts do it at the re-created Shantytown. The west coast is also rich in greenstone (nephrite jade) or *pounamu*, which was traded by the Maori from the earliest times. In the coastal town of Hokitika, skilled craftspeople still work this beautiful mineral.

Further south, the Westland coastline reaches an appropriate end in the pristine rainforests and coastal lagoons of the almost untouched World Heritage Area surrounding Haast.

The east coast, in comparison, is intensively cultivated. Lying between the plains and the pounding Pacific surf is the city of Christchurch, the second major gateway into New Zealand. To the southeast of Christchurch is the Banks Peninsula – a curious outcrop of land formed from the remnants of two sunken volcanoes – with many bays and

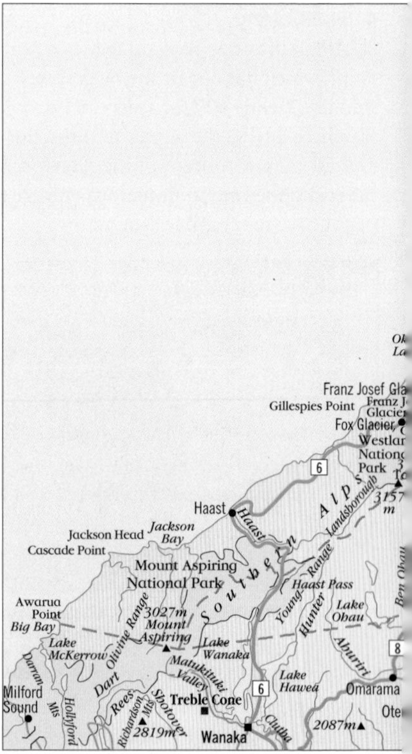

beaches to explore, and Akaroa, a former French settlement, the most southerly in the world.

Looping across the Canterbury Plains are many shallow, shingle-bed rivers that were almost impossible to navigate until a local engineer invented the jet-boat, now a common a feature of outdoor adventure in New Zealand. The Rakaia and Waimakariri rivers are popular for jet-boating.

Finally, there are the Southern Alps. Most visitor facilities here are in the breathtaking **Mount Cook National Park** and around the shores of the sparkling blue glacial lakes of Pukaki and Tekapo. Here, too, is the mightiest glacier in the Southern Hemisphere, the 27km **Tasman**, where ski-planes land on a regular basis. The more adventurous can ski down the glacier, weather conditions permitting, accompanied by a guide.

Central South Island

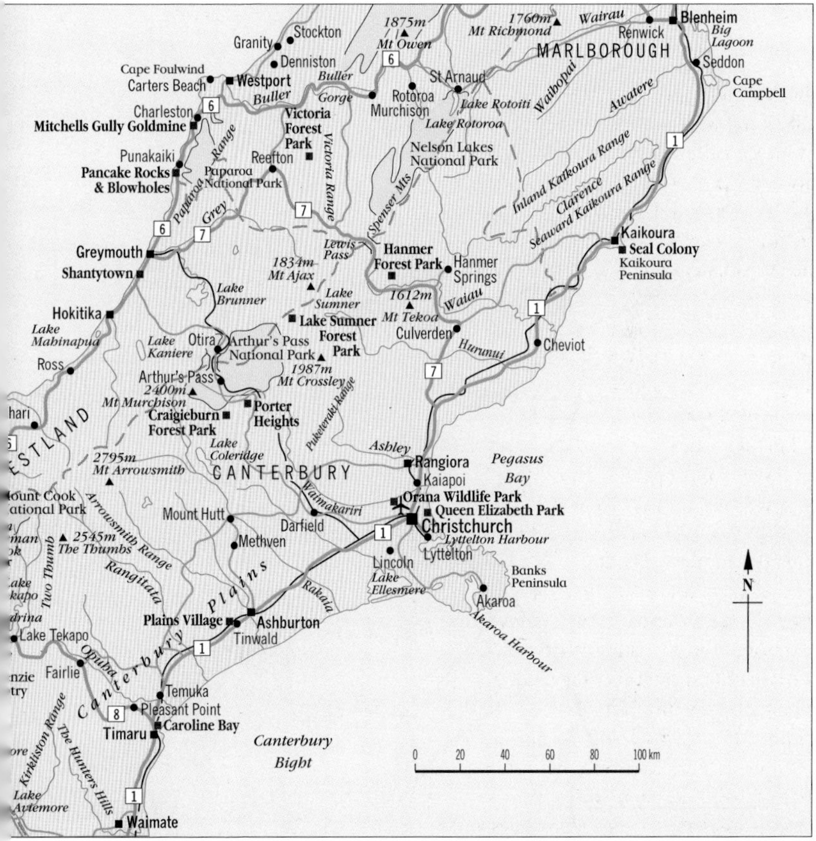

Christchurch

Christchurch is the South Island's largest city and is also one of the liveliest and most attractive in the country. It has long enjoyed the epithet of a 'garden city', with numerous leafy parks and gardens providing a relaxing backdrop to the well laid-out city centre. An added bonus is the delightful Avon River

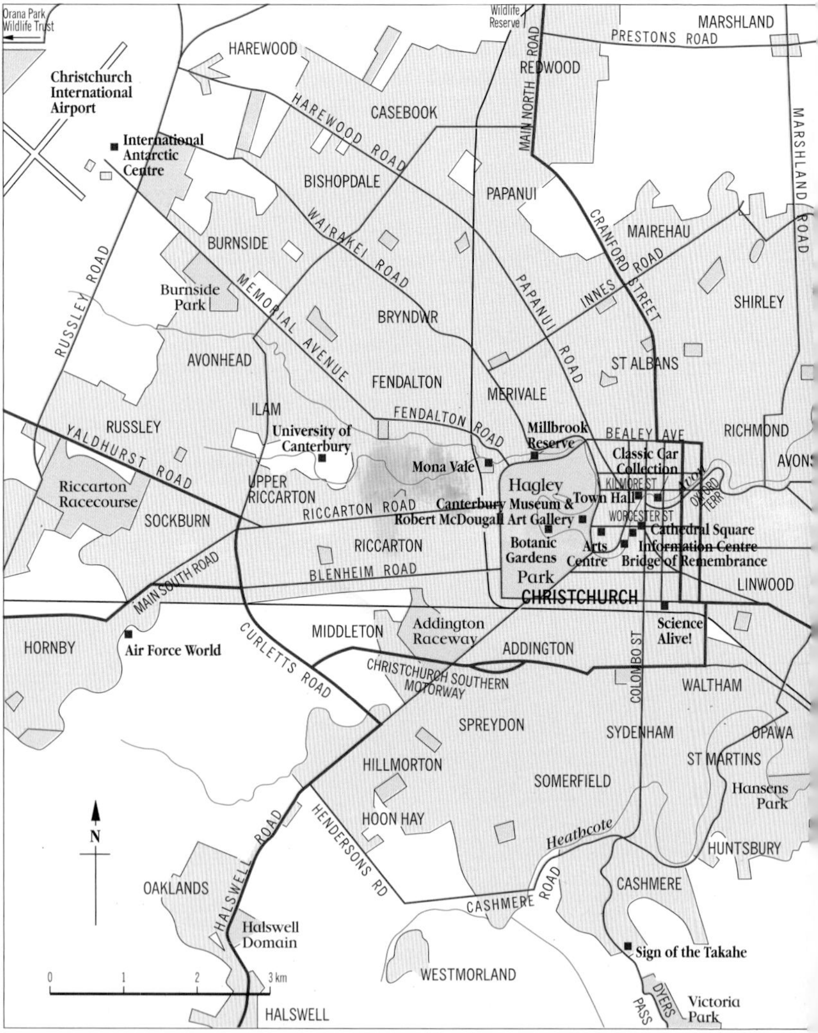

meandering between the city's Gothic stone buildings. Streetside cafés and trendy wine bars have mushroomed in recent years, adding to the vitality of streetlife, and complementing a vibrant arts scene with numerous festivals and

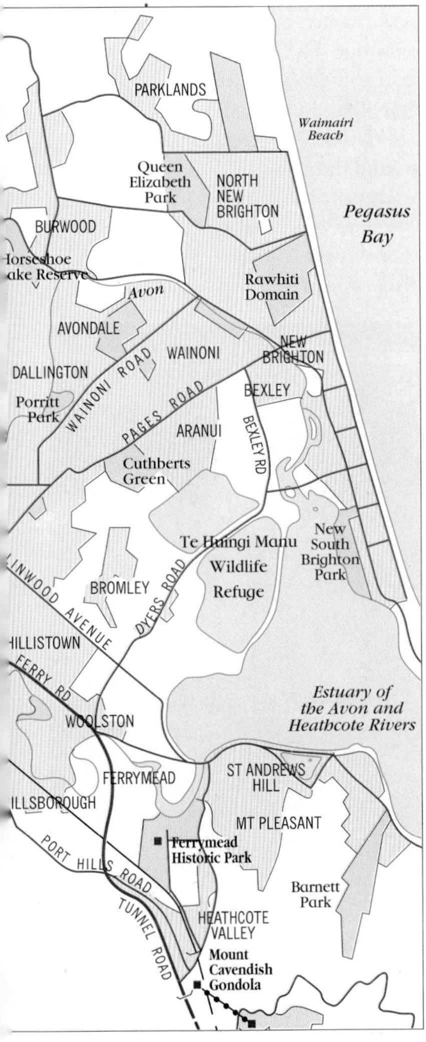

drama and music performances. Christchurch is also said to be the most English city in New Zealand. The first four ships carrying the so-called Canterbury Pilgrims arrived at Lyttelton Harbour in 1850, and the newcomers soon established clubs for the very English pastimes of rowing, archery, lawn tennis, and cricket.

Today, Christchurch has something of a reputation for breeding eccentricity and individualism. Creativity, however, is the flip side of the same coin, and the city has produced enormous numbers of talented craftspeople, whom you can see at work in the vast Arts Centre complex.

Christchurch is a city made for walking; many of the top sights are within easy reach of Cathedral Square. The historic tram network which follows a route around the central city is another option and there are also excellent bus services to outlying areas.

Outdoor enthusiasts reckon that, after Queenstown, there is no better place in the South Island than Christchurch to live in. Pacific Ocean beaches are close by, the Southern Alps are less than an hour's drive away for rock climbing, mountain biking, river rafting, and the like, and in the winter, there are 12 ski fields from which to choose. Taking advantage of the extensive Canterbury Plains to the west of the city, Christchurch has also become a major centre for hot-air ballooning.

Finally, Christchurch is the gateway to the Banks Peninsula (*see pp120–21*) and the starting point for the famous TranzAlpine Express rail route across the Southern Alps (*see pp124–5*).

Air Force World

This museum won a tourism design award in 1991 for the realistic-looking tableaux that surround many of the 28 classic aircraft exhibits. There are also plenty of hands-on exhibits, video shows, and a hall devoted to New Zealand military aviation.

Wigram RNZAF Base, Main South Rd. 20 minutes from downtown. Tel: (03) 343 9532. Open: daily 10am–5pm. Hangar tours: daily 11am, 1pm, & 3pm. Admission charge. Buses: 5, 51, 81, & 82.

Arts Centre

Housed in a rambling complex of Neo-Gothic buildings (once the home of the University of Canterbury), the Arts Centre is a lively mix of galleries, shops, studios and theatres, and cafés, bars and restaurants. You can wander around peering into small workshops or browsing in half a dozen galleries, then drop in on a lunchtime concert, a dance performance, or a foreign-movie screening. The festive weekend crafts market is also well worth visiting, with more than 100 arts and crafts stalls, live entertainment, and exotic foods from around the world.

Worcester Blvd. Tel: (03) 366 0989. Open: weekdays, summer 9.30am–5pm; winter 10am–4.30pm; weekend market 10am–4pm. Free admission.

A punt glides along the tranquil River Avon in the heart of Christchurch

A giant chess set in Cathedral Square

Avon River
Winding through the heart of the city, with oaks and willows lining its banks, the Avon adds immeasurably to the enchantment of Christchurch. A good way to get to know the city from this different viewpoint is on a sedate punting trip; alternatively, you can hire a canoe or paddle-boat.
Punt trips depart from behind the Information Centre. Tel: (03) 379 9629 for bookings. Canoes and paddle-boats may be hired at the Antigua Boat Sheds, 2 Cambridge Terrace. Tel: (03) 366 5885.

Botanic Gardens
The 30-hectare Botanic Gardens, bounded on three sides by the River Avon, are ideal for a relaxing stroll: extensive lawns and bedding displays provide the backdrop to a huge variety of exotic plants. The first trees were planted in 1863, and the collection now encompasses special sections for native plants, heathers, roses, herbs, water plants, primulas, plus a conservatory complex with exotic species.
Rolleston Ave. Tel: (03) 366 1701. Grounds open: daily 7am until one hour before sunset. Free admission. Conservatories open: 10.15am–4pm. Tours on a mini-train depart daily 11am–4pm from the northern end of the gardens, from where guided tours are also available. Admission charge.

Canterbury Museum
Housed within a historic building, the museum has displays on Antarctica (Hall of Antarctic Discovery) and New Zealand birds, an award-winning Maori gallery, and an Arts of Asia gallery. Being developed are Whalespace (with a magnificent blue whale skeleton), a second Maori gallery, and a section on colonial arts and costumes.
Rolleston Ave. Tel: (03) 366 5000. Open: daily 9am–5.30pm, until 5pm in winter. General admission free. Guided tours (donations) four times daily.

Cathedral Square
This spacious, pedestrianised square is a great place to while away a sunny day. This is where you will find the main Visitor Centre, at the Old Post Office, Cathedral Square (*tel: (03) 379 9629*). Atheists and the faithful mount their stepladders to battle it out verbally in front of amused crowds on the cathedral's steps – this is the city's free speech corner, where anything and everything goes. Watch out for the famous Wizard, so adept an orator-performer that he has been classified as a 'living work of art' (usually, not always, he turns up at 1pm every day). A regular crafts market and a clutch of stalls selling ethnic food add to the colour of the city's main focal point.

Christchurch Cathedral

Built over a period of 40 years and completed in 1904, the cathedral is in Neo-Gothic style and is worth visiting for the climb (133 steps) to the top of its bell tower, which has good views of the city centre.
Cathedral Square. Tel: (03) 366 0046. Guided tours: weekdays 11am & 2pm, Sat 11am, Sun 11.30am. Tower open: daily 8.30am–4pm. Admission charge to tower.

Ferrymead Heritage Park

The two separate sites of this park (linked by tramway) contain old locomotives and historic vehicles, a replica Edwardian township, a fire-fighting display, and other transport-related exhibits.
Ferrymead Park Drive. Tel: (03) 384 1970. Open: daily 10am–4.30pm. Admission charge. Buses 3H or H28 run from downtown.

International Antarctic Centre

Christchurch has been one of the principal gateways to the frozen south since Scott's famous expeditions, and the International Antarctic Centre (next to the airport) is now the main supply and administration base for the New Zealand, American, and Italian Antarctic programmes. The award-winning visitor centre within the complex includes a compelling and dramatic audio-visual show, a recreation of the current Scott Base, the world's only polar aquarium, the Antarctic Hägglund Ride Snowphone™, an ice cave, and plenty of hands-on exhibits. This is a highly recommended stop.
Orchard Rd, Christchurch Airport. 20 minutes by car from downtown. Tel: (03) 353 7798 or toll-free 0508 4846. Open: daily, summer 9am–8pm, winter 9am–5.30pm. Admission charge.

The Neo-Gothic cathedral dominates Cathedral Square in Christchurch

Mount Cavendish Gondola

The gondola scales the city side of the Port Hills to the 500m Mount Cavendish summit, from where you get spectacular views of Christchurch and the Banks Peninsula. Within the complex, the **Time Tunnel** recounts the history of the area with innovative displays, including a volcanic area which exudes hot air, and a superb mock-up (complete with musty smells) of below-decks in an immigrant ship. There is a shop and a licensed restaurant.
10 Bridle Path Rd, Heathcote. Tel: (03) 384 0700. Open: daily 10am until late evening. Admission charge. Regular shuttles from the Information Centre, or bus 28, or the City Circuit Bus.

Orana Park Wildlife Trust

This open-plan, 80-hectare zoo lies to the northwest of the city. There is a drive-through lion enclosure, and a huge 40-hectare African plains area. Catch the lion-feeding time at 2.30pm every day.

The Native Fauna and Flora Zone contains a kiwi house, a reptile house, and aviaries with rare species such as the Antipodes Island parakeet and the *kaka*.

McLeans Island Rd, Harewood, 20 minutes from downtown.
Tel: (03) 359 7109. Open: daily from 10am. Admission charge.

Science Alive!

Discovering science and technology through play and hands-on fun and experimentation is the key theme of this extensive display, aimed at all age groups from pre-teens to adults. Special exhibits often have a local flavour.

392 Moorhouse Ave. A 10-minute walk from the square. Tel: (03) 365 5199. Open: weekdays 9am–5pm, weekends 10am–6pm. Admission charge. Bus: 12 from Cathedral Square.

Willowbank Wildlife Reserve

This small, well laid-out park focuses on indigenous wildlife, although it also has monkeys, camels, and other introduced species, and a farmyard section containing rare breeds of colonial animals such as *kuni kuni* pigs. An unusual feature is the floodlit, night-time viewing, when you can see kiwis and other nocturnal species in their natural bush setting; There is an award winning restaurant and guided tours are free to dinner guests (*see p170*).

Hussey Rd, 15 minutes from downtown.
Tel: (03) 359 6226. Open: daily 10am–10pm. Admission charge.

A ride in the Mount Cavendish gondola provides spectacular views

Sheep

It is an often-quoted fact that there are 20 sheep for every person in New Zealand and, with nearly 45.5 million sheep compared with 3.5 million people, this figure is not far off the mark.

It was Captain Cook who landed the first sheep in New Zealand, but the two merinos didn't last long, and it wasn't until 1834 that the first sizeable flock arrived. The first major 'runs' (as ranches are called here) were in the North Island, but sheep farming developed even more rapidly in the South Island, where there was less forest to clear.

Fortunes had been made from wool exports, but falling prices in the 1880s jeopardised this lucrative commodity. However, refrigerated shipping was invented just in time, and when the Dunedin sailed for Britain in 1882 loaded with sheep carcasses, it marked a new era in the country's export trade. With the subsequent increase in meat exports, the merino was gradually replaced by hardy Romneys, great producers of fat lambs. As the wool of the Romney is far coarser than the fine fleece of the merino, production switched to those industries which require stronger, more resilient wools such as the carpet industry. The biggest farms today are in the South Island, spread over vast

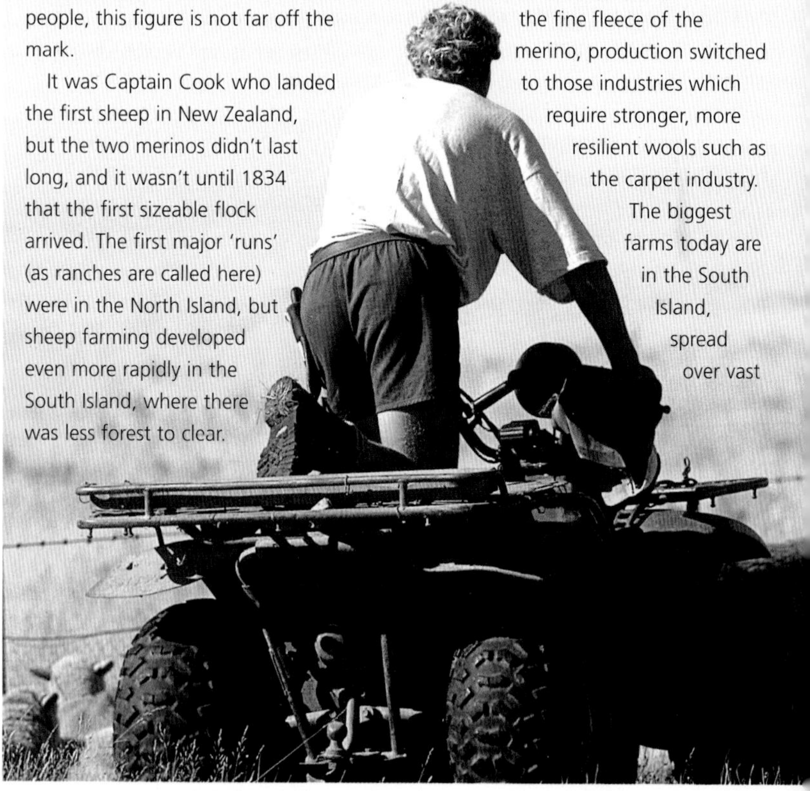

areas of comparatively poor land which supports low densities of sheep. These high-country stations often run up to 12,000 or more sheep, so mustering the flocks and bringing them down before the winter snows arrive is a major part of the farming calendar. Previously, this would have been done on horseback, but modern shepherds are more likely to use rugged, all-terrain motorbikes to get around.

Perched on the back of the bike or running alongside will be the shepherd's trusty sheepdogs. Descended from border collie stock, there are two main types: first, there is the 'heading' or 'eye' dog, which prowls silently around the sheep, fixing them with its stare and heading them in the right direction; second, there is the big, noisy 'huntaway', which controls the flocks by barking loudly. Finally, there are the all-important sheepshearers, who usually travel together in gangs from station to station. A good shearer can clip up to 300 sheep a day, although the record is an astonishing 831 sheep in nine hours. The average fleece yields around 4.5kg of wool.

Sheep farming is an important component in the New Zealand economy; agricultural shows have displays of a variety of breeds of sheep, as seen above

Franz Josef and Fox Glaciers

These two vast glaciers lie at the heart of the Westland National Park, which stretches from the coastline up to the highest peaks in New Zealand. The glaciers are unusual in that they extend right down through the forest into the temperate coastal zone, a phenomenon found nowhere else in the world.

The 12-km long Franz Josef (named after the Austrian emperor by explorer Julius Haast in 1864) and Fox (named after the country's prime minister, Sir William Fox, in 1871) are the two largest glaciers of the 140 that lie within the Westland National Park. Close to the bottom of each glacier are the respective villages of Franz Josef and Fox; the constant 'thud-thud' of helicopters taking off from helipads attests to the popularity of aerial sightseeing, with helicopter companies and ski-plane operators offering rides to the top of each glacier. A handful of restaurants,

A helicopter trip is a great way to experience the glaciers

motels, and shops provide for everyday needs alongside the helicopter booking offices.

From either village you can drive or walk out to the 'snout' of each glacier. Looming above, the towering blocks of ice (known as seracs) lie dramatically jumbled together, creaking and heaving as blocks split and tumble into the moraine below. The Franz Josef Glacier moves at an exceptionally fast rate of 1.5m to 3.5m per day, depending on the snowfall.

There are several interesting walks in the surrounding forests (details from the DOC centre), as well as twice-daily guided walks on to the glacier itself. The Fox Glacier is unusual in that blocks of ice remain buried beneath rock debris downstream of the terminal face, melting to create the milky grey or translucent blue kettle lakes – including the picturesque Lake Matheson (just south of the village along a short forest track) – that lie dotted around the bed of the Fox River. Stunning views of the peaks of Mount Cook and Mount Tasman are reflected in the waters.

Franz Josef is 172km south of Hokitika, and 273km north of Wananka. Fox is 25km further down Highway 6.

Guided walks on the glaciers (do not attempt them on your own) are run by Franz Josef Glacier Guides (tel: toll-free 0800 484 337) and Alpine Guides Fox Glacier (tel: toll-free 0800 111 600).

The Westland National Park headquarters in Franz Josef (tel: (03) 752 0796) has information leaflets on walks and a display on glaciers. Open: daily, Nov–Apr 8.30am–7pm; May–Oct 9am–5pm.

Helicopter 'flightseeing' available through Glacier Scenic Helicopters (Franz Josef, tel: toll-free 0800 800 732, & (03) 752 0755); Fox and Franz Josef Heliservices (tel: toll-free 0800 800 793); The Helicopter Line (tel: toll-free 0800 807 767). Mount Cook Ski Planes (tel: toll-free 0800 800 702, & (03) 435 10260) also operates ski-plane flights.

Hopeful visitors pan for gold at Shantytown, outside Greymouth

Greymouth

This former gold and coal centre, today the main commercial centre and largest town on the west coast, is known locally simply as 'Grey'; the tag can seem particularly appropriate on a typically rainy west coast day. **Shantytown**, just outside Greymouth, is a replica 1880s town set in native bushland on the site of a former goldfield. The township features an old bank, a bootshop, printing works, a blacksmiths', a fire station, a 'Chinese den', and a fascinating colonial hospital. Other attractions include a steam-train ride through the bush to an old wooden railway station,

gold panning, stagecoach, and a working replica sawmill.
Greymouth is 105km south of Westport on Highway 6, 256km from Christchurch. Shantytown, Paroa, is 10km from Greymouth, signposted off Highway 6. Tel: (03) 762 6634. Open: daily 8.30am–5pm. Admission charge.

Haast

Since Haast lies at the southernmost end of the Westland coastline, it is usually thought of as little more than a staging post for the Haast Pass across the Southern Alps into Otago. That's about to change, though, as the Haast area wins recognition for its magnificent rainforests, coastal lagoons, and wetlands (the most extensive in the country).

The region was designated the South West New Zealand World Heritage Area by UNESCO in 1991, and the excellent World Heritage Visitor Centre was opened on the banks of the Haast River in 1993. The centre has first-rate displays on early Maori settlers, the abundant local wildlife, swamp forests, and the unique sand-dune forests nearby. The staff also provides information on local walks, jet-boating on the Haast River, fishing (the coastal lagoons are renowned for their whitebait), hiking, and helicopter rides.
120km southwest of Fox Glacier, 345km southwest of Greymouth.
Visitor Centre: corner of SH6 & Jackson Bay Rd, Haast. Tel: (03) 750 0809. Open: daily 8.30am–4pm.

Hanmer Springs

These thermal springs, first discovered by Maori hunters who named them Waitapu or 'Sacred Waters', were rediscovered by a local farmer in 1859. By the turn of the 19th century, the springs were the focus of a popular sanatorium. Today, the springs are incorporated into a modern, open-air resort complex, the **Hanmer Springs Thermal Reserve**, located in the centre of this tranquil little alpine village. If you want some action and adventure before soaking away your aches and pains in the pools, the area offers an enormous number of activities from golf to rafting, fishing, bungee-jumping, climbing, and horse-trekking, and plenty of walking trails (details available from the information centre).
Hanmer Springs is 136km north of Christchurch.
Thermal Reserve: Jacksons Pass Rd, Hanmer Springs. Tel: (03) 315 7511. Open: daily 10am–9pm. Admission charge.

Jet-boating is just one of many adventure activities around Hanmer Springs

Hurunui Visitor Information Centre: 42 Amuri Ave West, Hanmer Springs. Tel: (03) 315 7128. Open: daily, summer 10am–6pm; winter 10am–4.30pm.

Hokitika

The next major town south of Greymouth is Hokitika, first settled by Maori in search of greenstone and later by Europeans in the gold rush of the 1860s. Today, life centres around farming, fishing, and tourism, although some gold-mining is still carried out.

Hokitika is an attractive town which has become a focus for local craftspeople and is also well known as a centre for greenstone carving. There are several workshops in town where you can watch these massive blocks being shaped and fashioned into intricate designs for pendants, sculptures, and so on; this is a fascinating process, and it costs nothing to wander about, watching the greenstone carvers at work. There are numerous other outlets in town for pottery, textiles, wood carvings, and hand-crafted jewellery made from gold nuggets found in the area.

The history of the area is narrated in the **West Coast Historical Museum**, where a well-constructed audio-visual show covers both greenstone and gold discoveries in the region, among the other displays.

Just south of town is the **Phelp's Gold Mine**. It has displays on old-time gold-mining, and on modern, large-scale mining. There are also bush walks through old mine workings and tunnels.

Hokitika is 46km south of Greymouth on Highway 6.
West Coast Historical Museum: Tancred St. Tel: (03) 755 6898.
Open: daily 9.30am–5pm.
Admission charge.
Phelp's Gold Mine: 2km south of town on Highway 6. Tel: (03) 755 7766.
Open: daily 9am–5pm. Admission charge.
Visitor Centre: corner of Hamilton & Tancred sts. Tel (03) 755 6166.

Open-air thermal pools at Hanmer Springs

Mount Cook National Park

Covering just over 70,000 hectares, the Mount Cook National Park runs in a narrow strip down the eastern side of the Southern Alps. Within this relatively small area are located 22 of New Zealand's 27 highest peaks, including, of course, the best-known, Mount Cook itself. This is an area of great natural beauty, where alpine scrub and forests are interspersed with glacial lakes that reflect the snow-capped crests soaring above. The park also includes the impressive 28-km long Tasman Glacier, the largest glacier in the Southern Hemisphere outside of Antarctica.

Known as Aoraki by the Maori, Mount Cook was renamed by Captain Stokes who sighted it from his survey ship in 1851. Rev. Green, an Irishman, was the first to attempt to climb the peak in 1882, but storms prevented him from reaching the summit; eventually three New Zealanders (Fyfe, Graham, and Clarke) conquered Mount Cook in 1894. Sir Edmund Hillary trained here before becoming the first man to climb Mount Everest in 1953.

This is one of the finest mountaineering regions in the world, with well-equipped high-level mountain huts for climbers' use. Walkers are restricted to the valley floor, but there are still some superb short walks near the base (*see pp122–3*).

The central focus of the national park is Mount Cook village, where there is a youth hostel, a campsite, self-contained chalets, and the famous Hermitage Hotel. The visitor centre can provide climbers with details on hut fees, routes, and weather conditions.

Inside Mount Cook National Park

More than 300 species of plants are to be found within the park, including the famed Mount Cook lily (*Ranunculus lyallii*), the largest buttercup in the world. Of the 40 species of birds, the most noticeable is the *kea*, known for pilfering hikers' belongings. Hunting of the Himalayan thar and European chamois (species of goat – both of which destroy vegetation) is encouraged.

Skiing is possible from July to October, but the only way up to the available slopes is by ski-plane or helicopter. The most spectacular run is the descent of the Tasman Glacier, suitable only for experienced and advanced snowboarders or skiers.

Aerial sightseeing is another popular option and provides opportunities for some breathtaking photographs of the peaks and glaciers. Mount Cook Airlines offers a number of options with snow landings, as well as a 'grand circle' tour which crosses the Alps over to the Franz Josef and Fox glaciers. Helicopter flights are also available.

333km west of Christchurch.

Visitor Centre: Bowen Drive, Mount

Cook. Tel: (03) 435 1895. Open: daily 8am–5pm, until 7pm in summer.
Department of Conservation: Mount Cook. Tel: (03)435 1186.
Air New Zealand: Mount Cook Airport. Tel: (03) 435 1849. Note: petrol can be obtained in Mount Cook only by credit card with a valid PIN number.

Paparoa National Park

The coastal road between Westport and Greymouth is at its most spectacular as it passes the fringes of the Paparoa National Park, located about halfway between the two towns. Created in 1987, the national park covers around 30,000 hectares.

On the coastal strip, steep limestone cliffs plunge down to the sea, creating a subtropical microclimate where tree ferns and *nikau* palms thrive. Inland, the park is a virtually untouched wilderness with unusual limestone karst formations, large caves, and waterfalls.

The undisturbed nature of Paparoa means that it is a good area for bird-watching (tuis, fantails, grey warblers, New Zealand pigeons, and bellbirds are commonly spotted).

At the heart of the park is the Paparoa Range, a rugged series of peaks and pinnacles covered in virtually impenetrable bush and often shrouded in clouds. The best-known walking route through the park is the Inland Pack Track, but there are also several short walks which start from Punakaiki. For details on the local DOC visitor centre and how to reach the park, *see* Punakaiki, *p118*.

Steep limestone cliffs border the coastal edge of Paparoa National Park

Punakaiki

Punakaiki is best known for its extraordinary Pancake Rocks, reached by a short, 15-minute walk from the main road, suitable even for wheelchairs. The stratified coastal limestone here has been weathered into a dramatic formation that looks just like a stack of giant pancakes; in rough conditions the sea forces itself up through fissures in the 'pancakes' to form spectacular blowholes.

The DOC visitor centre at Punakaiki provides details on short walks in the area which lead back into the rainforests of the Paparoa National Park (*see p117*).
Punakaiki is 57km south of Westport, 47km north of Greymouth on Highway 6. The DOC Visitor Centre is on the main road. Tel: (03) 731 1893. Open: daily 8am–4.30pm (closes later in summer).

Ross

Early prospectors descended on Ross in their thousands at the turn of the last century to fossick in the creeks running down from Mount Greenland. The Ross Historic Goldfields lie just off the highway through town. At the entrance of the old Bank of New South Wales building (1870) is the information centre. Just across from the centre is the **Miner's Cottage**, dating back to 1885.

The Jones Flat Walkway leads from the information centre up to the old workings. which include miles of intertwined water races and dams used to bring water to the sluicing claims.
Ross is 30km southwest of Hokitika. Information centre tel: (03) 755 4077. Open: daily 9am–4pm (until late in summer).

Tekapo

This small settlement straddles the road leading from the Mount Cook National Park back down to the coast, and where the Tekapo River drains out of the 20-km long Lake Tekapo, with the first of the hydroelectric stations linked to the Waitaki river system. Surrounded by tussock-clad hills, the milky turquoise lake is noted for its trout fishing.

On the edge of Tekapo is the famous **Church of the Good Shepherd**, a sublime stone-clad chapel erected as a memorial to pioneer farmers in the area.
105km west of Timaru.

Timaru

This large coastal port city, lying roughly midway between Christchurch and Dunedin, is famous for its annual carnival, which takes place on sandy Caroline Bay for three weeks at Christmas.
164km south of Christchurch, 202km north of Dunedin.

Twizel

This town, established as the centre for the upper Waitaki Valley hydroelectric development, lies just half an hour's drive from Mount Cook village, making it a convenient base for exploring the national park and the surrounding Waitaki River and Mackenzie Basin. The road from Twizel to Mount Cook runs alongside lovely Lake Pukaki, one of the four Mackenzie Basin lakes.

Just outside town is the Black Stilt (or *kaki*) Aviary, a DOC centre for a breeding programme aimed at saving this endangered species. Once common throughout New Zealand, the black

stilt's habitat is now confined to the Mackenzie Basin. One-hour guided tours include close-up views of captive stilts and explanations of the breeding programme and rearing aviaries.
Twizel is 162km west of Timaru Black Stilt Aviary, 3km south of town on SH8. Aviary open: summer, daily from 10am; closed on weekends in winter. Admission charge. Tours must be booked in advance at the DOC Visitor Centre, Wairepo Rd, Twizel. Tel: (03) 435 3118/0802.

Westport

Gold-mining, and later coal-mining, formed the basis of Westport's prosperity. If you are passing through, there are some good exhibits on coal-mining in the aptly named Coaltown Museum.

Nearby **Cape Foulwind** is one of six breeding colonies on the west coast for the New Zealand fur seal. Walkways lead to a series of wooden platforms on the cliff tops, from where you can get a clear view of the seals below without disturbing them.
Westport is 105km north of Greymouth. Coaltown, Queen St South, signposted from the town centre. Tel: (03) 789 8204. Open: daily 8.30am–5.30pm, winter 9am–4.30pm. Admission charge.
Cape Foulwind is 12km west of town on Highway 65A.

The Pancake Rocks at Punakaiki are one of the most striking features of Paparoa National Park

Tour: Banks Peninsula

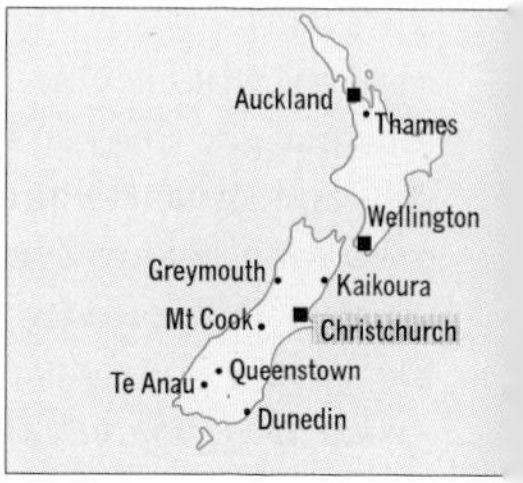

The Banks Peninsula is the site of the only attempt at a settlement by the French in New Zealand, and its offshore waters are home to one of the highest concentrations of the world's smallest and rarest marine dolphins, the Hector's dolphin.

Allow a full day for this 185km round trip from Christchurch.

Leave Christchurch on the SH75, following signs for Akaroa. Turning away from the sea past Little River, the road climbs up and over the crater rim, and descends into Barry's Bay.

1 Barry's Bay

Banks Peninsula was one of the first areas in New Zealand to produce cheese (commercial shipments were sent to Australia as early as the 1850s). This tradition continues today at the **cheese factory in Barry's Bay**, where you can watch cheese being made through the gallery window.

Continue around the bay to Akaroa.

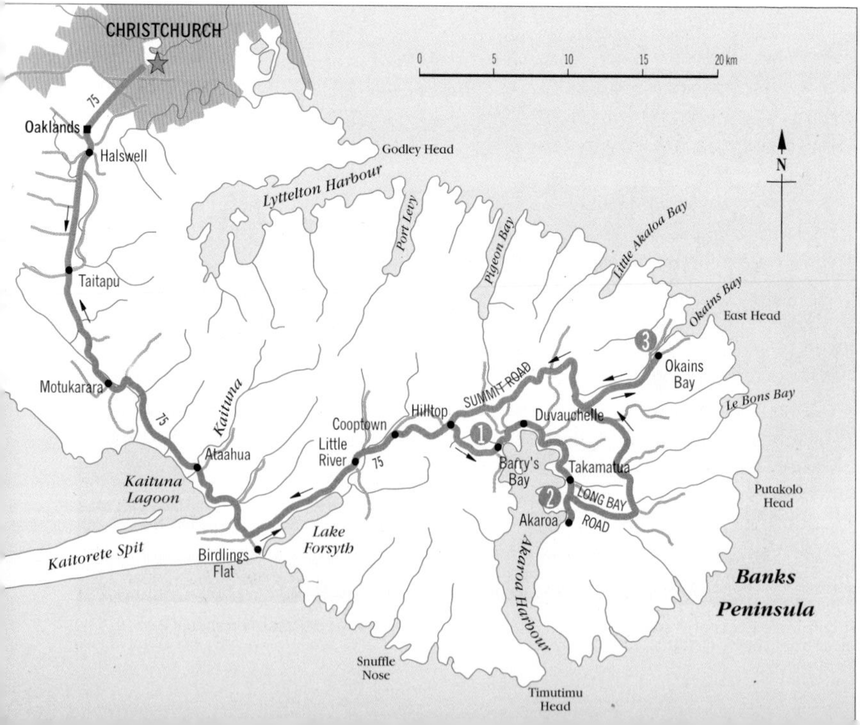

2 Akaroa

In 1838, Jean Langlois, captain of a whaling ship, negotiated to buy Banks Peninsula from the local Maori. He assembled a group of 63 colonists on his return to France, but by the time they arrived back in New Zealand the Maori had already ceded sovereignty to the British. The settlers still chose to remain, founding Akaroa. Today, this is a delightful township, with considerable emphasis placed on the French connection in the shops, bars, and restaurants.

One French colonist's home, the Langlois-Eteveneaux Cottage, now houses the small **Akaroa Museum**, with exhibits on Maori life on the peninsula and whaling. Further along the seafront, two plaques mark the landing site of the original settlers on 16 August 1840.

Nearby is a jetty from which you can take harbour cruises, with a reasonable chance of seeing some of the 600 to 700 Hector's dolphins that inhabit the harbour.

Turning back towards Barry's Bay, take Long Bay Rd, and follow the signs for Okains Bay, 19km from Akaroa.

3 Okains Bay

This lovely bay is a popular picnic spot, and the beach and lagoon provides safe, sheltered swimming.

In such a remote location it comes as a surprise to find a fascinating collection of artefacts in the **Maori and Colonial Museum**, located at the entrance to the village. This started as a private collection and has since grown to include a working blacksmith's shop, horse-drawn carriages, and an old 'slab cottage', built from large, adzed slabs of totara wood. The Maori collection is extraordinary and many rare objects are on display, including war weapons, flax cloaks, adzes, and an unusual and valuable 'god stick' dating back to AD 1400. There is also a war canoe (1867), and one of the only fully carved meeting-houses in the South Island.

Return to Christchurch along the panoramic Summit Rd, rejoining the SH75 at the Hilltop junction.

Rural surroundings of the Banks Peninsula

Barry's Bay Cheese Factory
Akaroa. *Tel: (03) 304 5809.* Open: weekdays 8am–5pm, weekends 9.30am–5pm, viewing only on alternate days between October and April.
Akaroa can also be reached on the Akaroa Shuttle (*tel: toll-free 0800 800 578*); twice-daily departures in each direction.

Akaroa Museum
Rue Lavaud and Rue Balguerie. *Tel: (03) 304 1013.* Open: daily 10.30am–4.30pm. Admission charge.

Maori and Colonial Museum
Okains Bay. *Tel: (03) 304 8611.* Open: daily 10am–5pm. Admission charge.

Walk: Hooker Valley

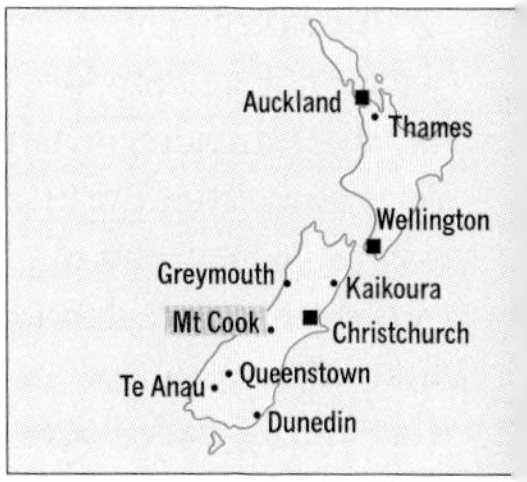

The Hooker Valley Walk is one of the loveliest walks in the Mount Cook National Park, with wonderful panoramas of the surrounding ranges and of Mount Cook itself. It runs along a gentle gradient, crossing the Hooker River twice on swingbridges, meandering through alpine pasturelands, and finishing at the lovely terminal lake below the Hooker Glacier. Most people return from here *(a 3- or 4-hour round trip)*, but if you haven't yet had your fill of views you can continue for a while longer up to the Hooker Hut *(allow another 2 hours)*.

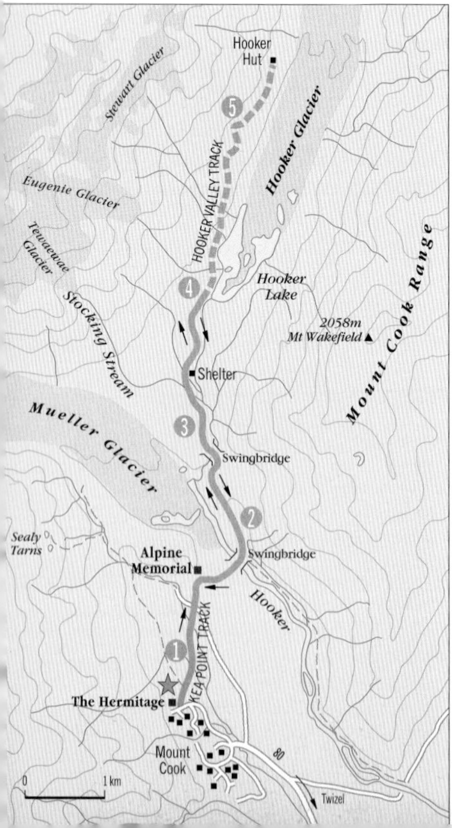

From the Hermitage, follow the Kea Point Track across the Hooker Flats, crossing the road and then joining the Hooker Valley Track.

1 Campsite to Hooker River

The path zigzags between tussock mounds past the site of the original Hermitage (1884–1913) before reaching the Alpine Memorial, which you can climb up to for good views of the Hooker Valley ahead. From the memorial, the track loops up and around low, hummocky hills of moraine (glacial debris), before arriving alongside the Hooker River. It should take you about an hour to complete this round trip.
Cross the first swingbridge.

2 Hooker Valley

Leading away to the left is the grey, debris-ridden expanse of the Mueller Glacier, with the mighty hanging glaciers and icefalls of Mount Sefton towering above it. The other peaks in the Main Divide of the Southern Alps curve round

on the north side of the Hooker Valley, with Mount Cook now visible at the head of the valley. The track continues beneath a series of small bluffs at the foot of Mount Wakefield before arriving at the second swingbridge. This is a two-hour round trip.
Cross the Hooker River again on the second swingbridge.

3 Alpine Pastures
The great ice faces of Mount Cook's southern flank dominate the view as the track leaves the Hooker River and crosses alpine pastureland to reach an open shelter at Stocking Stream, where there is an orientation table. Grasses and alpine plants cover the flatlands, with dense bushes clinging to the older moraine ridges above. In spring and summer these alpine meadows are a glorious profusion of buttercups (including the famous Mount Cook lily), giving way to daisies, and, in the autumn, gentians.
Continue on past the Stocking Stream shelter.

4 Hooker Lake and Glacier
A gentle climb alongside the river brings you to the terminal lake (the Hooker Lake) at the foot of the Hooker Glacier. Ice floes on the lake's waters create a photogenic foreground to the towering bulk of Mount Cook to the west.
Return the way you came or, if you have 4 hours for the round trip, continue up to the Hooker Hut.

5 Hooker Lake to Hooker Hut
The route follows the edge of the lake and then branches off diagonally upwards across the terminal moraine, marked by a series of cairns. The track crosses two side-streams on top of the moraine wall before zigzagging down to the hut in its sheltered basin. From here there are terrific views of Mount Cook, with the Noeline and Mona glaciers spilling down into the Hooker. The Hooker Hut is the starting point for the Copland Pass which crosses the Alps, but you should not proceed beyond here unless properly equipped.

Cairn beside the Hooker Glacier moraine lake with Mount Cook shrouded in clouds

Tour: TranzAlpine Express

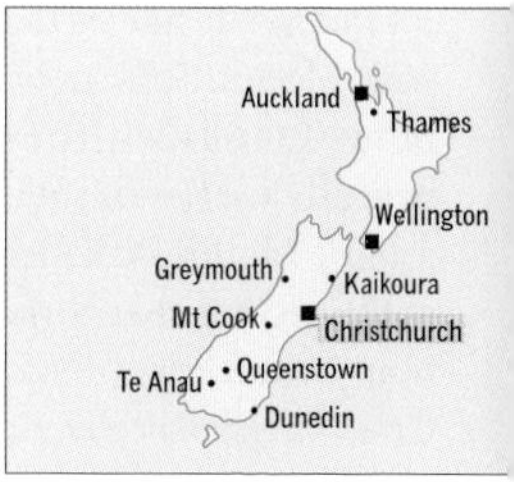

This 233-km journey from Christchurch to Greymouth is one of the classics of rail travel, connecting the two coastlines via the mountain passes of the Southern Alps on a narrow-gauge, single-track line which winds its way through tunnels and along impressive viaducts spanning deep canyons.

1 The Canterbury Plains

Leaving Christchurch station behind, the train crosses the rolling Canterbury Plains and passes through several small towns before halting at Springfield, the last stop before the climb into the mountains. The Southern Alps, dominated here by Mount Hutt (2,188m high), loom ahead.

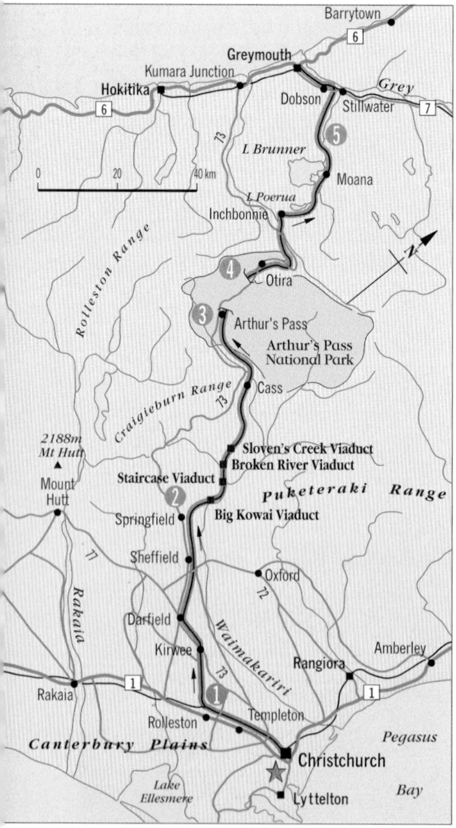

2 Springfield to Arthur's Pass

This is undoubtedly one of the most spectacular sections of the journey – try to get a seat on the right-hand side of the observation car if possible. The train soon crosses Big Kowai Viaduct, the first of five high viaducts that span rushing mountain torrents, and then enters the first of 16 tunnels chiselled through the rock. As you emerge from the sixth tunnel you will see the Waimakariri River way below, a raging blue-green snake twisting through the canyon. Next is Staircase Viaduct, the highest and most impressive on the line – at a height of 73m it could easily accommodate Christchurch Cathedral. All the tunnels on this route are relatively short (the longest, Tunnel 10, is just 600m long), although in the days of steam trains even these were long enough to nearly suffocate the footplate crews.

Once past Broken River Viaduct (with

spectacular views back down the Waimakariri River), the train clings to the northwest side of Broken River Gorge. Six tunnels are then passed in quick succession, before Sloven's Creek Viaduct is crossed and the broad, open valleys of the uplands are entered.

3 Arthur's Pass

This small township is the starting point for hikes into the surrounding Arthur's Pass National Park, and at 737m above sea level it is the highest railway station in New Zealand. Arthur's Pass was once the change-over point from steam to electric locomotives, as the next section is the steepest on the route.

4 Arthur's Pass to Otira

After a brief halt at Arthur's Pass, the TranzAlpine enters the 8.5-km long Otira Tunnel for the 400m descent to Otira; when it first opened in 1918 the tunnel was the longest in the British Empire, and seventh-longest in the world. The TranzAlpine cruises through in both directions with its diesel-electric locomotive, but coal trains making the long haul up from Greymouth to Arthur's Pass need up to four electric locomotives to overcome the gradient.

5 Otira to Greymouth

On the left after leaving Otira station you will see the escape track for runaway trains coming down from Arthur's Pass; this has been used at least twice, in 1957 and 1962, with locomotives failing to hold on the 1-in-33 grade track. From here on the contrast with the east coast landscapes is immediately apparent, the rainforests of Westland spreading out across the hillsides.

Arthur's Pass, a quiet but strategic halt on the TranzAlpine Express route

Skirting the edges of Lake Poerua and Lake Brunner, the TranzAlpine meets up with the west coast railway and follows the Grey River into Greymouth itself.

The TranzAlpine departs Christchurch at 9am daily, arriving in Greymouth at 1.25pm. The train stops at Arthur's Pass briefly at 11.27am, then continues on through the Otira Tunnel, returning to Christchurch approximately one hour after arriving in Greymouth. There is a full on-board buffet and bar service. Bookings can be made with any Tranzrail accredited travel agent or through Tranzrail central reservations (*tel: toll-free 0800 802 802*).

The Deep South

Known to the Maori as Muruhiku (the 'tail' of New Zealand), the Deep South encompasses a rich diversity of landscapes and attractions, ranging from the splendours of Milford Sound in the Fiordland National Park to the impressive architecture of Dunedin, historic gold-mining towns, and the rare wildlife of the Otago Peninsula and Stewart Island.

Almost the entire southwestern corner of the South Island is occupied by the massive Fiordland National Park, with its spectacular glaciated landscapes, inland lakes, and deep fiords.

The lakeside resort of Te Anau is one of the main access points to Fiordland, as is the busy resort of Queenstown on the shore of Lake Wakatipu. Outdoor adventures – from guided hiking to tranquil lake or fiord cruises – are well catered for, with Queenstown providing more thrills and spills than almost any other location in New Zealand.

Adjoining Fiordland is Southland, with the regional capital, Invercargill, serving as a springboard for Stewart Island (Rakiura), New Zealand's 140th and newest national park.

The Otago region has strong Scottish connections, a heritage evident in the well-preserved architecture of the regional capital, Dunedin. On the city's doorstep is the Otago Peninsula, where royal albatrosses and rare penguins can be seen at remarkably close quarters.

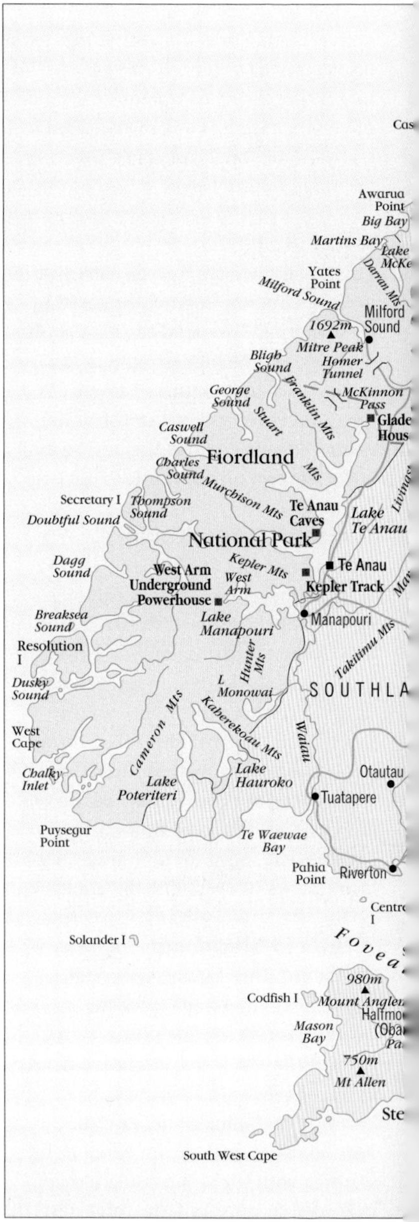

The Deep South

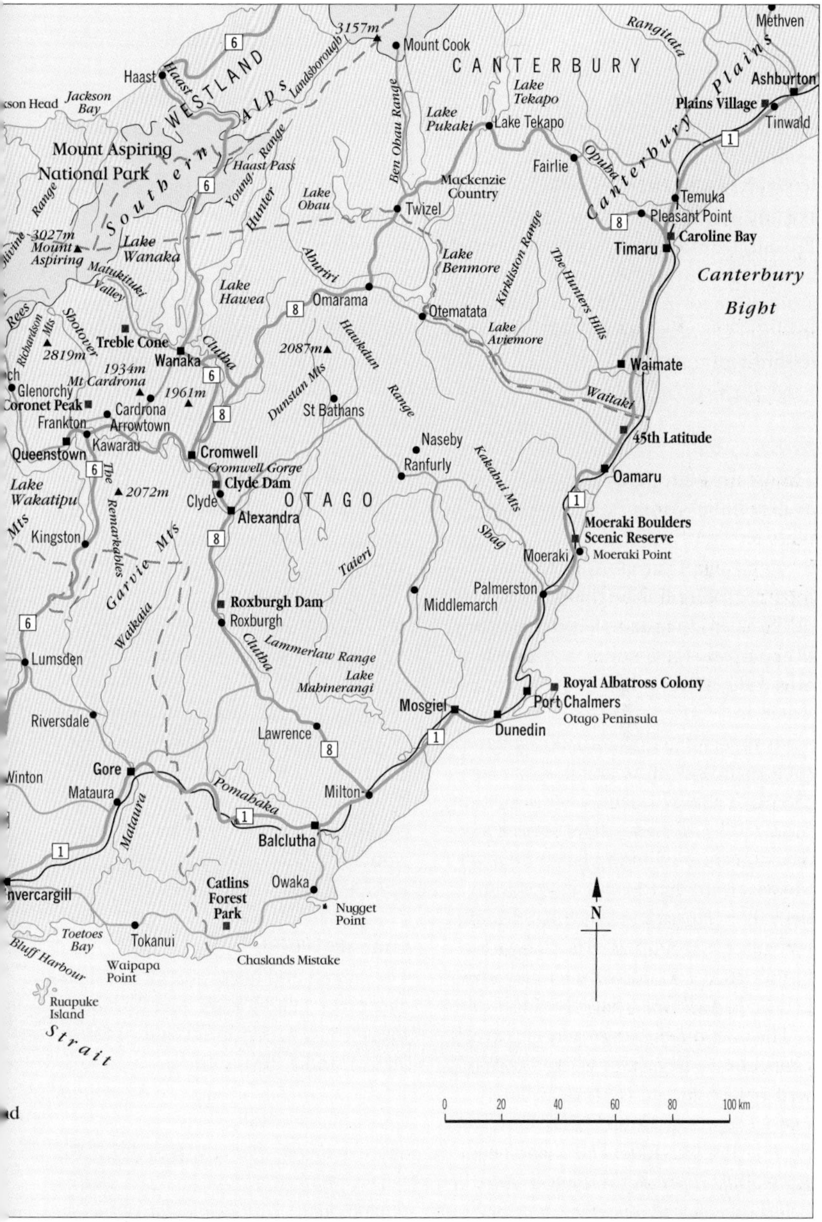

Alexandra

Built on the back of the Otago gold rushes, Alexandra later turned to fruit farming. It is a thriving service centre for the surrounding agricultural community. Tourism is also taking off, with adventure activities such as jet-boating and kayaking in the nearby Roxburgh Gorge, and mountain biking and 4WD tours in the rugged terrain around the town. Visitors can also see the local wineries and the country's first fresh water crayfish farm.
93km southeast of Queenstown.

Arrowtown

This picturesque gold-mining town is usually full of people taking snapshots of its old stone-miner's cottages and, in the autumn, of the glorious foliage on the trees lining Buckingham Street and the banks of the Arrow River. Ironically, the complete treelessness of the area forced the 1860s gold-miners to build in stone, and caused the later arrivals to plant non-indigenous broadleaved trees such as the sycamore and oak, which give Arrowtown its unique appeal today.

The story of those early pioneering days is recounted in the **Lakes District Museum**, where you can also pick up the leaflet 'Historic Arrowtown' which will guide you around over 40 historic buildings in the township – many are private houses, seen only from the street.
Arrowtown is 21km northeast of Queenstown. Regular tours on the Double Decker Red Bus. Tel: (03) 442 6067. Lakes District Museum: 49 Buckingham St. Tel: (03) 442 1806. Open: daily 9am–5pm. Tours: daily 10am & 2pm. Admission charge.

Dunedin

Sprawling in a horseshoe shape around the head of the deep-water inlet of Otago Harbour, Dunedin is an attractive, solidly-built city that was originally founded by Scottish settlers. It grew prosperous on the back of the 1860s' gold rush in Central Otago and was the wealthiest city in New Zealand at the turn of the last century. The legacy of those days is visible in the numerous well-preserved Victorian and Edwardian buildings that dot the city, such as the University of Otago (1869), the Railway Station (1906), the Municipal Chambers (1880), and the Otago Boys' High School (1885).

Dunedin retains a distinctive Scottish heritage. It has the country's only whisky distillery. Scottish Week is celebrated with bagpipe-playing and highland flings in March, and you can even arrange a *haggis* ceremony or buy a kilt here.

The South Island's second-largest city is also a thriving university town and cultural centre, and makes the world-famous Cadbury chocolate. Also, the city is a convenient base for visiting the wonderful Otago Peninsula (*see pp132–3*) right on its doorstep.

Cadbury World

The secrets and history of chocolate and chocolate making is all here. Exhibits are followed by a 45 minute tour of the factory and a visit to the store. In early July you can catch the annual Cadbury Chocolate Festival.
280 Cumberland St. Tel: (03) 467 7967; www.cadburyworld.co.nz Open: daily 9am–3.30pm. Admission charge.

The Octagon

Dominated by a statue of the Scottish bard Robbie Burns, the Octagon is the focal centre of the city and has a clutch of lively cafés and restaurants along its eastern side. On the western side you will find the visitor centre (housed in the old Municipal Chambers) and the Anglican St Paul's Cathedral, built from Oamaru stone in 1919.

Olveston

Built at the start of the 20th century, Olveston is a gracious Jacobean stone mansion with a wealth of decorative detail, furnishings, treasured artefacts, and paintings collected by the Theomin family who lived here.
42 Royal Terrace. Tel: (03) 477 3320. Open: daily 9.30am–4pm; 6 one-hour guided tours daily. Admission charge.

Otago Settlers Museum

Just a short distance west of the station is the Otago Settlers Museum. This museum houses New Zealand's leading collection of colonial memorabilia, priceless archives, manuscripts, and photographs.
31 Queens Gardens. Tel: (03) 477 5052.
Open: daily 10am–5pm.
Admission charge.

Otago Museum

Founded in 1868 and renowned for its Maori and Pacific Island artefacts, the museum also has a good natural history section. Discovery World has numerous hands-on science exhibits for children.
419 Great King St. Tel: (03) 474 7474. Open: daily 10am–5pm. Free admission to museum; admission charge to Discovery World.

Speights Brewery Heritage Tour

This one-hour tour introduces you to the story of beer in New Zealand, and includes 'The Pride of the South' Tour.
200 Rattray Rd, Dunedin.
Tel: (03) 477 7697; www.speights.co.nz
Tours: daily 10am, 11.45am & 2 pm, Mon–Thu also at 7pm.

A statue of Robert Burns in the university town of Dunedin

Fiordland National Park

Spread over 1.2 million sq km in the most remote corner of the South Island is Fiordland, New Zealand's largest national park, and one of the world's largest. The park's serrated coastline is punctuated by beautiful fiords which reach back into the bush-clad hills and mountains. In the hinterland, deep, branching lakes – also carved out by glaciers – add further allure to this stunning region. The impenetrability of Fiordland's rainforests and rugged mountains have kept intruders at bay for centuries, and much of the region remains an unspoiled wilderness where rare species – such as the blue duck and the *takahe* – have managed to retain a foothold. The high annual rainfall creates hundreds of cascading waterfalls, often leading to dramatic landslips as it washes away whole hillsides of vegetation.

The most northerly of the 14 fiords along the coast is Milford Sound, dominated by the majestic Mitre Peak. The hanging valleys that flank the fiord drain Milford's phenomenal annual rainfall (at average 6,526mm per annum, the country's highest) into a series of spectacular waterfalls, while the fiord's sheer walls (rising 1,200m vertically from the sea) dwarf even the biggest visiting cruise liners as they make their way down the sound.

Milford is the most accessible and heavily visited of the fiords. You can reach it by coach tour, drive there from Te Anau (*see pp140–41*), or fly in by helicopter or light aeroplane. Another option is to walk in along the famous Milford Track.

A beautiful alpine stream flowing through the Fiordland National Park

The main gateway to Fiordland is the lakeside township of **Te Anau**, which has a wide range of accommodation and activities on offer. The 53-km long Lake Te Anau is the largest in the South Island, and cruises across to the Te Anau Caves are popular; accessible only by boat, these feature underground waterfalls and a glow-worm grotto.

To the south of Te Anau lies beautiful **Lake Manapouri**, once threatened by a hydroelectric scheme. The huge public outcry that greeted this plan led to the idea being vetoed; although a power plant was still built, it was sited underground to placate the protesters. Tours of the giant **West Arm Underground Powerhouse** (200m underground and reached via a 2-km long spiral access tunnel) can be combined with a trip onwards over the mountains across the Wilmot Pass to **Doubtful Sound**. This fiord is home to fur seals, dusky and bottlenose dolphins, and the Fiordland crested penguin.

Te Anau lies 167km from Queenstown. The main agency for tours and activities is Fiordland Travel, Lake Front, Te Anau.

Tel: toll-free 0800 656 501. Tours to the Caves depart daily 2pm & 8.15pm. Lake Manapouri & power station tours depart twice daily; morning departure continues to Doubtful Sound. Fiordland Travel Pearl Harbour Manapouri tel: toll-free 0800 656 502; (03) 249 6602.

Invercargill

This is the southernmost city in New Zealand, and the main gateway to Stewart Island (*see p136*). If you are passing through, the **Southland Museum and Art Gallery** (housed inside a giant pyramid) is a must: the exhibits span hundreds of years of cultural and natural history, including New Zealand's sub-antarctic islands, with stunning photography and audio-visual effects.

Invercargill is also the starting point (or the finish, depending on which way you're travelling) of the excellent Southern Scenic Route, which traverses the remote southeastern coastline up to Balclutha. This 172-km route encompasses the untouched coastal forests of the **Catlins** (home to many rare birds) as well as the fossilised remains of 180-million-year-old trees at Curio Bay and colonies of seals, yellow-eyed penguins, gannets, and sooty sheerwaters.
Invercargill is 225km southwest of Dunedin.
Southland Museum and Art Gallery: Queens Park. Tel: (03) 218 9753. Open: weekdays 9am–5pm, weekends 10am–5pm. Admission charge.

Rugged peaks and deep glacial valleys are characteristic features of Fiordland

Moeraki

Just outside this small fishing port is the Moeraki Boulders Scenic Reserve, a small area of beach on which lie several spherical boulders. These geological curiosities were formed in the surrounding mudstone some 60 million years ago when North Otago was covered by the ocean; there are around 50 boulders along this section of coast, the largest more than 2m in diameter. A boardwalk runs around the low cliffs and along the beach.

38km south of Oamaru, 78km north of Dunedin. The Reserve is signposted off the main road (SH1), with open access.

A church in Oamaru, noted for its pure Oamaru stone

Oamaru

Oamaru is the main coastal town in North Otago and best known for its exceptionally pure, creamy white limestone, used to good effect in fine public buildings in the 19th century, including, on the tree-lined Thames Street, the National Bank, the Bank of New South Wales (now an art gallery), and the first Post Office (now a restaurant).

The Old Harbour area is gradually being restored as a typical Victorian waterfront village, with some huge old warehouses and grain and wool stores being converted for use by craft-workers and others. Oamaru is noted for its extensive **Public Gardens** set up in 1876, including a wallaby park, featuring fountains, statues, and floral displays.

Just outside Oamaru is a blue penguin colony; from two viewing platforms you can see the penguins return to their nesting sites each night. The yellow-eyed penguin colony is on Bushy Beach.

Oamaru is 250km south of Christchurch, 116km north of Dunedin.
One-hour tours of the Old Harbour area starting 2pm daily can be booked through the Visitor Centre, Thames St, tel: (03) 434 1656.
Oamaru Public Gardens: Chelmer St. Tel: (03) 434 8060. Details on viewing times and access regulations to both penguin colonies are available from the Oamaru Blue Penguin Colony: Breakwater Rd, Oamaru (tel: (03) 434 119) or Penguin Express Bus (tel: (03) 434 7744).

Otago Peninsula

Jutting out from Dunedin and protecting its harbour from the Pacific Ocean is the Otago Peninsula, remarkable for the variety of wildlife concentrated here, close to the city centre. New Zealand fur seals are numerous around the coastline, and colonies of yellow-eyed and blue penguins nest on several beaches. The peninsula's scenic inlets are also home to large numbers of wading and water fowl, and, to cap it all, **Taiaroa Head** boasts the only royal albatross nesting site in the world which exists this close to civilisation.

The peninsula also has its man-made attractions, prime among which is **Larnach Castle** in its spectacular setting overlooking the sea and the peninsula. The castle is the legacy of William Larnach, whose family had a colourful history. (Larnach committed suicide in 1898 after a series of financial disasters.) Built between 1871 and 1887, the castle has a huge ballroom, a skilful Georgian hanging staircase, several fine Italian marble fireplaces, and elaborately decorated ceilings. The castle is surrounded by 14 hectares of attractive gardens.

Another popular spot is the **Glenfalloch Gardens** on the seashore, with 12 hectares of rhododendrons, azaleas, magnolias, fuchsias, and roses. Further along the coast road, the **New Zealand Marine Studies Centre and Trustbank Aquarium** (the largest marine research centre in the country) has a public aquarium in its basement which houses some unusual and fascinating species that can be found around the rocky coastlines of the peninsula, and a touch tank where you can handle invertebrates and other animals.

For more details on wildlife and other attractions in the area, *see pp138–9.*

Larnach Castle: Camp Rd, Dunedin. 15km from central Dunedin, off Castlewood Rd, 9km from central Dunedin on the Portobello Rd. Tel: (03) 476 1616. Open: daily 9am–5pm. Admission charge.

Glenfalloch Gardens: 430 Portobello Rd, Dunedin. Tel: (03) 476 1006. Open: daily dawn–dusk. Entry by donation.

New Zealand Marine Studies Centre: Hatchery Rd, Portobello, Dunedin. Tel: (03) 479 5826. Open: daily noon–4.30pm. Admission charge.

The Moeraki Boulders look like giant marbles on the seashore

Queenstown

The wonderful natural setting of Queenstown on the shores of the Lake Wakatipu, with the dramatic Remarkables mountain range rising up behind it, would be a tremendous draw in itself even if the town had no other assets – but it does, by the bucketload. Queenstown is New Zealand's premier tourist resort, offering a remarkable range of activities for visitors to choose from: sensational helicopter adventures, white-water surfing, flightseeing in an old DC3 and jet-boating, tandem parachute or parapente jumps – and AJ Hackett's famous bungee-jumping enterprise (*see pp146–7*).

The TSS *Earnslaw* is a vintage steamer which still plies the lake waters daily

The ultimate Queenstown thrill is the 'Awesome Foursome', an adrenalin-pumping day that combines a helicopter ride with jet-boating, white-water rafting, and a bungee jump. Less hair-raising activities include sedate lake cruises, back-country tours, or horse-trekking; in winter, the nearby Coronet Peak and Remarkables ski fields (among the best in the country) are very busy.

Efficient, computerised booking offices line Queenstown's main street. Relax in one of the town's 100 or so restaurants, bars and eateries, many of which have live music. The resort's excellent range of shops stay open until 9pm, seven days a week. More than 40 hotels and motels, and 26 guest houses and hostels cater for the annual influx of over half a million visitors.
For details on individual adventure activities, see pp146–9.

Central Otago Wine Trail

Less than an hour's drive from Queenstown along State Highway 6 are the world's most southerly vineyards, and the start of the Central Otago Wine Trail. There are 24 wineries in this fertile countryside, including **Gibbston Valley** (Pinot Noir), **Black Ridge Wines** (reisling), and **Rippon Vineyard**.
Gibbston Valley: Main Cromwell-Queenstown Highway. Tel: (03) 442 6910. Open: daily 10am–5pm.
Black Ridge Wines: Conroys Rd, Alexandra. Tel: (03) 449 2059. Open: daily 10am–5pm.
Rippon Vineyard: Mt Aspiring Rd, Lake Wanaka. Tel: (03) 443 8084. Open: Dec–Apr 11am–5pm, Jul–Nov 1.30pm–4.30 pm. Closed: May & Jun.
The Queenstown Wine Trail departs daily at 12.30pm from the centre of town and allows you a full afternoon for wine tasting. Tel: (03) 442 3799.

Kiwi and Birdlife Park

The park has a nocturnal kiwi house, as well as aviaries, ponds, and landscaped

gardens where you can see other native birds too.
Bevan St. Tel: (03) 442 8059.
Open: daily, summer 9am–7.30pm; winter 9am–5pm. Admission charge.

Motor Museum

More than 80 well-preserved classic cars and motorcycles make up this historic collection.
Brecon St. Tel: (03) 442 8775. Open: daily 9.30am–5.30pm. Admission charge.

Skyline Gondola and Kiwi Magic

A good way to orientate yourself when you first arrive here is to take the Skyline Gondola, which rises 790m above sea level from central Queenstown and offers stunning views of the lake, the mountains, and the town from the restaurant/viewing platform at the top of Bob's Peak. In a wide-screen viewing theatre inside the complex, catch a regular screening of a short film, *Kiwi Magic*, which takes you on a realistic tour by helicopter, jet-boat, biplane, ski-sled, and raft through some of New Zealand's most beautiful scenery.
Brecon St. Tel: (03) 441 0101.
Open: daily 9am–midnight. Admission charge. Kiwi Magic *is screened on the hour, 11am–9pm. Admission charge.*

TSS Earnslaw and Walter Peak Farm

The vintage TSS *Earnslaw* is the last of the coal-burning steamers that once plied the lake to supply outlying sheep stations; lovingly restored, the venerable steamer now cruises for pleasure only.

In the afternoons the steamer calls in at **Walter Peak**, a high-country farm on the other side of the lake, where refreshments are served, and where you can see sheepdog and sheep-shearing demonstrations.
TSS Earnslaw *is operated by Fiordland Travel, 4–14 Steamer Wharf. Tel: toll-free 0800 656 503. Cruises depart three times daily Oct–Apr, with barbecue lunch options on several departures. Visit Walter Peak by launch also at other times (bookings through Fiordland Travel).*

Queenstown, one of the country's busiest resorts, lies on the shores of Lake Wakatipu

Stewart Island
This triangular-shaped island is a naturalist's paradise, now New Zealand's newest national park. The park has 157,000 hectares of protected native bush and rainforest, 750km of indented coastline with hundreds of hidden beaches and sandy bays, and a mere 20km of roads!

There is just one township, Halfmoon Bay (Oban), and a permanent population of only 400 people.

Stewart Island has a rich Maori history, and the harvesting of *titi* (fledgling chicks of the sooty sheerwater, also sold in fish shops as mutton birds) continues on the tiny islands around its coastline as it has done for centuries.

Cook sailed around the southern tip in March 1770, but mistakenly thought it was a peninsula. Twenty years later, Captain Chase on board the *Pegasus* brought a sealing gang to these shores and attempted to set up a shipyard on an inlet on the southeast coast (still named Port Pegasus). The island was named after his first officer, William Stewart, who charted the inlet.

Today, commercial fishing – principally for *paua* (puff oysters), crayfish, and blue cod – is the lifeblood of most islanders, with tourism now playing an important part as hikers, hunters, divers, and fishermen seek out Stewart Island's wild places. Hikers should arrive well equipped: the North West Circuit (around the top half of the island) takes 10 days, while the Rakiura Track (closer to Oban) takes at least three days.

Native birds include the kiwi, *kaka, tui,* bellbird, robin, tomtit, fantail, and the long-tailed and shining cuckoo. One of the great attractions of the island is the chance to see kiwis in their natural habitat – unusually, the Stewart Island brown kiwi forages during the daytime (they are particularly numerous at Mason Bay on the North West Circuit). Launch trips also depart from Oban to watch kiwis foraging for sand-hoppers on Ocean Beach during the evenings.
Stewart Island can be reached on a 20-minute flight (four times daily) with Southern Air from Invercargill (tel: (03) 218 9129; toll-free 0800 843 475).
There is also a 60-minute catamaran service, the Foveaux Express, from Bluff (tel: (03) 212 7660).
Kiwi-watching trips are operated every second night by Bravo Adventure Cruises, Stewart Island (tel: (03) 219 1144; book well in advance).

Te Anau
See p130.

Wanaka
This more laid-back version of Queenstown is set in similarly stunning scenery on the edge of Lake Wanaka, with the peaks of the Mount Aspiring National Park rising up in the background. Wanaka's waterfront is at its most majestic in the autumn, when poplars and willows in shades of gold and red frame the alpine views.

Though Wanaka's less commercialised than Queenstown, outdoor adventure is the town's main business, and plenty of thrills are on offer: paragliding, rafting, mountain-biking, jet-boating, four-wheel-drive tours, and cruising on the lake by hovercraft. For something unusual, take a ride in a vintage Tiger Moth biplane.

Wanaka is a major fishing centre, and both coarse fishing on the lake and fly fishing on nearby rivers are available. Hikers are also well catered for as numerous tracks run through the Mount Aspiring National Park; shorter walks in the vicinity include the Diamond Lake Track (2½ hours) and Mount Roy Track (5–6 hours return). In the winter, skiers head for the renowned Cardrona and Treble Cone ski fields.

For a gentler form of entertainment, don't miss the Stuart Landsborough's **Puzzling World and Great Maze**; built in 1973, it started a trend which led to the creation of numerous mazes throughout New Zealand. The split-level maze has over 1.5km of passageways, whilst the Tilted Towers complex will confuse you even further. Next to the tearooms is the Puzzle Centre, housing a huge collection of mind-bending puzzles and the Illusions Gallery.

Wanaka is 120km north of Queenstown (recommended route via Cromwell; extra care is necessary if using Crown Range road during the winter months). Details on activities are available from the Visitor Centre, corner of Ballantyna Rd. Tel: (03) 443 1233. Hiking information is available from the DOC information centre in the Visitor Centre building. Tel: (03) 443 7660.

Stuart Landsborough's Puzzling World and Great Maze: Main Highway, 2km outside town on SH8A to Cromwell. Tel: (03) 443 7489. Open: daily 8.30am–5.30pm. Admission charge.

You could spend ages trying to find your way out of this maze in Wanaka

Tour: Otago Peninsula

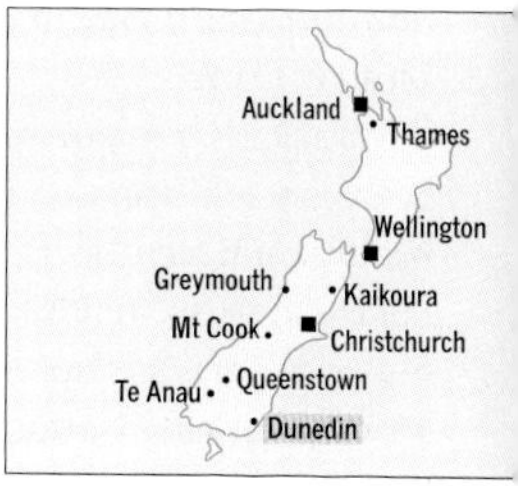

This tour around the peninsula is a wildlife extravaganza of sea birds and marine life, with a historic castle thrown in for good measure. Ideally, you should plan to arrive at the Royal Albatross Colony between noon and 2pm; book your tour before leaving Dunedin, and also make sure you are booked into the Penguin Place Yellow-Eyed Penguin Conservation Reserve for the 4pm tour.

Allow a full day.

From the Octagon, head down Princes St and take a left turn down Andersons Bay Rd. After 5km, turn left down Silverton Rd and follow the signs to Larnach Castle (see p133) along the ridgetop road. After visiting Larnach return to the Highcliff Rd. You should then turn left, continuing down to Hoopers Inlet, and eventually following Sheppard Rd to the Papanui Inlet.

1 Hoopers and Papanui Inlets

Both of these lovely inlets are home to a variety of wading and water birds. The innermost part of Hoopers Inlet is a wildlife sanctuary – a plaque by the roadside illustrates the birds that can be seen here at different times of year.

Take Weir Rd to Portobello Bay and continue along the coast road, stopping

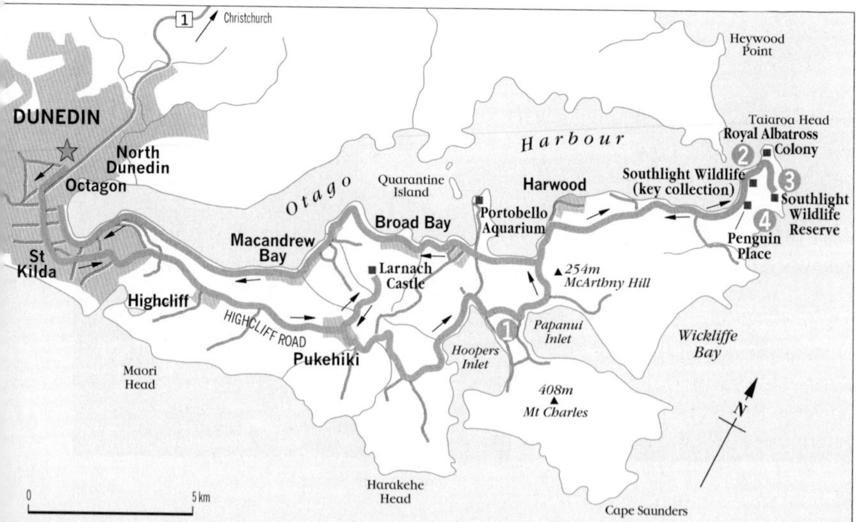

at Southlight Wildlife to collect the key for the reserve itself. Continue on to Taiaroa Head.

2 Royal Albatross Colony

This reserve is one of the most special wildlife zones in New Zealand, and the only mainland albatross colony of its kind in the world. The area has been protected since 1937, and public viewing started in 1972. The Albatross Centre has displays and an audio-visual presentation on these magnificent birds, and from here you are led by trained guides up to the hide overlooking the nesting sites on the hill top.

Winging in from Antarctic waters, the albatross build their nests in late September and, once all the eggs have been laid (usually by 24 November), the colony is open to the public. The tasks of incubation and guarding the new-born chicks are shared by both parents, with hatching taking place between January and February. The fluffy albatross chicks remain at Taiaroa until they are ready to set off in late September.

Continue past the car park, through the gate and along the cliff top road to Southlight Wildlife Reserve.

3 Southlight Wildlife Reserve

Yellow-eyed penguins come ashore in the late afternoons to nest above the beach here, but you won't get as close to them as you will in the Penguin Place Reserve. There are plenty of fur seals to photograph at close quarters, and, at the end of the beach, a spotted shag colony.

Return along the coast road to Penguin Place. If you have time, you could also detour back to the Trustbank Aquarium (see p133).

A royal albatross at Taiaroa Head on the tip of the peninsula

4 Penguin Place Yellow-eyed Penguin Conservation Reserve

This is by far the better of the two penguin reserves. Following a brief introductory talk at the farm headquarters, you are ferried over the hill to the penguin beach where a series of crafty tunnels and hides allows you to pop up within a metre or two of the many nesting sites in this colony.

Return to Dunedin around the shoreline.

Royal Albatross Colony Tairoa Head Dunedin. *Tel: (03) 478 0499*. Open: daily 9am–dusk. Closed: mid-Sep–late Nov. Reservations essential. Tours operate daily except Tuesdays, on the hour in winter, and half-hour in summer. Admission charge.

Southlight Wildlife 932 Harrington Point. Tel: *(03) 478 0287*. Open: daily dawn–dusk. Admission charge.

Penguin Place Yellow-eyed Penguin Conservation Reserve Harrington Point. *Tel: (03) 478 0286*. Open: daily 9am–dusk. Admission charge.

Tour: Milford Sound

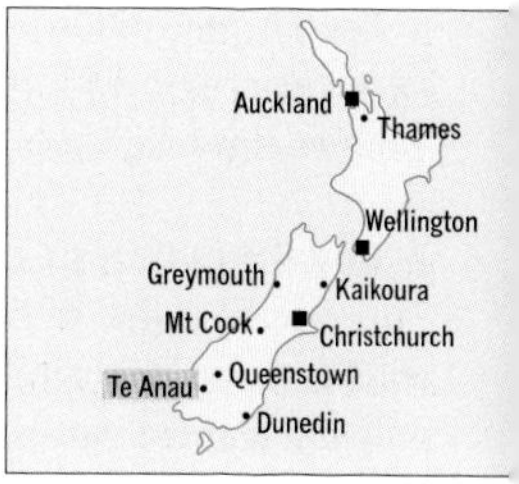

This tour starts and finishes in Te Anau, following the Milford Road, with several interesting stop-offs before arriving at Milford itself, where you have a choice of cruise options on the Sound. If you are based in Queenstown it is better to do the trip by coach or cruise excursion so that someone else drives the six hours involved.

Allow a full day to complete the tour at a leisurely pace.

From Te Anau, follow signs for Milford Sound.

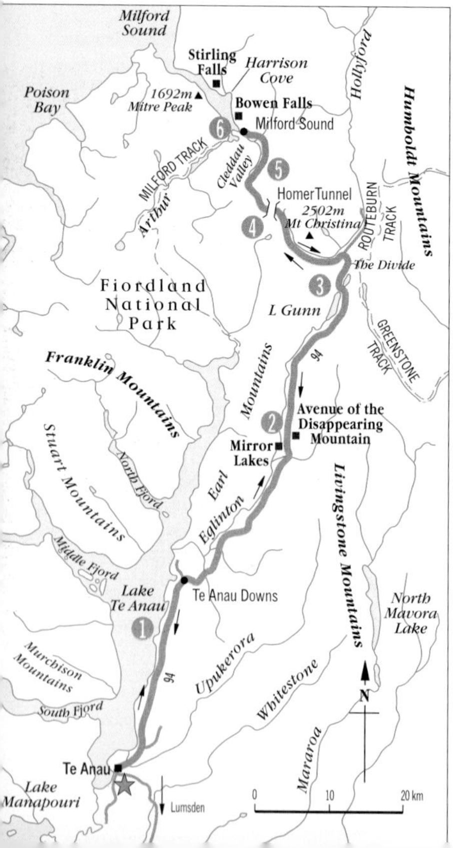

1 Lake Te Anau

The road skirts Lake Te Anau, with views across to the Murchison Mountains, before arriving at Te Anau Downs and then heading away from the lake up towards the Livingstone and Humboldt mountains.

At the 40km mark you pass the entrance to the Fiordland National Park; after 58km you arrive at the Mirror Lakes.

2 Mirror Lakes

A boardwalk from the road leads around the edge of two small, sheltered lakes which mirror the mountains opposite – hundreds of day-trippers pour off their tour buses to capture this famous scene on film. Shortly afterwards, you drive along the Avenue of the Disappearing Mountain, so called because the peak at the end of the road seems to diminish in perspective the closer you get to it.

At 76km, the road skirts Lake Gunn.

3 Lake Gunn

Lake Gunn sometimes also has a mirror image of the mountains, although less reliably so than the Mirror Lakes. This large lake is named after an early

explorer, George Gunn. From the road a loop track leads through red beech forest to the lakeside (a pleasant half-hour's ramble). Shortly afterwards you pass The Divide, the lowest east-west pass (534m) across the Southern Alps and the departure point for the Routeburn and Greenstone tracks.
Continue on to the Homer Tunnel (101km).

4 Homer Tunnel

The tunnel was started in 1935 when just five men set to the mountain with picks and shovels. Not surprisingly, it wasn't completed until 1952, and at the cost of five lives. Hewn out of solid rock, the tunnel is narrow and unlined, dropping along a gradient of one in 11 over its 1.2-km length. You can't help but drive through with extreme caution.

5 Cleddau Valley

As the road emerges from the Homer Tunnel it spirals down the Cleddau Valley, with dozens of waterfalls tumbling over the sheer sides of the valley. Further down, the Cleddau River plunges beneath a natural rock bridge to create another spectacular waterfall.
At the 120km point you arrive at Milford Sound, from where cruises depart down the Sound to the Tasman Sea. A visitor centre with facilities is available.

6 Milford Sound

The rainfall is practically incessant in Milford Sound (averaging over 6,526mm per year with more than 200 rainy days), giving it an almost permanent misty, moody atmosphere and contributing to the dozens of spectacular but temporary waterfalls that tumble down the sheer rock faces into the sea. Most cruises take a similar route down the 16-km long sound, first passing by Mitre Peak (1,692m) and then nosing in for a spray-filled view of the Bowen Falls before approaching a fur seal colony and heading up to the Tasman Sea. On the return journey, your captain will point out hanging glacial valleys and other features, and will try to seek out schools of dolphins. The boat passes the wind-lashed Stirling Falls, Harrison Cove, and, once again, the **Bowen Falls** before docking back at the visitor centre jetty.
Return to Te Anau along the same route.

Dramatic scenery in the Milford Sound

The Routeburn Track

Weather and Hazards

The Routeburn is a well-used and clearly marked path, with tracks, huts, and bridges maintained efficiently by park staff. Most people walk the track during the summer months (mid-November to March), though autumn (April to mid-May) can also be excellent, with less people on the trail. Remember that advance booking is essential. Mountain flowers are at their best from November to January. Rainfall can be high during midsummer, so the best views are often to be had from February to April.

The main hazard is the southerly or northwesterly storms which come in from the Tasman Sea any time of year. Be prepared for adverse conditions with waterproofs and warm clothing.

Guided Walks

Guided walking is a comfortable and pleasant option which allows anybody of average fitness to enjoy this wonderful area, even if they have had no previous hiking experience. Routeburn Walk Ltd has its own private mountain lodges with comfortable accommodation and hot showers. All meals are prepared by the guides and the lodge managers, which means that during the day you have only to carry a light day pack with your clothing and other requirements. The friendly and knowledgeable guides will ensure a safe journey and allow you

The Routeburn Track is one of the most popular walks in the South Island

Tramping is almost a national pastime, and facilities are well organised

to make the most of this superb walk. *For full details on costs and bookings, contact: Routeburn Walk, PO Box 568, Queenstown. Tel: (03) 442 8200: toll-free 0800 659 255. Departures: Jan–Mar daily, Nov-Dec & Apr weekdays only.*

Independent Walking

Public transport is available from both ends of the track, and hut wardens are in residence from November to May. *Maps and information can be obtained from the Fiordland National Park Visitor Centre, Lake Front Drive, Te Anau (tel: (03) 249 7924; open: daily, summer from 8am; winter from 9am; call for closing times), or the DOC office, corner of Mull & Oban sts, Glenorchy. (tel: (03) 442 9937; open: Nov–Apr daily 8.30am–5pm; weekdays only in winter).*

Walk: The Routeburn Track

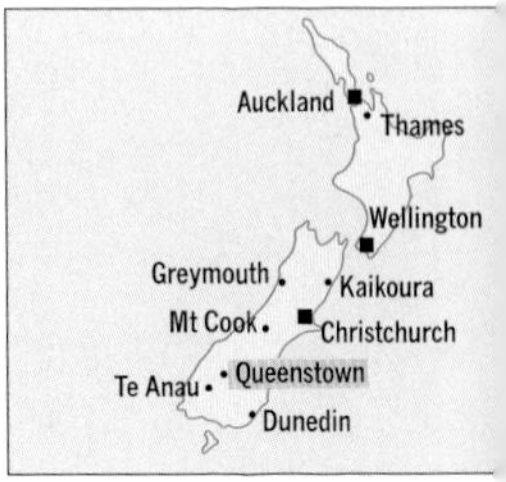

This is one of New Zealand's great walks, a relatively easy, well-marked track passing from the Fiordland National Park over the Harris Saddle and into the Mount Aspiring National Park. It is a popular route, with spectacular alpine panoramas along much of its 39km length. The track can be walked independently in either direction, or on a guided tramp from west to east, as described here. For practical details, *see pp142–3*.

Allow three days, two nights.

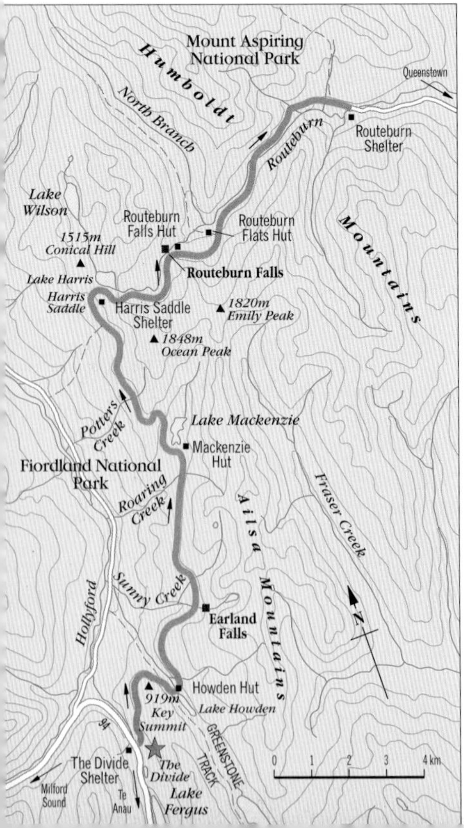

Your trek begins with a coach ride from Queenstown, through Te Anau and along the Milford Highway to The Divide, from where you start walking.

Day One: The Divide to Lake Mackenzie

The track climbs gently through magnificent silver-beech forests, where the gnarled trunks of larger trees are cloaked in moss, lichen, and epiphyte. Emerging above the tree-line, detour briefly (30 minutes) up to Key Summit (919m), a small, rocky knoll surrounded by a swampland of bogs and tarns, with extensive views of the peaks and valleys of Fiordland. From here it is a quick descent to Lake Howden, where you break for lunch. The afternoon's walk is a steady, gentle climb from the Lake Howden to the Lake Mackenzie, passing the dramatic Earland Falls on the way. The track goes almost directly underneath these 100-m high falls; the surrounding rocks and ferns are drenched in spray. Further along, you get occasional glimpses of the snow-capped peaks and glaciers of the Darren Range. A last, rocky descent through silver-beech forest comes out at the Mackenzie Hut, where you stop for the night.

Day Two: The Divide to Lake Mackenzie

After breakfast you set off alongside the Lake Mackenzie, which on a calm day will reward you with a breathtaking image of Emily Peak (1,820m) reflected in its emerald depths. The track zigzags steeply up above the tree-line before levelling out and hugging the Hollyford Face for the next two to three hours; from here there are magnificent views across the valley to the Darren Range. A brief ascent brings you to the Harris Saddle (1,217m), where you pass from the Fiordland National Park into the Mount Aspiring National Park.

From the shelter at Harris Saddle it is well worth making the extra effort to climb Conical Hill (1,515m). There are awe-inspiring views from its summit of the Routeburn Valley leading down to Lake McKerrow, Martins Bay, and the Tasman Sea.

Beyond Harris Saddle the track skirts Lake Harris, emerging into the fragile tussock and swampland of the Harris Basin. The track then follows the Routeburn River down to the Routeburn Falls, well known as a haunt for mischievous *keas*. Your hut for the night is within earshot of the falls.

Day Three: Routeburn Falls to Routeburn Shelter

The track descends through silver-, mountain- and then red-beech forest. At the Routeburn Flats, the river winds placidly across the grass-covered plains, with Mount Somnus (2,294m) dominating the view. After you have crossed the Routeburn on a suspension bridge, a gentle downhill amble along the river's forested banks leads you to the Routeburn Shelter, from where you will be transported back to Queenstown.

Looking down Routeburn Valley from Routeburn Falls

Getting Away From It All

Many people come to New Zealand specifically for its wide open spaces and unspoiled natural environment, and since New Zealanders themselves are equally keen on the great outdoors there is no shortage of opportunities to get away from it all. The activities listed here form just a sample of the options available *(see also pp160–63)*, but they can be enjoyed by anyone and are, in their own way, typically Kiwi ways to escape – whether only for a few seconds on a bungee jump or several days on a rafting or walking trip.

Taking the plunge with bungee-jumping

Ballooning

Canterbury Plains is the biggest centre for hot-air ballooning in New Zealand, thanks largely to the ideal conditions provided by the rolling countryside; balloons drift quietly high above the sheep and farmlands. The scenery is spectacular: the Southern Alps rear up to the west, and to the east the Pacific coastline stretches off into the distance. Most balloon flights start at dawn (to take advantage of calm conditions), but the trauma of having to get up so early is soon forgotten in the excitement of clambering into the basket and lifting off. After the initial roar of the gas burners you can settle back to enjoy your hour-long flight. Champagne is always served on landing (a tradition with balloonists worldwide), followed by a hearty breakfast.

Aoraki Balloon Safaris: Methven. Tel: toll-free 0800 256 837; (03) 302 8172.
Sunrise Ballooning Adventures: Queenstown. Tel: (03) 435 0100.
Up, Up, and Away: PO Box 36014, Christchurch. Tel: (03) 381 4600.

Bungee-Jumping

Jumping off high places with nothing but a piece of elastic tied to your ankles is perhaps one of the oddest adventure sports ever invented, but at least 70,000 people a year are now taking the plunge.

The attraction lies partly in conquering your inner fears sufficiently to throw yourself off, partly in the exhilaration of the 'drop', and partly in the relief that floods through you as the bungee cord drags you back up again, and you bounce gently in mid-air before being hoisted aboard a raft on the river below.

Bungee-jumping was invented by a New Zealander, AJ Hackett and started as a commercial operation in Queenstown in 1988 with the Kawarau Bridge jump (43m). You can also try the Nevis Highwire, the highest at 134m, or The Ledge, an urban jump of 47m over Queenstown.

Also, the jump at the Skippers Canyon Suspension Bridge (71m) and at other locations such as Lake Taupo. It is surprising how many people come back

for more, and there is no age limit either – over-65s go free, and the oldest person ever to have jumped was 89. The whole organisation is highly professional (the sport has an excellent safety record), and motorised cameras and videos capture your jump on film so that you can astound your friends later.
AJ Hackett Bungy: Shotover St, Queenstown. Tel: (03) 442 4007; toll-free 0800 2864 95867. It is essential for you to book ahead.

Jet-Boating

Jet-boats were invented by the Kiwi engineer and farmer, Bill Hamilton, to operate on the shallow and otherwise unnavigable rivers of the South Island. Unlike normal boats, the propeller on the jet-boat is on the inside of the hull, driving water out through a nozzle at the rear with tremendous force.

The nozzle also steers the boat, giving it incredible manoeuvrability: jet-boats can execute high-speed, 360-degree turns almost on their own axis. High-speed 'jet-spins', 'flick turns', and other manoeuvres provide thrills and excitement for the majority of passengers on rivers such as the Shotover and Kawarau, but the real benefit of jet-boats is that they can venture far into the wilderness up shallow river systems as they can operate in just 10cm of water.

If you can, take a jet-boat safari up through the beautiful **Dart River Valley** or somewhere similarly remote; you will find jet-boats for hire at many riverside localities throughout the country.
Dart River Safari, Box 76, Queenstown. Tel: (03) 442 9992.
Huka Jet: Wairakei Park, Taupo. Tel: toll-free 0800 4852 538.
Shotover Jet: Arthurs Point, Queenstown. Tel: (03) 442 857; toll-free 0800 746 868.

Hot-air balloons are a thrilling and luxurious way of seeing the urban and rural landscape

Walking

There is no better way to experience New Zealand's wild and beautiful backcountry than by spending a few days walking on one of the many long-distance tracks that traverse the country. Forests, mountains, lakes, beaches, volcanoes – each track has its own special characteristics, most taking two to five days to complete. Tramping, as it's called in New Zealand, is one of the most popular (and certainly one of the best value) activities for getting away from it all.

The network encompasses more than 100 tramping tracks, although most visitors opt for one of the four main tracks listed below. The best season for walking runs from October to March.

Abel Tasman

Rated the easiest tramp of its length in New Zealand, this is a good choice if you have never tramped before and want to give it a go. The track is well marked and well graded – almost a gentle amble – and passes beach after beach along a seashore backed by native forests. This is considered to be one of the most beautiful coastal walks in the world, through an area renowned for its mild, sunny weather. Not surprisingly, it is the most popular track in the country; boats also ferry walkers between the beaches.

50km, three to four days. Marahau to Totaranui or Wainui, or vice versa. Easy. Daily bus connections to/from Nelson.

Kepler

This is the newest and certainly the best-planned tramping track in New Zealand, and was designed to take the pressure off other Fiordland tramps; as a result, the Kepler has become a classic in its own right. The track follows a circular route, passing through stunning alpine landscapes of lakes, mountains, and beech forests. Steep gradients make this a tougher walk than the Routeburn or the Milford.

67km, four days. Start and finish near Te Anau. Difficult.

A variety of ferns greet walkers in the woods

Milford

This is New Zealand's best-known track, and for this reason is the only one that requires pre-booked hut accommodation.

Although highly regulated (you can walk only in one direction, and must complete it in the time allotted, so there are no breaks for bad weather), the walk is still worth doing for its spectacular views of alpine meadows, forests, and waterfalls – including **Sutherland Falls**, the highest in the country at 580m. Although the track can be rough in

places, it is within the capabilities of the averagely fit.
53km, three to six days. Lake Te Anau to Milford Sound. Medium.
Book well in advance during the peak summer months with DOC, PO Box 29, Te Anau. Tel: (03) 249 8514.

Routeburn
See pp142–5. 39km, three to four days. Lake Wakatipu to Upper Hollyford Valley, or vice versa. Medium.

Other Major Tracks
The most frequently used tracks in the North Island are the Tongariro Crossing in the Tongariro National Park, the shoreline track around Lake Waikaremoana, and the Coromandel State Forest Park Walk.

Popular tracks in the South Island include the Heaphy and Wangapeka in the North-West Nelson Forest Park (which comes within the Kahurangi National Park), the Travers-Sabine Circuit in the Nelson Lakes National Park, and the Rees-Dart, Hollyford, and Greenstone-Caples Tracks in Fiordland. The Northern Circuit-Rakiura Track on Stewart Island is also classified as one of the 'great walks'.

Independent Tramping
Your first stop for information should be the Department of Conservation (DOC) information centres. The DOC maintains thousands of kilometres of tracks and over 900 huts. The department also publishes a number of useful brochures, including *The World at Your Feet – Tramping in the New Zealand Backcountry* and *Exploring New Zealand's Parks*, plus individual brochures on most tramping tracks.
Head Office, DOC, PO Box 10–420, Wellington. Tel: (04) 471 0726.

Guided Tramping
If you are not used to carrying a large backpack for several days, a guided tramp allows you to experience some tracks by staying in privately owned, comfortable huts en route and carrying just a day pack.

Such tramps are more costly than going it alone, but may suit inexperienced or more elderly walkers.
Milford Track Guided Walk: *PO Box 185, Te Anau. Tel: (03) 249 7411; toll-free 0800 659 255.*
Routeburn Guided Walk and Greenstone-Caples Guided Walk: *PO Box 568, Queenstown. Tel: (03) 442 8200.*

Trampers (hikers) on top of Mount Rakeahua looking towards Masons Bay

White-water Rafting

Given the number of rivers and rapids in New Zealand, it is hardly surprising that rafting is one of the most popular outdoor adventures for visitors. There are more than 50 rafting companies in the country, which between them offer a wide range of trips to suit everyone from beginners to more experienced rafters looking for wild and wet adventures.

The season usually runs from late October to March, although many trips now operate year round, with rafters simply donning thicker wetsuits.

Queenstown is the main focus of rafting in the South Island, with half-day trips available on the nearby Shotover and Kawarau rivers, and two-day expeditions to the beautiful Landsborough River which flows through deep gorges from its source in the Mount Cook National Park. The Buller, Clarence, Waimakariri, Rakaia, and Rangitata are other well-known rafting rivers in the South Island. The most challenging white-water rafting in the South Island is on the Karamea, a grade 5 river which runs down from the Tasman Mountains in Nelson; you need to go by helicopter to get to the start-point.

In the North Island most rafting takes place on the Mohaka, Rangataiki, Rangitikei, and Motu rivers. The Wairoa is also popular, although its grade 5 ride is only possible on 26 days of the year as the river is controlled by hydroelectric

Some of the calmer rivers are excellent for jet-boating

The thrills and spills of white-water rafting are open to everyone

schemes. The ultimate rafting sensation in the Rotorua area is the upper Kaituna River (grade 5+), which drops 7m over Hinemoa's Steps – the highest commercially rafted waterfall in the world.

Buller Adventure Tours
Half-day tours on the Buller and full- or three-day adventures on the Karamea (including helicopter flight).
Buller Gorge Rd, Westport.
Tel: (03) 789 7286.

Queenstown Rafting
Winners of the 1999 award for best Activity Adventure Operator. Ride the Kawaran and Shotover.
35 Shotover St, Queenstown.
Tel: (03) 442 9792.

River Rats
One of the largest North Island rafting companies, wide choice of rivers, including the Kaituna.
Te Ngae, Rotorua. Tel: (07) 345 6543.

Shopping

New Zealand is not renowned for bargain shopping. While there are locally produced goods of excellent quality, these can be fairly pricey: a recent survey showed that thousands of tourists were leaving the country with money still in their wallets because the things they wanted to buy were too expensive. So, be warned that you may have to dig deep for that coveted item. The best buys are sheepskin, crafts, and greenstone. For shop opening times, *see pp185–6*.

What to Buy

Arts and Crafts

Craftspeople seem to thrive in New Zealand, and if you like hand-crafted items you will be spoilt for choice. Many souvenir shops stock handicrafts, but you can find better bargains by buying directly from studios. In major craft centres such as Nelson, Golden Bay and the Coromandel you can pick up 'Craft Trail' leaflets listing the locations, opening times, as well as specialities of local studios.

Pottery and wood-carvings are perhaps the most widely available products, although you can also find glassware, hand-weaving, metalwork, patchwork, wooden toys, jewellery, bone-carvings, decorative boxes, and much more. Traditional and contemporary Maori woodcarvings are also widely available.

Jewellery and other souvenirs made from iridescent *paua* (abalone) shell are also worth looking at. In comparison to elsewhere in the world, greenstone or jade is excellent value, particularly smaller items such as finely carved *tiki* good-luck charms. Larger sculpted pieces, which may take many months to work, can run into thousands of dollars.

Clothing and Sheepskin

Rugged outdoor clothing (such as jackets and bushwacker hats) is worth looking at, particularly classic designs made with deerskin, sheepskin, leather, or suede. Hand-knitted sweaters and other

TAXES AND SHIPPING

All goods and services are subject to the 12.5 per cent Goods and Services Tax (GST), which is always included in the price displayed. Apart from this unitary tax there are no other local taxes. Visitors cannot reclaim this tax, though if a supplier agrees to export a major item to a visitor's home address, GST will not be charged on either the goods or freight.

Souvenirs and other goods can be bought without paying GST if the supplier ships them home for you. With some items – sheepskins or fragile crafts such as ceramics – this is often more convenient anyway.

In major centres such as Wellington, Auckland, Christchurch, Queens-town, and Rotorua, there are duty-free outlets in the downtown areas. Take your airline ticket and passport with you when purchasing goods; and the shop then arranges for them to be waiting for you at the airport on the day of your departure.

woollen items are expensive but worth splashing out on.

One of the best known labels for leisurewear is Canterbury of New Zealand, whose colourful, all-cotton rugby shirts are a good buy; other good-quality brands include Jackson Bay, Action Down Under, T&Ski, and MacKenzie Country Knitwear.

Sheepskin is turned into everything from bedroom slippers to car seat covers and floor rugs; the leading manufacturer is Bowron. Lambskin, luxuriously soft since it has only been shorn once, is particularly popular.

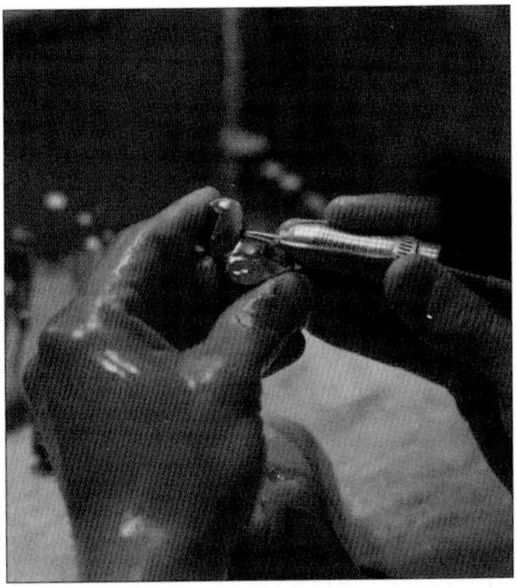

A master craftsman carves a piece of jewellery

Other Specialities

Wines, cheeses, pre-packed Bluff oysters and honey scented with native flowers are further options if you want to take home a taste of New Zealand. CDs and cassettes of Maori songs make appealing souvenirs, and are usually sold at Maori concerts as well as record and souvenir shops.

Charms, pendants, and other greenstone items are popular souvenirs

Where to Buy

NORTH ISLAND

Auckland

Auckland Museum
Excellent quality Maori arts and crafts, as well as jewellery and other well-designed souvenirs. Good selection of Maori CDs and tapes.
The Domain.
Tel: (09) 306 7067.
Open: daily 10am–5pm.

Parnell
Probably the best up-market shopping area in Auckland, with dozens of high-quality craft shops, art galleries, antique shops, and fashion boutiques that spread out into the streets surrounding the quaint shopping arcade known as Parnell Village.
Parnell St and environs.

Queen Street
Auckland's main shopping street, with a mix of department stores, fashion outlets, souvenir shops, and jewellers. The side streets on the east side (such as High Street and Vulcan Lane) are worth a look, with interesting bookshops, boutiques, and cafés.

Victoria Park Market
Has a good selection of off-beat arts and crafts, as well as T-shirts and reasonably priced leather and sheepskin goods.
Victoria St West and corner of Wellesley St.
Tel: (09) 309 6911.
Open: daily 9am–6pm.

Rotorua

As one of the country's premier tourist destinations, Rotorua has numerous souvenir and duty-free shops.

Agrodome
Like Rainbow Springs (*below*), Agrodome is geared towards a huge through-put of package tourists, and all the usual sheepskin, woollen, and leather goods can be purchased here.
Ngongotaha.
Tel: toll-free 0800 339 400, or (07) 357 1050.
Open: daily 9am–5pm.

New Zealand Arts and Crafts Institute
Authentic hand-crafted Maori carvings from workshops where the traditional styles are taught.
Hemo Rd, Whakarewarewa.
Tel: toll-free 0800 494 252.
Open: daily 8.30am–5pm.

Rainbow Springs
The recently rebuilt international shopping complex here claims to be the largest souvenir shop in New Zealand, and stocks a huge range of items including knitwear, sheepskin, leather goods, bone- and woodcarvings, and opal and *paua* (abalone shell) jewellery.
Fairy Springs Rd, Auckland Highway (SH5).
Tel: toll-free 0800 724 626, or (07) 347 9301.
Open: daily 8am–5pm.

SOUTH ISLAND

Christchurch

There is a good selection of shops in central downtown Christchurch, with pedestrianised or enclosed malls radiating outwards from Cathedral Square.

Arts Centre
The Arts Centre, with its numerous small workshops and galleries, is one of the best places in the South Island for crafts; there is even more choice at the centre's weekend markets.
Arts Centre, Worcester St.
Tel: (03) 363 2836.
Open: weekdays 8.30am–5pm, weekends 10am–5pm. Market open: weekends 10am–5pm.

New Regent Street
One block north of the square (leading off from Gloucester Street) is New Regent Street, a quaint

row of pastel-painted shops which formed the first 'shopping mall' in the country when it opened in 1931. You can find crystals, antiquarian books, fashion, and herbal remedies here.

Hokitika

Westland Greenstone
High-quality, individually designed greenstone (jade) ornaments.
25 Tancred St.
Tel: (03) 768 0700.
Open: 8.30am– 8.30pm; up to only 5pm in winter.

Mountain Jade
Exquisite jade carvings, sculptures, and jewellery.
41 Weld St. Tel: (03) 755 8007. Open: daily 9am–7pm (till 6pm in winter).

Westland Greenstone
One of the largest processors of greenstone, with a wide range of items available.
34 Tancred St.
Tel: (03) 755 8713.
Open: daily 8am–5pm.

Queenstown

Queenstown has an excellent range of shops, and is the only place in New Zealand where major stores and boutiques stay open until 10pm, seven days a week. Jewellery, leatherwork, sheepskin shops, and a huge range of fashion and outdoor clothing stores all lie within a few minutes' walk of each other in the pedestrianised streets parallel to the Mall in the downtown area.

Wellington

The main shopping street is Lambton Quay, with many covered arcades and some small, speciality shops on its north side. Further on, three streets – Willis, Manners, and Cuba – all have a similar mix of shops. A good place to look for crafts, posters, clothes, and so on is Wakefield Market (corner of Jervois Quay & Taranaki St), which is open Fridays, weekends, and public holidays. A good area for craft souvenirs, jewellery, and antiques and art galleries, is Tinakori Road.

Shopping in Parnell Village, Auckland

Entertainment

New Zealand is a farming country, so every town holds an annual agricultural show – known as A&P, for agricultural and pastoral – well worth a look. However, there is much else besides to occupy you when you have had your fill of sightseeing.

Cultural events are staged throughout the year

Classical Music, Dance, and Theatre

The main classical orchestras are the New Zealand Symphony Orchestra (based in Wellington) and the Auckland Philharmonic Orchestra, which give regular concerts from their home bases and in regional centres. The Royal New Zealand Ballet (based in Wellington) also tours extensively, often with visiting soloists. Despite the fact that New Zealand boasts such talented opera stars as Dames Kiri Te Kanawa and Malvina Major, grand opera is staged regionally in only the four main centres, but it is of a high standard. Dame Kiri does, however, sometimes perform at outdoor concerts and other events.

Theatre has proliferated in New Zealand, with many professional and semi-professional theatre groups staging productions in the major centres.

Other Entertainment

The most internationally renowned pop group to have come out of New Zealand was Split Enz, now disbanded. Plenty of aspiring rock bands do, however, perform on the pub circuit, as do blues, jazz, and folk musicians. Auckland, Wellington, Christchurch, and Queenstown are the best places for live music, and there are also discos in the major centres. Most towns and cities have cinemas, with new films shown soon after their international release. Out-of-town multiplex cinemas are also common.

Maori Concerts

Although most Maori concerts are presented principally for the tourist trade, they still present a genuine example of the culture – indeed, many young Maori have rediscovered their traditions and re-learnt old skills via these shows. They are also highly professional, with many of the concert groups touring overseas. A typical performance will start with a *wero* (challenge), followed by a *powhiri* (welcoming), and a *hongi* (a greeting which involves the touching of noses), all of which are explained. These introductions will then be followed by various songs and dances, such as the *haka* or *poi* (*see pp22–3*), usually with some entertaining audience participation. Many concerts are also followed by a *hangi* feast.

Daytime concerts are held at the Auckland Domain (*see p33)* and at the Whakarewarewa Thermal Reserve in Rotorua (*see p67*). Several large hotels in Rotorua (such as the Sheraton, the Lake

Plaza, and the THC Rotorua Hotel) put on evening concerts, but by far the best way to experience authentic Maori culture is to go to a concert and *hangi* held on a *marae*. These are run by the following Maori groups: **Tamaki Tours**: *PO Box 1492, Rotorua. Tel: (07) 346 2823;* **Matariki Hangi & Concert**: *Tutanekai St. Tel: (07) 346 3888. Daily at 6.30pm.*

Events

New Zealand stages a huge range of events and cultural activities each year, from gumboot-throwing competitions to internationally acclaimed arts festivals. The best source of information is the annual *Special Events* brochure produced by the tourism board. Some of the regular annual events include:

January
Annual Yachting Regatta, Auckland.
Summer City Mardi Gras, Wellington.

February
6th: Treaty of Waitangi Celebrations.
1st weekend: Speight Coast to Coast Race.
Last weekend: Devonport Wine and Food Festival, Auckland.
Late Feb: Kapa Haka Fest, Orakei Marai, Auckland.
2nd Sat: NZ International Festival of the Arts, Wellington (biennial – even years).

March
2nd weekend: Wild Foods Festival, Hokitika.
Mid-Mar: New Zealand Cheese Festival, Auckland.
Waiheke Jazz Festival, Auckland.

April
Easter weekend: Silverstone Race to the Sky, Cardona.

May
1st fortnight: TV2 International Laugh Festival, Wellington.

June
Auckland Winter Festival.
International Car Rally, Auckland.

July
Wellington International Film Festival.
Canterbury Winter Carnival, Christchurch.

August
2nd weekend: Jazz and Blues Festival, Bay of Islands.
Mid Aug: Queenstown Winter Festival.

September
The Great NZ Craft Show, Christchurch.
Annual Citrus Festival, Te Puke.
Russell Oyster Festival, Russell, Bay of Islands.

October
1st weekend: Kaikoura Seafest.
World Festival of Golf, Canterbury.
Mid-Oct: Wellington International Jazz Festival.

November
Cup Carnival Week, Christchurch.
Rhododendron Festival, Taranaki.
3rd week: Ellersie Flower Show, Botanic Gardens, Manurewa, Auckland.

December
Summertime Festival, Christchurch.

Children

New Zealand is in many ways a family-oriented country, and children will be made to feel welcome almost everywhere. There are no problems with language, strange food, or culture shock, and no dangerous animals or poisonous insects! Adequate protection from the sun is absolutely essential as New Zealand has high levels of damaging ultraviolet rays. Supplies of baby foods, nappies, and other essentials are widely available, and the water is clean and safe to drink everywhere.

Children's farms are a feature of many zoos

There are plenty of parks and playgrounds where children can run wild, and as well as enjoying purpose-built attractions such as funfairs (the biggest are Splash Planet in Hastings and Rainbow's End in Auckland), they will be enthralled by natural wonders such as volcanoes, glaciers, and bubbling, smelly mud pools.

Adventure Sports

Older children will enjoy adventure sports such as sea kayaking and river rafting, and some companies offer family discounts. Jet-boating is perfectly safe for kids of any age, and, if you can afford it, a helicopter ride will no doubt prove to be a highlight of the trip. The youngest person ever to bungee jump off the Kawaru Bridge near Queenstown was only seven!

Unless you have considerable experience, hiking with children is not advisable, although you could certainly walk short sections of the Abel Tasman Coastal Track, where there are regular boat shuttles to and from various beaches. There are plenty of short bush walks and nature trails all over the country.

Boat Trips

Scenic cruises are very popular. There is a huge choice of such cruises, from old sailing ships in the Bay of Islands to catamarans on the Marlborough Sounds and old steamships on Lakes Taupo, Rotorua, and Wakatipu. Many single-day yacht charters from Auckland include stops for swimming, snorkelling, and beach picnics.

Museums and Science Centres

New Zealand has some exceptionally well-designed museum exhibits which make the past come alive in an entertaining way. The Time Tunnel at the top of the Mount Cavendish Gondola in Christchurch, for instance, has volcanoes that blast hot air and a below-decks scene in an immigrant ship that even smells realistic; the National Maritime Museum in Auckland also has a convincing mock-up of a ship's interior.

Other top spots for children include: Kelly Tarlton's Antarctic Encounter and Underwater World (Auckland); the Sky Tower (Auckland); the International Antarctic Centre (Christchurch); and there is plenty to see at Air Force World (Christchurch) and at the Museum of Transport Technology and Social History (Auckland). But by far the best and most innovative of such centres in New Zealand is Capital Discovery Place (Wellington).

The Museum of New Zealand/Te Papa Tongarewa is the country's first national museum and covers every aspect of New Zealand's life – past, present, and future.

Swimming

There are opportunities for swimming in the ocean, rivers, and lakes almost everywhere, as well as in swimming-pools in most major towns and cities. Swimming outdoors is, however, only practicable from late October to early March – except in the north.

Not all the country's beaches are safe for swimming, and you should always check locally for hazardous conditions. Surf life-savers operate patrols at popular beaches during the summer. If children spend too long near lakeshores in the summer months, they may develop 'duck itch', an unpleasant but harmless irritation caused by a parasite that is carried by ducks.

Wildlife

There are numerous opportunities for getting close to wildlife, particularly on the east coast of the South Island where seal and penguin colonies can be reached after just a short walk. Whale-watching (in Kaikoura) or swimming with dolphins (Bay of Islands and Whakatane) will provide memorable experiences.

Most wildlife centres have nocturnal houses where you can spot kiwis. If native bird aviaries don't appeal, there are always bigger, more exotic animals in places such as Auckland Zoo, Wellington Zoo, and the Orana Park Wildlife Trust (Christchurch), which also have children's farms.

Riding a big bull at Walter Peak Station, near Queenstown, is quite an experience

Sport and Leisure

New Zealand is a nation of sports and fitness fanatics, with more than 35 per cent of the population belonging to a sporting club of some kind. National teams and individual competitors are followed with considerable pride, and television coverage of sport is extensive. The country has no less than five museums devoted entirely to sport!

Fly fishing

Competitive Sports

Rugby football is the most popular sport in the country, with more than 119,000 registered players and many more supporters. The national team, the All Blacks, is held in high esteem (the team-members are probably better known to most New Zealanders than elected politicians) and its progress in international matches is followed avidly.

During the winter, netball (a sport in which New Zealand has several times been world champion), soccer, and hockey are also played. During the summer months, cricket takes over from rugby as the focus of national aspirations abroad. Lawn bowls is incredibly popular, more than sports such as tennis, squash, softball, and basketball.

New Zealanders are also passionate about horse-racing; over 70 tracks around the country feature 'the gallops' by day and 'the trots' by night.

Cycling

With its scenic attractions and uncrowded roads, New Zealand is ideal for cycling – but be warned, distances between destinations can be considerable, and, of course, the country is also fairly mountainous. If you are heading into the hills or off the beaten track, a mountain bike is essential for the unmetalled side-roads. There are, as yet, very few dedicated off-road routes. Several local cycle-touring guidebooks are available if you want to go it alone, or you can join a group tour with accommodation (or tents) and meals provided, and with a mini-bus back-up. Mountain bikes can be hired in many resort areas.

Adventure South
PO Box 33–153, Christchurch.
Tel: (03) 332 1222.
Mountain Bike Adventure Company
Tel: toll-free 0800 424 534.
Adventure Cycles
Tel: (09) 309 5566.

Fishing

Unpolluted rivers and miles of clean, accessible coastline make New Zealand a fisherman's mecca. Licences for inland fisheries are available from fishing-tackle and sports shops for daily, weekly, or monthly periods; sea fishing requires no licence. A special tourist licence, valid for the whole of the country for one month, is also available.

The introduction of trout and other species such as salmon and perch has given New Zealand some of the best dry-fly fishing in the world, and reputable and experienced fishing guides can be hired locally. Lake Taupo is the main centre for trout fishing, but numerous rivers and lakes on both islands are stocked with brown, rainbow, and brook trout. Quinnat salmon is caught in the rivers on the east coast of the South Island between January and March.

New Zealand is also well known for its big-game fishing, particularly around the east coast of the North Island where marlin, broadbill, shark, yellowfin tuna, and other pelagic species abound. The main season runs from January to May. Surfcasting and boat fishing are also very popular. Contact:

NZ Professional Fishing Guides Association
PO Box 16, Motu, Gisborne Tel: (06) 863 5822; www.flyfishing.net.nz/nzpfga.html

Golf

Golfers will find no shortage of places to play – with around 400 golf-courses, New Zealand has more per head of population than anywhere else in the world. Many of the courses are set in beautiful scenery and may even include hazards such as boiling mud pools or sheep! Golf is a year-round activity and visitors are welcome at most clubs.

New Zealand Golf Association
Level 7, 49 Boulcott St, PO Box 11 842, Wellington. Tel: (04) 385 4330; www.nzga.co.nz

Horse-Riding

There are numerous opportunities for horse-riding, with half-day, full-day, or longer treks available for all abilities. Most stables will supply all gear if necessary. Many country lodges and farmsteads offer their guests horse-riding.

New Zealand Equestrian Federation
PO Box 6146, Wellington.
Tel: (04) 801 6449; fax: (04) 801 7701; www.nzhorses.co.nz

Mountain bikes can be hired for those heading off into the hills

Hunting

Whereas it might be frowned upon elsewhere, recreational hunting is considered an important method of controlling the damage to native forests caused by New Zealand's large mammals. A permit is required to hunt in national parks. Some of the world's best deer-stalking is found in New Zealand, with autumn (March to May) being the optimum season. Chamois, thar, goats, pigs, opossums, rabbits, hares, and wallabies can also be hunted.

Fish and Game New Zealand
PO Box 13–141, Wellington.
Tel: (04) 499 4767; fax: (04) 499 4768; www.fishandgame.org.nz

Conservation Department of Hunting
Permits, Hut Passes, Walking Tracks details available from the department office.

Skiing

New Zealand is proud of its skiing facilities. Because of the low prices of lift passes, lessons, ski hire, and so on, one in every ten New Zealanders can ski. And since the cost of reaching virgin, high-altitude runs by helicopter is very reasonable, heli-skiing is also very popular. There are nearly 25 ski fields, mostly along the Southern Alps.

The biggest winter resort is Queenstown: the nearby Coronet Peak and Remarkables ski fields have a wide variety of runs, all with fabulous views. The Cardrona and Treble Cone ski fields near Wanaka offer terrains suitable for all skiers, beginners or advanced.

Mount Hutt, inland from Christchurch, has the longest season in the country (late May–early November); other nearby fields include Porter Heights, Dobson, Ohau, and the country's newest ski area, Mount Lyford.

On the North Island, the main ski fields are Whakapapa and Turoa, both on the volcanic slopes of Mt Ruapehu, in the Tongariro National Park. (Look up *The Official New Zealand Ski Guide,* published by the Tourism Board.)

Canoeing and kayaking are popular with both locals and visitors alike

Watersports

With its numerous lakes and rivers, and over 10,000km of coastline, New Zealand has tremendous opportunities for virtually every kind of watersport. Apart from rafting and jet-boating (*see p147 & pp150–51*), canoeing and kayaking are also popular, particularly sea kayaking in the sheltered waters of the Bay of Islands, the Marlborough Sounds, and along the coast of the Abel Tasman National Park. One of the most popular canoeing rivers is the Whanganui, which has both rapids and long stretches of calm water. Rentals and/or organised tours are available in all these locations.

Surfing is possible all year round. In the North Island, the most frequented beaches are in the Auckland area: Raglan (west of Hamilton), around New Plymouth, Gisborne, and Mount Manganui in the Bay of Plenty. In the South Island, the beaches near Dunedin, Kaikoura,and Westport are popular.

Scuba diving takes place mostly off the North Island where the sea is warmer, especially the Poor Knights Marine Reserve off Whangarei, which supports a wide variety of marine life.

Other good spots include the Bay of Islands Maritime Park (where the wreck of the Greenpeace ship *Rainbow Warrior* was resunk after it was destroyed by the French secret service in Auckland Harbour), Marlborough Sounds, the Hauraki Gulf, Stewart Island, and even Fiordland.

Yachting

Yachting seems to be in the lifeblood of most New Zealanders. Charter boats of all kinds are available to visitors. The classic sailing areas include the Hauraki Gulf, Bay of Islands, Marlborough Sounds, and Coromandel Peninsula.

The popular America's Cup series is being defended by last time's winner, Team New Zealand, in the year 2003 (races start in February).

New Zealand Canoeing Association
PO Box 284, Wellington.
Tel: (04) 560 3590.

New Zealand Underwater Association
PO Box 875, Auckland. Tel: (09) 623 3252; www.nzundewater.org.nz

Yachting New Zealand
PO Box 33–789, Takapura, North Shore.
Tel: (09) 488 9525;
www.yachtingnz.org.nz

Lakes and harbours present numerous opportunities for messing about in boats

Food and Drink

The kiwifruit is just one of numerous succulent fruits which thrive in New Zealand soil

It has become something of a cliché to say that New Zealand has witnessed a 'culinary revolution' in recent years, nonetheless, this is true. You might still find plenty of stodgy food, meat pies, and overdone steaks, but there are also hundreds of restaurants, wine bars, and hotels where you can eat the best local produce cooked with imagination and flair.

Natural Ingredients

The raw ingredients have always been here, and it was only a matter of time before Kiwi chefs developed their own distinctive cuisine. The rich pasturelands and mild climate produce excellent beef and lamb, and deer are now also farmed extensively (local venison appears on menus as 'cervena', and has a much milder, less gamey taste than wild venison). Dairy products such as butter, cheese, milk, yoghurt, and cream have always been of top quality.

New Zealanders are particularly partial to what the Maori call *kai-moana* (meaning 'food from the sea'), and some of the best eating fish include blue cod, snapper, orange roughy, John Dory, *tarakihi*, and *hapuka* (grouper). Shellfish are plentiful, and include rock lobsters (known as crayfish), scallops, Bluff oysters, and green-lipped mussels. Whitebait is a much-prized delicacy, particularly on the West coast, usually served in fritters or sandwiches. You will also find salmon on the menu, but never trout, as it is illegal to buy or sell it.

Fresh fruit and vegetables grow in abundance, and apart from the usual standards such as apples, apricots, cherries, grapes, peaches, pears, nectarines, raspberries, and strawberries, you should also try boysenberries, feijoa, and tamarillos – not forgetting, of course, the ubiquitous kiwifruit.

For the sweet-toothed, New Zealand has excellent ice creams, flans, and pastries, as well as the national dessert of pavlova, a rich concoction of meringue, whipped cream, and fresh fruit.

Eating Places

Almost every town and village has at least one tea shop serving refreshments and snacks. If you are in the middle of nowhere, the worst you can expect are plain meat pies and dry, lifeless sandwiches, but elsewhere, pies, scones, pastries, and sandwiches are often fresh, home-made and quite delicious.

Take-aways all over the country churn out fish and chips, pies and the like, often highly variable in quality. Pub food follows more or less the same format, although in cities and tourist areas some pubs have evolved into far more trendy places where you can get a decent meal in civilised surroundings.

Restaurants are either fully licensed (selling wines and spirits), licensed (wine and beer only) or BYO (bring your own alcohol, in which case a small corkage charge is added to the bill); some are both licensed and BYO. Wine bars and licensed cafés have also proliferated in recent years, and you will find plenty of places where you can enjoy a meal and a drink outdoors at pavement tables, Mediterranean-style.

Ethnic cuisine has had its impact and although Chinese take-ways are by far the most frequented, there are also Greek, Italian, Mexican, Thai, and Indian restaurants.

Vegetarian food is widely available and usually very good.

Maori Feasts

You should try a Maori *hangi* at least once. This is a feast of meat, seafood, and vegetables (including the delicious *kumara*, or sweet potato, a Maori staple) steamed on heated stones in an 'earthen oven' (the *hangi*). The best *hangi* are those that follow an authentic Maori concert, although some hotels offer their own versions.

Beer and Wines

Beer is practically the national drink, and the New Zealand lager, Steinlager, has won many international awards. Lion and DB are the two main brands

Try a *hangi* – a traditional Maori feast

served in pubs, but recently there has been a proliferation of 'boutique' or 'micro' breweries that produce excellent beers in small quantities.

In recent years, New Zealand wines have begun gaining international renown. The first vines were planted by the British Resident, James Busby, in his back garden at Waitangi in the 1840s, but it has only been during the last decade that the New Zealand wine industry has come of age.

White Wines

New Zealand's relatively cool climate is well adapted to vine-growing, with the long autumn giving the grapes a chance to ripen slowly, concentrating their flavour to the full.

These conditions are ideally suited to Sauvignon Blanc, the slightly tart, 'grassy' grape which originates in France's Loire Valley. Nearly 60 per cent of Sauvignon comes from the Marlborough region.

The Chardonnay grape has also done very well here, producing a subtle, full-bodied wine. Gisborne is one of the prime Chardonnay areas, and the local wine-growers have many medals to their credit. Other successful white varieties are Gewürztraminer, dry Riesling, and Müller-Thurgau.

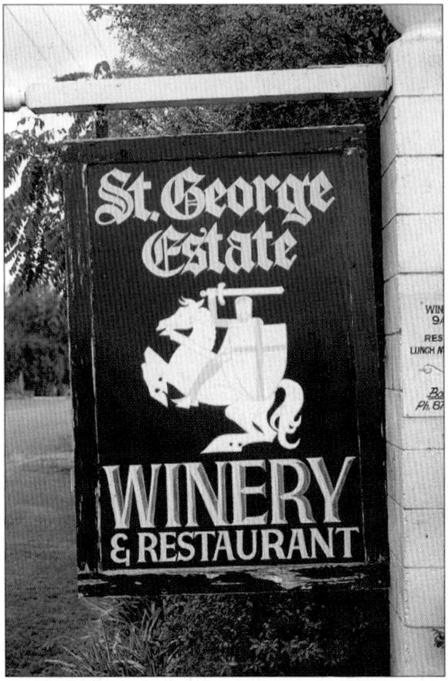

New Zealand wines are now exported worldwide

Wine Trails
In the major wine-growing areas, local tourist offices provide 'Wine Trail' brochures detailing the locations and opening hours of vineyards you can visit to taste and buy wines.

Familiar signpost to a winery

Red Wines

Although New Zealand is well known for its white wines, progress has been slower with the reds. However, Cabernet Sauvignon seems to have found a natural home in the Hawke's Bay area. Pinot Noir, a notoriously fickle variety, is also doing well in the Martinborough district north of Wellington.

A wine cellar at Gibbston Valley winery

Where to Eat

In the following list of selected restaurants, the star ratings indicate the approximate cost of a meal for one person, not including drinks:

★	up to NZ$15
★★	NZ$15–25
★★★	Over NZ $25

NORTH ISLAND

Auckland

Cin-Cin on the Quay ★★★
Busy brasserie on the quayside; extensive menu, New Zealand and Pacific dishes cooked with flair and imagination. Good portions, efficient service. Reservations advised.
Auckland Ferry Building, 99 Quay St.
Tel: (09) 307 6966.

The Loaded Hog ★/★★
Cavernous bar and restaurant with good selection of snacks and main meals, all freshly prepared. The own-brand beers come from a micro-brewery visible through glass screens at the back.
Viaduct Quay, corner of Hobson and Quay sts.
Tel: (09) 366 6491.
Other branches in Wellington, Christchurch, and Timaru.

Tony's ★★/★★★
Popular steakhouse with a wide selection of perfectly cooked cuts. Also lunches and other meals available.
32 Lorne St.
Tel: (09) 373 2138.
Also at 27 Wellesley St.
Tel: (09) 373 4196.

Paihia

Kelly Tarlton's Tui ★★
Unusual café-restaurant on the barque *Tui* (*see p44*). Good food, welcoming, and informal. Licensed.
By the bridge.
Tel: (09) 402 7018.

Tides ★★
Homely bistro specialising in venison, mussels, fresh fish, and lamb dishes.
Williams Rd.
Tel: (09) 402 7557.

Lake Taupo

The Bach ★/★★
Café-wine bar. Comfortable environs and good food, especially gourmet pizza, complemented by an extensive wine list.
Corner of Lake Terrace and Pataka Rd.
Tel: (07) 378 7856.

Finch's Bar & Brasserie ★★★
Classic 'new wave' Kiwi cuisine prepared by an award-winning chef. Licensed.
64 Tuwharetoa St.
Tel: (07) 377 2425.

Prawn Park ★★★
Prawns from the restaurant's own ponds feature in every conceivable combination. Bookings essential. Licensed.
Prawn Park.
Tel: (07) 374 8474.

Rotorua

Fishpot Cafe ★★
'One bite and you'll be hooked' is the claim made by this licensed seafood restaurant. The whitebait. fritters are recommended.
1123 Eruera St.
Tel: (07) 349 3494.

Mitas Restaurant ★★
The best of 'East meets West'. Authentic Indonesian cuisine.
1114 Tutanekai St.
Tel: (07) 349 6482.

Mr India ★★
A family-owned chain across the lower North Island. Delicious *tandoori* cuisine, coupled with good service.
1161 Amohau St.
Tel: (07) 349 4940.

Pig & Whistle City Bar ★★
Serves generous portions of food and brews its own ales. Also offers live entertainment on Friday and Saturday evenings.

Corner of Haupapa & Tutanekai sts.
Tel: (07) 347 3025.
Open: 11.30am–late.

Roundabout Bar & Café ★
Lively, informal café-bar with a good range of bar snacks, soups, salads, steaks, burgers, and vegetarian dishes. Generous portions, excellent value.
83 Arawa St.
Tel: (07) 347 2553.

Sirocco Bar Café ★/★★
Cosy eating-house with a trendy, Mediterranean-style atmosphere. Serves a variety of bar snacks (*nachos*, sandwiches, soups) and main-course pasta, seafood, and salads. Delicious desserts and good coffee. Licensed. Good value.
1280 Eruera St.
Tel: (07) 347 3388.

Zanelli's Italian Café & Restaurant ★★
Unpretentious, no-frills Italian restaurant where the emphasis is on well-cooked, well-presented classic dishes.
1243A Amohia St.
Tel: (07) 348 4908.

Wellington

Fresco Express Café ★
Fresh-cooked, home-made pasta and filled breads, cakes, and sammies galore.
Cable Car Lane Centre, Lambton Quay.
Tel: (04) 473 0542.

The Backbencher Pub ★★/★★★
Light, airy pub opposite Parliament with a jovial atmosphere (plenty of political cartoons and so on). A fun theme pub.
Corner of Kate Shepherd Place and Molesworth St.
Tel: (04) 472 3065.

The Malthouse ★★
Spacious bar in the heart of the city with a terrace and conservatory. The adjoining carvery has five different roasts on offer daily, plus a blackboard menu. Good food, reasonable prices.
41 Willis St.
Tel: (04) 499 4355.

Cin-Cin on the Quay, popular with the Auckland smart set

One of the excellent restaurants in Christchurch

SOUTH ISLAND

Christchurch

Canterbury Tales ★★★
Located in the city's top hotel, this elegant restaurant (with tapestries depicting Chaucerian scenes on the walls) has an extensive menu and is deservedly popular. Bookings essential.
Parkroyal Hotel, corner of Durham & Kilmar sts.
Tel: (03) 365 7799.

Gloucester Street Café & Bar ★/★★
Good value for light meals, with reasonably priced daily blackboard specials and imaginative vegetarian dishes. Licensed.
96 Gloucester St.
Tel: (03) 379 8298.

Mainstreet Café & Bar ★/★★
Rated as one of the best vegetarian restaurants in New Zealand, with tasty and imaginative food at reasonable prices. Licensed and BYO.
840, corner of Colombo & Salisbury sts.
Tel: (03) 365 0421.

Oxford on Avon ★/★★
Good value meals are the order of the day in this pub-restaurant situated beside the River Avon.
794 Colombo St.
Tel: (03) 379 7148.

Willowbank ★★/★★★
This excellent licensed restaurant is part of a wildlife reserve *(see p109)*, and you can view the wildlife at night after eating. Guided tours are free to diners, and offer the chance to see kiwis and other nocturnal species in their natural (floodlit) bush habitat.
Willowbank Wildlife Reserve, Hussey Rd.
Tel: (03) 359 6226.

Dunedin

High Tide ★/★★
Quiet waterfront restaurant that serves meat and seafood dishes.
29 Kitchener St.
Tel: (03) 477 9784.

Homestead Restaurant ★★/★★★
This restaurant is situated amid magnificent woodlands at 'the hidden valley' of Glenfalloch. Fine cuisine; BYO and licensed. By arrangement.
430 Portobello Rd.
Tel: (03) 476 1006.
Ten minutes from the city centre.

Lone Star ★/★★
Lively atmosphere, part of

a highly popular chain of Tex-Mex restaurants. Licensed.
417 Princes St.
Tel: (03) 474 1955.
Other branches in Christchurch and Queenstown, Wellington.

Queenstown

Avanti ★
Better than average selection of pizzas, soups, and Italian dishes is on offer in this cheerful and reasonably cheap restaurant.
20 The Mall.
Tel: (03) 442 8503.

The Cow ★/★★
Very cosy and popular pizza and spaghetti house in an old stone building, with a roaring fire. Book in advance or expect a long wait.
Cow Lane.
Tel: (03) 442 8588.
Open: noon–late hours.

Fishbone Bar & Grill ★★/★★★
Good seafood and fish dishes in an unpretentious, café-style setting. Oysters, mussels, calamari, crayfish, fish fillets, and so on, are served in generous portions, so go with a hearty appetite if you want more than one course.
Beach St.
Tel: (03) 442 6768.

McNeills Cottage Brewery, Bar, and Restaurant ★★
Great atmosphere; real beer served.
14 Church St.
Tel: (03) 442 9688.

Decorated with kitsch, the Lone Star Café is immensely popular

Hotels and Accommodation

New Zealand has a huge range of accommodation to suit every budget, ranging from campsites in national parks to stylish country retreats and smart city business hotels. There is rarely a problem, even in the most remote location, of finding a clean, comfortable room, although during the peak summer season (mid-December to January) you may need to telephone ahead to make reservations in popular tourist centres such as Rotorua and Queenstown.

Moderately-priced motels are found in almost every corner of the country

Advance reservations are also necessary for up-market country lodges and places with very limited accommodation options, such as the Mount Cook National Park.

One of the more useful publications, covering numerous options all over the country, is the *New Zealand Where to Stay Guide,* published by the tourism board in conjunction with the New Zealand Automobile Association (NZAA). A classification system for accommodation, developed jointly by the tourism board and the New Zealand AA, has been introduced under the 'Qualmark' logo, by which hotels and all other lodgings are graded with a one- to five-star rating system.

Luxury Hotels

International chain hotels such as Sheraton, Regent, and Hyatt are found in the major cities and resorts, alongside locally owned hotel chains such as the Pacific Park Group and Scenic Circle Hotels. Many of the prime tourist hotels in the country that were once part of the government-owned Tourist Hotel Corporation are now operated by Southern Pacific Hotels. The cost of a room in an international-standard hotel ranges from around NZ$200 to over NZ$1,000 a night for deluxe suites.

Retreats and Sporting Lodges

Wilderness hideaways are something of a New Zealand speciality, and if your budget allows it, you should certainly try to stay in one of these exclusive, highly individual retreats for a few days. Exceptionally high standards of accommodation, coupled with good food, plenty of atmosphere, and first-class facilities are the hallmarks of this type of lodge. Many concentrate on hunting and fishing, with professional guides on tap (the world-renowned Huka Lodge and Tongariro Lodge, both near Lake Taupo, are sports-oriented), while others are remarkable for their beautiful natural surroundings – such as the Puka Park Lodge in the Coromandel and Moose Lodge on Lake Rotoiti. Around two dozen lodges are described in *The Lodges of New Zealand*, from the tourism board.

Motor Inns, Motels, and Other Hotels

Although there is quite a lot of overlap between these categories, motor inns usually have more facilities than motels, with a house bar, swimming pool, and licensed restaurant. They include chains such as Flag Hotels, Best Western, Quality Inns, and Manor Motor Inns. Expect to pay NZ$80–200 per night.

Motels are located everywhere and provide one of the best options for mid-market, independent travellers. The clean, comfortable units usually have one or more bedrooms, a lounge and a reasonably well-equipped kitchen. Some also have swimming pools, spa pools, in-house video channels, laundry rooms, and other facilities. You can often find motel rooms from NZ$70 in the off-season. Many motels are affiliated to booking chains, as at Jason's, Flag Hotels, and Best Western.

New Zealand also has numerous independent hotels, often older buildings in town or city centres. Budget rooms in these hotels are invariably one of the cheapest options (apart from hostels or backpacker accommodation), costing from around NZ$30–40. However, standards vary widely and at these prices your room is unlikely to have a private bathroom. Some historic hotels (such as the Brian Boru in Thames) have been renovated to higher standards and still represent good value for money.

Around 50 historic hotels and country pubs are listed in the *Pub Beds Guide* (available from Pub Beds, PO Box 32–332, Auckland; *tel: (09) 443 0888; enclose SAE*).

Accommodation throughout the country is covered in the AA Accommodation Guide *Jason's Motels and Motor Lodges* (NZ$9.95 from bookshops or free when you stay in a listed property).

Backpacker hostels catering for young travellers often have good facilities

Guest Houses and Bed and Breakfast Accommodation

Staying in a private guest house or B&B is a good way to meet people and find out about the locality. Again, standards vary widely: a room in a basic guest-house costs from NZ$30 per person, while one in a more comfortable B&B establishment where breakfast (usually huge!) is included will set you back around NZ$40–60, per person. The New Zealand *Bed & Breakfast Book* by J and J Thomas (Moonshine Press, Wellington) is a good source of information.

Farmstays and Homestays

The difference between farmstays and B&Bs is that at the former you usually get the chance to take part in day-to-day activities and learn about the Kiwi way of life; you will be staying in a real family home and will usually share home-cooked meals with your hosts.

On farmstays, you can help out with activities such as shearing and milking, and a range of other outdoor activities (bush-walking, fishing, cycling, and so on) is usually available. Homestays are an urban version of the farmstay.

An upmarket variation on farmstays are high-country sheep stations; these have purpose-built facilities where you can stay in complete luxury and take part in almost anything you want, from hunting expeditions to heli-sking. Some (such as the Mount Hutt Station Resort) even have international-standard restaurants and conference facilities!

You can arrange accommodation at farmstays for just one night or for a whole holiday, and your room may either be in the family home or in a separate unit or farm cottage. Rates start as low as NZ$20–30 for shared, self-catering units, reaching around NZ$70–80 for full board and rooms with private facilities. There are several agencies which specialise in bookings:

Friendly B&B establishments are common

Rural Holidays New Zealand Ltd
PO Box 2155, Christchurch.
Tel: (03) 366 1919; fax: (03) 379 3087.
New Zealand Farm Holidays Ltd
PO Box 256, Silverdale, Auckland.
Tel: (09) 426 5430; fax: (09) 426 8474.
New Zealand Home Hospitality
PO Box 309, Nelson. Tel: (03) 548 2424; fax: (03) 546 9519.

Hostels and Backpacker Accommodation

Hostels are as common in New Zealand as motels, providing clean, basic accommodation almost everywhere tourists are likely to go – and a few more places besides. While there are numerous 'official' hostels (run by the YHA, YMCA, and YWCA), there are also hundreds more private hostels – usually called 'backpackers'.

Gone are the days of segregated dormitories and lights out by 10pm: hostels now have private rooms as well as a more liberal attitude. Communal facilities usually include kitchens, lounge areas, laundries, and so on, and although you may sometimes have to provide your own bedding this can often be hired for a small charge. Nightly costs are around NZ$12–20.

Numerous sources of information, including *New Zealand Budget Backpackers Accommodation*, *Backpackers Guide to New Zealand*, and the *New Zealand Backpackers Hotels* information booklet, are available from information centres and hostels.

Camping and Motorcamps

There are well equipped campsites all over the country. Some also have cabins and/or 'tourist flats' attached. Campsite costs start at around NZ$8 per adult, while powered sites for motorhomes are around NZ$9–10 per adult.

The Camp and Cabin Association (CCA) leaflet, *Holiday Accommodation Parks*, gives details on sites operated by its members, who have to meet certain minimum standards. The leaflet is available from the CCA, PO Box 394, Paraparaumu.

The *AA Accommodation Guide* offers detailed listings of motor camps and caravan parks (costs are NZ$8–23 for a standard cabin).

The Department of Conservation (DOC) maintains a network of huts and campsites in national parks and other wilderness areas. Facilities range from the basic minimum to fully serviced campgrounds with hot showers, laundry facilities, lighting. Costs are minimal (NZ$2–9). Locations and facilities are given in *Conservation Campsites*, available at DOC information centres or from the DOC, PO Box 10420, Wellington.

A campervan will give you the flexibility of your own home on wheels

On Business

Since the mid-1980s, the New Zealand economy has undergone a programme of wide-ranging reforms designed to create an open, more competitive business environment. Economic growth in the 1980s remained sluggish as the reforms were pushed through by successive governments but by 1994 had risen to 7 per cent per annum. In 1997 there was again a recession following a drought and downturn in tourism. Since 1998, however, the economy has been revived, and in the first half of 2002 it grew by a robust 4 per cent.

Wellington is New Zealand's business capital

Business and Investment Environment

Foreign investors are welcomed in New Zealand, particularly in sectors contributing to foreign exchange earnings such as tourism and the export of locally manufactured processed goods. Businesses are now subject to much less regulation than they used to be, and the transfer of funds in and out of the country is not restricted. The sale of major national assets to foreign investors has been encouraged, and similar policies are still being pursued; there are no ceilings on the level of non-resident ownership of privatised state enterprises.

Incentives are sometimes available to foreign investors, and investment is widely promoted through bodies such as the Tourist Development Board and the New Zealand Import Export Corporation. Foreign investment is monitored and controlled by the Overseas Investment Commission (OIC), but consent is not required for investments below a value threshold of NZ$10 million – unless they are related to broadcasting, commercial fishing, or rural land. Stock exchanges operate in Auckland, Wellington, Christchurch, and Dunedin.

Business Etiquette

New Zealand's business culture lies somewhere between that of Britain and the United States, with a fast-growing entrepreneurial sector which has a highly positive outlook on the economic future. You will generally find the people are helpful, efficient, and straightforward in their dealings.

Business Hours

Offices and businesses operate Monday to Friday, 8.30am–5pm. Trading banks open Monday to Friday, 9.30am–4.30pm.

Communications

(*See* Telephones *on pp188–9* and Post Offices *on p186*). Internet cafés are found in all cities and large towns and conference calls and satellite links can easily be arranged. Luxury hotel chains are equipped with modern business facilities.

Conferences

The largest conference centres are the Auckland Convention Centre, Christchurch Town Hall, the Wellington Festival and Convention Centre, the new Rotorua Convention and Exhibition Centre, the Trafalgar Centre in Nelson, and the Dunedin Centre, all of which have single room capacities of over 2,000 people. Hotels such as the Carlton, Sheraton, and Hyatt in Auckland have facilities for over 1,000 people, and there are numerous other venues around the country capable of accommodating anything from 10 to 500 people. Professional Conference Organisers (PCOs) are available to help plan and manage conventions on any scale.

Further details can be had from: **The New Zealand Convention Association**, PO Box 331202, Takapuna, Auckland. *Tel: (09) 486 4128; fax: (09) 486 4126. www.nzconventions.co.nz*

Secretarial Services

A full range of secretarial and business services is available in the main cities, where you will also find short- or long-term serviced office space to rent. Hotels catering specifically for executive travellers, such as the Regent in Auckland, have business centres with all the usual facilities.

Further Information

The international accountancy firm Ernst & Young produces the book *Doing Business in New Zealand*, which provides details about taxation laws, company structures, financial reporting, and the like. The book is available from the company's overseas branches or from:

Ernst & Young, National Mutual Centre
37–41 Shortland St, Auckland.
Tel: (09) 377 4790; fax: (09) 309 8137.

Another useful address is:

Ministry of Foreign Affairs and Trade
Stafford House, 38–40 The Terrace, Private Bag 18901, Wellington.
Tel: (04) 494 8500; fax: (04) 494 8512.

Auckland's central business district and waterfront, with Sky Tower

Practical Guide

Arriving

By Air

Auckland is the main international gateway for passengers arriving in New Zealand, although increasing numbers of airlines are also flying into Christchurch in the South Island. Wellington only handles flights to and from Australia. Air New Zealand, the national carrier, has flights to Australia, Japan, Singapore, Malaysia, Hong Kong, Taiwan, the USA, and Europe, either directly or via the Pacific Islands. Around 17 international airlines operate scheduled services to New Zealand.

Auckland's international terminal has all the usual visitor facilities and information centres for accommodation reservations, sightseeing, and onward travel arrangements. Special elevators and toilet facilities are available for the disabled. Auckland airport (AKL) lies 22km from the city centre, and taxis are fairly expensive (around NZ$40). At least three companies operate shuttle buses (costing NZ$9 one way) which pick up at both the domestic and international terminals and drop off at any city-centre hotel and other major locations. Christchurch (10km north-west) and Wellington (8km southeast) airports have similar facilities.

An airport departure tax of NZ$22 is payable by all passengers leaving on international flights.

By Sea

There are no regular passenger services but some round-the-world cruises call in at New Zealand. Arriving by yacht is a distinct possibility, since many cruising yachts take on casual crews at various points in the South Pacific before visiting New Zealand.

Customs

There are no exchange controls or restrictions on the import or export of currency. Aside from personal effects, visitors are allowed to bring in 200 cigarettes, 250g tobacco or 50 cigars, one bottle of spirits, and 4.5 litres of wine.

New Zealand has remained largely free of most plant and animal diseases, and there are strict controls on the import of foodstuffs and plant and animal material. If you are carrying walking boots, these may be confiscated, but returned to you cleaned!

If you are planning to go fishing, you may bring your own rods, but lures or flies containing feathers will need to be fumigated. Hunters should check firearms regulations with their nearest embassy before departure *(see p182)*, but in general, hunting rifles may be brought in. A firearms permit is compulsory, obtainable from the police after a declaration to customs officers upon arrival.

The import of narcotics is prohibited, and sniffer dogs are used regularly in arrival halls.

Documents

No vaccination certificates are necessary. Passports must be valid for at least three months beyond your intended departure date. Visitors may be granted entry for up to three months, although this can be extended for up to a year for genuine tourists. Visitors must hold fully paid onward or return tickets, and sufficient funds to keep themselves while in the country. Everybody has to complete an arrival card. Visas are normally only required for visitors intending to work or study, or if you are being sponsored during your visit by a friend, relative, or business organisation.

Camping

Camping may be permitted on any suitable public open space (apart from those designated 'No Camping') or on private property subject to the owners' permission. For details on campsites, *see p175.*

Children

See pp158–9.

Campsites are often on the edge of wilderness areas

Climate

The seasons in New Zealand are the reverse of those in the Northern Hemisphere: summer runs from December to March, autumn from March to May, winter from June to August, and spring from September to November. However, seasonal variations are not extreme, and a mild winter can often lead to spring growths appearing at the end of July; conversely, autumn weather often carries over well into June in northerly latitudes.

Because the sun is in the northern sky, temperatures are highest in the far north (where summers are subtropical) and lowest in the far south (where winters are closer to sub-antarctic, but only for short periods). Average daily sunshine figures are seven to eight hours in summer, and four to five hours in winter. Most places get around 2,000 hours of sunshine a year, with the north of the North Island and the north of the South Island slightly above average, with around 2,350 hours or more.

Rainfall is spread fairly evenly throughout the year, averaging 600 to 1,200mm. The prevailing winds are westerly, and the backbone of mountains, which runs right through the country, ensures that the western side therefore receives a much higher rainfall than eastern areas; this is particularly marked in the South Island, where the altitude of the Southern Alps means that rain falls on the western coast almost constantly. The highest rainfall is in Fiordland, and although it doesn't rain every day here it does tend to bucket it down. Snow falls on the mountains and hills (particularly in the South Island) during winter.

Auckland and the far north have the hottest and most humid summers, while those around Marlborough and Nelson are comfortably hot and dry. The coldest winters and hottest summers are found

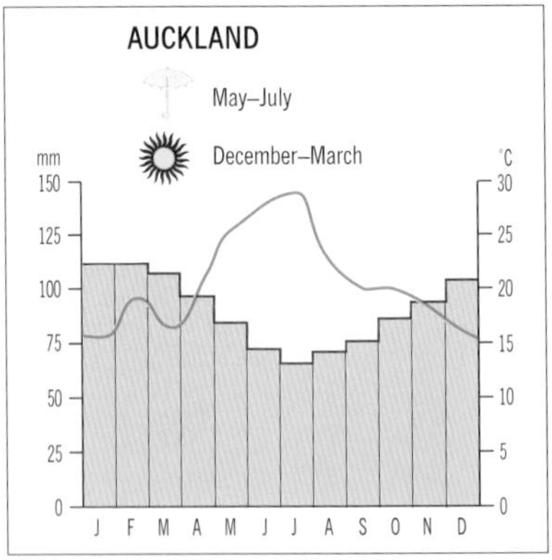

Weather Conversion Chart
25.4mm = 1 inch
°F = 1.8 x °C + 32

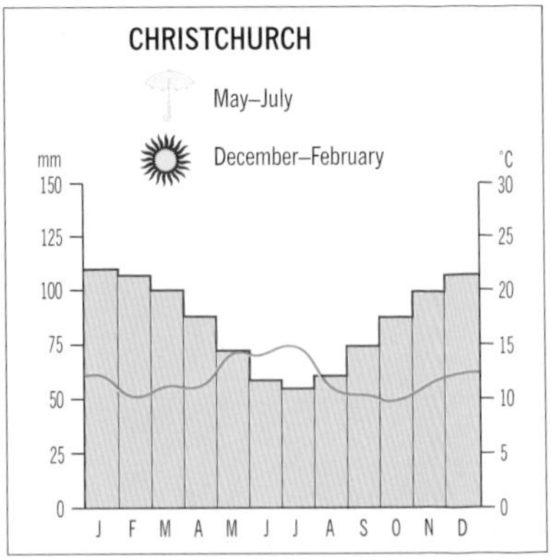

in central Otago. Wellington is exposed to southerly winds off the Cook Strait (which keep the temperature down all year), as well as occasional gales.

Although seasonal variations aren't dramatic, the weather is highly changeable and may alter several times during the course of the day in any one place, so be prepared for both rain and sun almost all year round. When the sun does shine (even behind cloud cover), it can burn very quickly (*see pp28–9*).

Climate

See tables opposite.

Conversion Tables

Clothes and shoe sizes in New Zealand follow the standard sizes used in the UK.

Crime

Although New Zealand doesn't have a high level of serious crime there has been a noticeable increase in recent years in assault, rape, and petty theft.

Take the same precautions you would anywhere else: avoid dark city backstreets at night; don't leave valuables on view in parked cars; don't leave your car unlocked; make use of hotel safes; and, finally, make sure you are fully insured for loss or damage.

Electricity

The electricity supply is 230–240 volts/50 hertz. Hotels and motels provide 110-volt AC sockets for shavers only (rated at 20 watts). For all other equipment you need an adaptor for flat, three- or two-pin plugs (readily available in major hardware stores), but check that it can operate on 230–240 volts first.

Conversion Table

FROM	TO	MULTIPLY BY
Inches	Centimetres	2.54
Feet	Metres	0.3048
Yards	Metres	0.9144
Miles	Kilometres	1.6090
Acres	Hectares	0.4047
Gallons	Litres	4.5460
Ounces	Grams	28.35
Pounds	Grams	453.6
Pounds	Kilograms	0.4536
Tons	Tonnes	1.0160

To convert back, for example from centimetres to inches, divide by the number in the third column.

Men's Suits

UK	36	38	40	42	44	46	48
Rest of Europe	46	48	50	52	54	56	58
USA	36	38	40	42	44	46	48

Dress Sizes

UK	8	10	12	14	16	18
France	36	38	40	42	44	46
Italy	38	40	42	44	46	48
Rest of Europe	34	36	38	40	42	44
USA	6	8	10	12	14	16

Men's Shirts

UK	14	14.5	15	15.5	16	16.5	17
Rest of Europe	36	37	38	39/40	41	42	43
USA	14	14.5	15	15.5	16	16.5	17

Men's Shoes

UK	7	7.5	8.5	9.5	10.5	11
Rest of Europe	41	42	43	44	45	46
USA	8	8.5	9.5	10.5	11.5	12

Women's Shoes

UK	4.5	5	5.5	6	6.5	7
Rest of Europe	38	38	39	39	40	41
USA	6	6.5	7	7.5	8	8.5

Embassies and Consulates

New Zealand Embassies Overseas

Australia Commonwealth Avenue, Canberra, ACT 2600.
Consulate: *Tel: (612) 6270 4211.*

Canada Metropolitan House, Suite 727, 99 Bank Street, Ottawa, Ontario KIP 6G3. *Tel: (613) 238 5991.*

UK New Zealand House, 80 Haymarket, London SW1Y 4TQ. *Tel: (020) 7930 8422.*

USA 37 Observatory Circle NW, Washington, DC 20008. *Tel: (202) 328 4848.* There are also consulates across the USA.

Foreign Representation in New Zealand

American Embassy 29 Fitzherbert Terrace, Wellington. *Tel: (04) 472 2068.*

Australian High Commission 72 Hobson St, Thorndon, Wellington. *Tel: (04) 498 7103.*

British High Commission 44 Hill St, Thorndon, Wellington. *Tel: (04) 924 2889.*

Canadian High Commission ICI House, 61 Molesworth St, Wellington. *Tel: (04) 473 9577.*

Irish Consulate 6th Floor, 18 Shortland St, Auckland. *Tel: (09) 302 2867.*

Emergency Telephone Numbers

Dial 111 and ask for police, fire, or ambulance.

Getting Around

By Air

The major towns, cities, and tourist destinations in New Zealand are served by flights on Air New Zealand, Qantas, and Origin Pacific Airways.

The three main airlines offer travel passes for overseas visitors (with discounts on normal tickets), either for a set number of sectors or for a limited period of time (usually one month).

Air New Zealand's air pass must be bought overseas before you travel to New Zealand. In addition, Air New Zealand offers Thrifty Fares (40 per cent discount; must be purchased overseas) and Off-Peak Saver fares (20 per cent discount; may be bought at the time of flying) on off-peak domestic flights.

Domestic Airlines

Air New Zealand
Tel: toll-free 0800 737 000.

Qantas *Tel: toll-free 0800 808 767.*

Origin Pacific Airways
Tel: toll-free 0800 302 302.

By Rail

See pp187–8.

Car Hire

All the big international agencies have rental depots in the major cities and tourist areas. You need a current national or international driving licence; the minimum age for rentals is 21 years. Insurance is compulsory, and is usually included in hire charges.

Hire charges can be fairly expensive (standard high-season charges are NZ$90 per day or NZ$80 a day for a week). If you plan to tour the whole of New Zealand by car you could negotiate discounts with the companies direct.

Campervans are another alternative for small groups or families, giving a great deal of flexibility on accommodation. Rates start from around

NZ$144 per day in low season for a two-berth van, to NZ$228 per day for a four to six berth in high season. The main agency is **Maui Tours**.
Avis 17/19 Nelson Street, Auckland. *Tel: (09) 526 2847, or toll-free 0800 655 111.*
Budget 83 Beach Road, Auckland. *Tel: (09) 976 2220, or toll-free 0800 652 227.*
Hertz 154 Victoria Street West, Auckland. *Tel: (09) 367 6350, or toll-free 0800 654 321.*
National Car Rental Auckland Airport. *Tel: (09) 275 0066, or toll-free 0800 800 115.*

Thomas Cook Holidays *Signature* has flexible packages for UK-based travellers which include car rental, rail pass, and accommodation options – or fully inclusive tours, at good rates (contact a branch of Thomas Cook).

Driving
New Zealand has an excellent, well-signposted road network and (apart from urban areas) traffic is light. Drive on the left. Speed limits: 100kph on motorways and the open road, 50kph in built-up areas; other limits may be indicated. In backcountry areas and forests, the roads – known as gravel or unmetalled roads – are often unsealed.

Restrictions may apply in some areas if you have a rental car, although these are usually ignored (there's not much point in hiring a car here if you can't take it to some of the most unspoiled wilderness areas!).

Take extra care driving on unsealed roads, and watch out for the large

A mural in MacKenzie Country, below the Southern Alps. Tourists are made to feel welcome

grading machines. Heavy rains may also cause a 'washout' or road slump, which leaves hazardous holes on the edge of the road.

Breakdowns

Many rental companies will include free breakdown services as part of the package. Members of the Automobile Association in the UK are offered free reciprocal membership of the AA in New Zealand, including breakdown assistance, the provision of maps, touring advice, and accommodation guides.

In the South Island in particular, it is always a good idea to fill up with petrol as the next service station may be some distance away. If you do run out (or even think you are about to run out), rural cafés and shops usually have emergency petrol for sale in small quantities.

Hitch-hiking

Hitch-hiking is perfectly acceptable (and legal) in New Zealand, and although it is far safer here than in many other countries you should still exercise common sense and reasonable care in accepting lifts. Women should not hitch-hike alone.

Health

New Zealand is a clean, healthy country and tap water is safe to drink everywhere. However, the parasite giardia has been found in some lakes, rivers, and streams, and can cause diarrhoea if it gets into your system. The probability of catching giardia is remote, but if you are camping it is best either to boil water for three minutes and then add iodine solution or chlorine bleach, or use a giardia-rated water filter.

Public and private health-care facilities operate to high standards, and in case of illness, your hotel or motel will be able to arrange a local doctor (otherwise, see 'Doctors and Medical Services' at the front of telephone directories).

If you have an accident you will be covered by the Accident Compensation Scheme and entitled to make a claim to the Accident Compensation Corporation, irrespective of blame. Allowable benefits include some medical and hospital expenses and compensation for permanent disability – but not for loss of earnings outside the country. The existence of this scheme means that it is not possible to sue for damages in the courts for accidental injury or death.

Like every other part of the world, AIDS is present.

Insurance

A comprehensive personal travel-insurance policy is highly advisable. Despite the Accident Compensation Scheme (*see above*), make sure your policy covers personal accidents as not all costs will be covered. Cover for loss of personal possessions and travel delay is also recommended.

Note that most policies automatically exclude adventure sports such as white-water rafting and skiing, so if you are planning to take part in these activities, you might want to arrange for an extension to the cover. You should contact a specialist travel insurance company who will normally provide cover for most sporting activities considered 'dangerous', except bungee jumping.

Lost Property

Always inform the police as soon as possible if you lose any valuables. If you need to make an insurance claim for valuable items, remember you will need to obtain a copy of your statement from the police. Lost credit cards or traveller's cheques should always be reported within 24 hours to the issuing company.

Media

Television and Radio

There are four main television channels: Television One for current affairs and sport; Television Two for light entertainment; and TV3 and Channel 4 feature a variety of programmes. All channels carry commercials. Sky TV is also available (including CNN News) in hotels and motels. Also VHF channels broadcasting in many areas with various topic channels.

There are many FM radio stations; also two non-commercial stations: the AM National Programme (mainly news, documentaries, drama, and the like); and the FM Concert Programme (classical music).

Tourist FM Radio (in English on 88.2MHz) provides visitors with 24-hour information on history and culture, local activities, and attractions.

Newspapers and Magazines

There is no national newspaper as such, although the *New Zealand Herald* (published in Auckland) has the highest daily circulation, closely followed by the *Dominion* (published in Wellington). In addition, there are a handful of regional morning and evening dailies, plus two national Sunday newspapers. Tourist newspapers are also produced in resort areas.

International magazines are widely available. The best local magazine is Auckland's *Metro*, published monthly. The fortnightly *Te Maori News* is mostly written in English. One of the best current affairs magazines is the monthly *North and South.*

Money Matters

The New Zealand dollar (NZ$) is divided into 100 cents, with notes in denominations of $5, $10, $20, $50, and $100; and coins of 5, 10, 20, 50 cents, $1, and $2.

Banks are open Monday to Friday, 9.30am–4.30pm, except public holidays. Bureaux de change, which can be found in most major resorts, are open longer hours and often at weekends. Automated teller machines (ATMs) are widespread and can be used with international PIN numbers to obtain cash.

Traveller's cheques can be changed in banks, hotels, and in large stores in cities, and in tourist areas. All international credit cards (American Express, Diners Club, JCB, VISA, and MasterCard) are widely accepted.

Opening Hours

Shops are usually open Monday to Friday, 9am–5.30pm, with late-night shopping until 8.30 or 9pm one or two nights a week (usually Thursday or Friday). Some shops close at 12.30–1pm

Watch out for single-lane bridges, which are found even on the main highways

on Saturdays (4.30pm in larger centres), while others stay open all day. Many tourist shops and some travel agents are open longer hours. Many supermarkets, grocery stores, and some retail chains are also open on Sunday. Local food shops (known as dairies) are usually open seven days a week, 7am–10pm. Petrol (gas) stations are also open longer hours (many are open 24 hours), except in rural areas, and stock food and other sundries.

Pharmacies

Known by the English term 'Chemists', pharmacies are open during normal shopping hours and most cities also have urgent dispensaries that open outside these hours (listed under 'Hospitals' in the front of telephone directories). Pharmacies also stock a wide range of other products such as sunblock, cosmetics, photographic film, and so on.

Places of Worship

The major Christian denominations are Anglican, Presbyterian, Methodist, Baptist, and Roman Catholic, each with places of worship in most towns and cities. There are also synagogues and mosques in the larger cities. Your hotel reception will be able to advise on the times of services.

Police

Dial 111 for the police, fire, and ambulance.

Post

Post shops are open Monday to Friday, 9am–5.30pm, and stamps can also be bought in grocery shops, bookshops, and stationers. The two main types of postal service are standard post (which delivers the next day across town and in two to three working days nationwide), and fast post (international mail, plus next-day delivery between major towns and cities within the country). A poste restante service is available at many branches.

Public and School Holidays

Most businesses and all banks are closed on public holidays; all shops are closed on Christmas Day and Good Friday except for a few convenience stores and petrol stations.

1 & 2 January New Year
6 February Waitangi Day
March/April Good Friday and Easter Monday
25 April Anzac Day
1st Monday in June Queen's Birthday
4th Monday in October Labour Day
25 December Christmas Day
26 December Boxing Day

There are also regional holidays which

correspond to the founding days of each of the country's 12 provinces.

During school holidays you are strongly advised to book ahead for accommodation in the more popular holiday resorts.

Summer mid-December to the beginning of February
April middle two weeks
Mid-term early July
September/October late September/early October 2 weeks.

Public Transport

Coaches

The InterCity network, Newmans Coaches, Mount Cook Landlines, and Magic Bus services between them connect most towns and cities in the country. All the operators offer coach passes, either with discounts on various sectors or for periods ranging from seven to 35 days.

Several companies offer backpackers 'alternative' coach services, either within a particular region or across the whole country, which stop off at places of interest. You can hop off some of these services and rejoin the next one that comes along if you want to stay somewhere longer. One of the better known companies offering these services is Kiwi Experience, which has five different routes all over the country.

InterCity Travel Centre PO Box 26 601, Epsom. *Tel: (09) 913 6100.*
Kiwi Experience 170 Parnell Rd, Parnell. *Tel: (09) 366 9830.*
Johnston Coaches Queen St, Auckland. *Tel: toll-free 0800 800 287.*
Magic Bus Union House, 136–138 Quay St, Auckland. *Tel: (09) 358 5600.*
Newmans Coaches SkyCity Coach Terminal, 102 Hobson St, PO Box 90-821, Auckland. *Tel: (09) 913 6200.*

Ferries

The main form of transport between the North and South Islands is the Inter-Island ferry, or fast ferry, *The Lynx,* which operates between Wellington and Picton three or four times daily, with a crossing time of just over three hours. The ferry offers a roll-on, roll-off service for cars, and although passenger bookings are rarely necessary, cars should be pre-booked in peak periods (December to February and on public holidays). Make bookings through any travel agent, at the railway station, or on *toll-free tel: 0800 802 802.*

Rail

Tranzrail operates daily Auckland-Wellington services, in the North Island, and between Christchurch and Picton and the TranzAlpine to the West Coast at Greymouth. There are four different price bands for rail tickets: Standard, Economy, Saver, and Super Saver, the last three of which offer various discount levels if tickets are purchased in advance (within the country).

New Zealand Rail Private Bag, Wellington. Central reservations: *Tel: (09) 498 3003,* or *toll-free 0800 802 802* from outside New Zealand.

New Zealand Travelpass

As well as the individual travel passes that are available for air, rail, and coach travel, you can also buy a combined travel pass for trains, coaches, and ferries (a 3-in-1 Travelpass) or one which also includes an air travel sector on Air New Zealand (a 4-in-1 Travelpass). The variations of packages for the 3-in-1 and 4-in-1 Travelpasses range from 5 days travel over 10 days, to 22 days travel over 8 weeks. These passes can be bought outside New Zealand or on arrival. Contact Travelpass New Zealand, PO Box 785, Auckland (*tel: (09) 357 8400*). For InterCity Travel Centre, *see* Coaches, *p187.*

Senior Citizens

There are few limitations for senior citizens travelling in New Zealand; in fact, the Kiwis' innate sense of hospitality and general helpfulness means that they will probably find it an easier destination than many others. The main discounts are on the railways, where senior citizen fares offer a saving of around 30 per cent on standard tickets for those over 60 (proof of age required).

Student and Youth Travel

Being a young nation itself, New Zealand is well geared up to cater for the needs of student and youth travellers. A wide range of youth and student discounts on internal travel is available through the Student Travel Agency (STA), which has branches throughout the country; it also issues International Student Identity Cards. InterCity offers a range of discounts on rail, ferry, and coach travel: a YHA Travel Card (NZ$30 and NZ$3 p+p) will give up to 15 per cent discount on coach services and 20 per cent on Tranzscenic fares; and the VIP Backpacker Card (NZ$35) gives discounts on coach travel, Air New

Blue penguins nest near Oamaru

Zealand, Kiwi Experience, and car rental. Mount Cook Landlines and Newmans offer similar deals for coach travel.

STA International Travellers Centre
10 High St, Auckland.
Tel: (09) 309 0458.

Youth Hostels Association 28 Worcester St, PO Box 436. *Tel (03) 379 9808.*
The *Youth Hostels Guide* contains a list of addresses, phone numbers, and maps.

Telephones

Telecom New Zealand, still the major provider, offers both national and international services and operates two types of payphones, colour-coded:
card phone booths – green;
credit card booths – yellow.
The majority of public telephones now use phonecards, which are available from newsagents, supermarkets, petrol stations, and other retail outlets. There are also around 200 credit card

telephones around the country. You can make direct-dial inter-national calls from most telephone boxes; as elsewhere in the world, hotels and motels impose surcharges for international calls.

Travellers can obtain Telecom calling cards which charge the calls to your home telephone bill. The international dialling code for New Zealand is *64*.

Emergencies *111*
Local Operator *010*
International Operator *0170*
Local Directory Assistance *018*
Internatonal Directory Assistance *0172* (NZ$1.50 fee)
International Access Code *00*
International Dialling Codes Australia *(00) 61*; Canada *(00) 1*; Ireland *(00) 353*; UK *(00) 44*; USA *(00) 1.*

Time

Local time is GMT (Greenwich Mean Time) plus 12 hours; Australia plus 2–4 hours; Canada plus 15–20 hours; and USA plus 17–22 hours. New Zealand Summer Time runs from the beginning of October to the third Sunday in March, during which period local clock time is one hour ahead.

Tipping

It is a long-established part of the country's egalitarian culture that tips and gratuities are not expected for service anywhere. This includes restaurants and bars.

Toilets

Public conveniences are found in information and visitor centres, tourist attractions, shopping malls, hotels, bars, petrol stations, public libraries, and urban parks.

Tourist Offices

New Zealand Tourism runs a large number of Visitor Information Centres. The main ones are:
Wellington Corner of Victoria and Wakefield streets. *Tel: (04) 802 4860.*
Auckland 287 Queen Street. *Tel: (09) 979 2333.*
Christchurch Old Chief Post Office, Cathedral Square. *Tel: (03) 379 9629.*
Australia 8th floor, 35 Pitt Street, Sydney, NSW 2000. *Tel: (02) 9247 5222.*
UK New Zealand House, Haymarket, London SW1Y 4TQ. *Tel: (020) 7930 1662.*
USA 501 Santa Monica Boulevard, Suite 300, Santa Monica, Los Angeles CA90401. *Tel: (310) 395 7480; toll-free 1800 388 5494.*
780 3rd Avenue, New York, Ny 10017-2024, Suite 1904. *Tel (212) 832 8482.*

Travellers with Disabilities

In most respects New Zealand compares favourably with other countries in its provision of facilities for the disabled which are available at airports and in public places such as shopping malls and theatres (you can even do a bungee jump in a wheelchair!). Most major tourist attractions are accessible to the disabled. Booklets such as the *New Zealand Where to Stay Guide* (*see p172*) list accommodation options for wheelchair users. Contact:
The Disability Resource Centre
PO Box 24-042, Royal Oak, Auckland
Tel: (09) 625 8069; fax: (09) 624 1633; e-mail: drc@disabilityresource.org.nz

A
Abel Tasman coastal track 148
Abel Tasman National Park 92, 162
AC Baths 70, 71
accommodation 172–5
adventure sports 146–7, 150–51, 158
also see sport
aerial sightseeing 24
agricultural shows 156
Agrodome 64, 154
Air Force World 106
airports and air services 25, 178, 182
Akaroa 121
Akaroa Museum 121
Alberton 38, 39
Alexandra 128
Aranui Cave 72
Arawa 62
Arrowtown 128
Art and History Museum, Rotorua 62, 63
Arthur's Pass 125
Artist's Palette 66
Arts Centre, Christchurch 106, 154
arts and crafts 152
Atia Point 101
Astronomy Centre 88
Auckland 32–7, 154, 168
Auckland Domain 33
Auckland War Memorial Museum 33
Auckland Zoo 34
Avenue of the Disappearing Mountain 140
Avon River 107

B
ballooning 146
banks 185
Banks Peninsula 102–3, 105, 120–21
Barry's Bay 120
Bath House 62
Bay of Islands 31, 44–5
Bay of Plenty 52, 54–5
beaches 24, 40, 75
bed and breakfast 174
beer 165–6
Bethells 40
Big Kowai Viaduct 124
birdlife 12–13, 24, 78, 94, 117, 118, 119, 132–3, 136, 138, 139
Black Stilt Aviary 118–19
Blenheim 90, 92–3
Blue Baths 62, 63
boat trips 158
Botanic Gardens, Christchurch 107
Botanic Gardens, Wellington 88, 89
Bowen Falls 141
Brayshaw Historic Museum Park 93
Broadgreen House 98
Brooklands 80
Brooklyn Wind Turbine 87
Browns Bay 40
bungee-jumping 70, 146–7
business travel 176–7

C
Cable Bay 46
Cadbury World 128
camping and motorcamps 175, 179
Canterbury Museum 107
Canterbury Plains 102–3, 124, 146
Cape Foulwind 119
Cape Kidnappers 59
Cape Reinga 31, 46
Cape Road 75
Capital Discovery Place 84
car hire 25–6, 182–3
Carter Observatory 88
Cathedral Square, Christchurch 105, 107
Catlins 131
caves 72–3, 96, 101
central North Island 52–75
central South Island 102–25
Champagne Pool 66
Chateau Tongariro 72
children's entertainment 158–9
Christchurch 102, 104–9, 154–5, 170–71
Christchurch Cathedral 108
Christ Church Cathedral, Nelson 98
Christ Church, Russell 44–5
Church of the Good Shepherd 118
City Art Gallery, Auckland 34
City Art Gallery, Wellington 84
Claphams Clock Museum 49
classical music, dance and theatre 156
Cleddau Valley 141
climate 6, 180–81
clothing and sheepskin 152–3
coach services 25, 187
Collingwood 94, 95
Colonial Cottage Museum 84–5
Colville 56, 75
Conical Hill 145
conversion tables 181
Cook, Captain James 28, 46, 50, 58, 78
Cook Strait 82
Cooper, Whina 18, 19
Cooper's Beach 46
Coromandel 52, 56–7, 74–5
Coromandel Mining and Historical Museum 56
Coromandel Stamper Battery 56
Craft Habitat 98
Craters of the Moon 70, 71
crime 181
cruising 24, 178
cuisine 164–71
culture 20–21
currency 185
customs regulations 178–9
cycling 160

D
Dart River Valley 147
Deep South 126–45
Devonport 42–3
disabilities, travellers with 189
Doubtful Sound 130
Doubtless Bay 46
dress code 28
driving 25–6, 183–4
Driving Creek Railway and Potteries 56
Dunedin 126, 128–9, 170–71

E
Earland Falls 142
East Cape 58
East Head 101
eating out 164–5, 168–71
economy 7, 176
ecotourism 14–15
Edwin Fox Museum 99
electricity 181
Egmont National Park 78
Elms Mission House 54
embassies and consulates 182
emergencies 182
entertainment 156–7
environmental planning 14–15
etiquette 27, 176
events and festivals 157
Ewelme Cottage 39
explorers 50–51

F
Fairy Springs 65
Fantail Bay 75
Farewell Spit 94, 95
farmstays and homestays 174
Ferry Landing 57
ferry services 187
Ferrymead Heritage Park 108
Fiordland National Park 126, 130–31
fishing, commercial and recreational 160–61
Flagstaff Hill 45
Fletcher Bay 75
flora and fauna 10–13, 65, 78, 97, 101, 133, 159
food and drink 164–71
forests 10–11
Fox Glacier 112–13
Franz Josef Glacier 112–13
Frying Pan Lake 66
Fyffe House 96

G
gemstones 74, 102, 155
geography 6–13
geothermal energy 8–9, 70, 71
gifts and souvenirs 152–3
Gisborne 50, 58–9
Glenfalloch Gardens 133
Gold Mine and Stamper Battery 57
gold mines 56, 57, 118
Golden Bay 94–5
golf 157, 161
Goods and Services Tax (GST) 152
governance 18–19
Govett-Brewster Art Gallery 80
Great Barrier Island 40
Greymouth 102, 113–14, 125
guest houses 174
guided walks and tramps 142–3, 144–5, 149

H
Haast 114
Hamilton 59
hangi (Maori feasts) 156, 165
Hanmer Springs 114–15
Hastings 52, 59
Hauraki Gulf 40, 52
Hauraki Gulf Maritime Park 40
Havelock 95
Hawke's Bay Museum 60
health advice 28–9, 184
Hell's Gate 64
Highwic 38, 39
historic houses 38–9
Historical Museum, Thames 56
history 16–17
hitch-hiking 184
Hokianga Harbour 46
Hokitika 50, 102, 113, 115, 155
Hooker Glacier 122, 123
Homer Tunnel 141
Hooker Hut 123
Hooker Lake 123
Hooker Valley 122–3
Hoopers Inlet 138
horse-riding 161
hostels and backpacker accommodation 174–5
hot-air ballooning 105, 146
Hot Water Beach 57
hotels 172, 173
Houhora 46
hunting 162, 178
Hurworth 80

I
Inferno Crater 66
information centres 26
insurance 184–5
International Antarctic Centre 108
Invercargill 126, 131
Isel House 98
itineraries 24

J
jet-boating 147

K
Kaikoura 90, 96
Kaikoura Museum 96

Kaikoura Peninsula
Walkway 100–101
Kaitaia 46
Katherine Mansfield
Birthplace 85
Kawau Island 40–41
Kelburn Cable Car 85
Kelly Tarlton's Antarctic
Encounter and
Underwater World
34–5, 44
Kemp House 47
Kepler Track 148
Kerikeri 31, 46–7
Key Summit 144
Kiwi and Birdlife Park 134–5
Kiwi House, Napier 60
Kiwi House and Native
Bird Park, Otorohanga
60, 61
Kiwi Magic 135
Kiwifruit Country 55
kiwis 12, 136
Kiwis (New Zealanders)
21, 26
Kohimarama 40
Kupe 46, 50, 82

L
Lady Knox Geyser 66
Lake Gunn 140–41
Lake Howden 144
Lake Mackenzie 144–5
Lake Manapouri 130
Lake Matheson 113
Lake Pukaki 118
Lake Rotoiti 99
Lake Rotoroa 62, 99
Lake Taupo 9, 70–71, 168
Lake Te Anau 130, 140
Lake Tekapo 118
Lake Waikaremoana 61
Lakes District Museum 128
landscapes 6
Lange, David 18
Langlois-Eteveneaux
Cottage 121
language, Maori 69
Larnach Castle 133
lost property 185
Lower Hutt 77

M
Mangonui 46
Mansfield, Katherine 85
Mansion House, Kawau
Island 40–41
Maori 18–19, 21, 50, 68–9
Maori and Colonial
Museum 121
Maori concerts 33, 156–7
Maori culture and society
22–3, 27, 68–9, 78
Maori Leap Cave 96
Marahau 92
Marineland, Napier 60
Maritime Museum,
Gisborne 59
Marlborough, *see* Nelson
and Marlborough
Marlborough Sounds 90
Marlborough Sounds
Maritime Park 90
Martinborough 77
Masterton 76
Matakohe Kauri Museum 48
Mataraua 48
media 185
medical treatment 184
Milford Sound
14, 126, 130, 140–41
Milford track 149–50
Mineralogical Museum
56–7
Miner's Cottage 118
Mirror Lakes 140
Mission Bay,
Kohimarama 40
Moeraki 132
Mokoia Island 62
money 185
MOTAT (Museum of
Transport and
Technology) 37
motor inns and motels 173
Motor Museum 135
Motueka 98
Mount Aspiring National
Park 136
Mount Bruce National
Wildlife Centre 77, 78
Mount Cavendish
Gondola 108
Mount Cook National
Park 103, 116–17
Mount Eden 35
Mount Maunganui 54
Mount Moehau 74–5
Mount Taranaki/Egmont
78–9
Mount Victoria 42–3
Mount Victoria Lookout 86
Muldoon, Sir Robert 18
Muriwai 40
Museum and Arts Centre,
Gisborne 59
Museum of Caves 73
Museum of Shipwrecks 44
Museum of Transport
Technology and Social
History 37
Museum of Wellington City
and Sea 85
museums 24, 158–9
MV *Waipa Delta* 59

N
Napier 60
Napier Aquarium 60
National Archives 89
National Maritime Museum,
Auckland 24, 34
Needles 75
Nelson (city) 98–9
Nelson and Marlborough
90–101
Nelson Lakes National Park
91, 99
New Plymouth 76, 79–80
New Zealand Maori Arts
and Crafts Institute
67, 154
New Zealand Marine Studies
Centre and Trustbank
Aquarium 133
New Zealand,
Museum of 83, 86
Ngauruhoe 72
Ninety Mile Beach 46
North Egmont 79
North Head Historic
Reserve 43
North Island 6, 30–49, 52–89
Northland 30–49

O
Oamaru 132
Oamaru Bay 75
Octagon, Dunedin 129
Ohaki Maori Village 73
Ohakune 72
Ohinemutu Marae 62
Okains Bay 121
Old St Paul's Church 89
Olveston 129
Omapere 46
One Tree Hill 35
opening hours 185–6
Opononi 46
Orana Park Wildlife Trust
108–9
Orewa 40
Otago Settlers Museum 129
Otago Museum 129
Otago Peninsula
126, 128, 132–3, 138–9
Otari Native Botanic
Gardens 86–7
Otira 125
Otira Tunnel 125
Otorohanga 60–61

P
pa sites, Maori 35, 101
Paihia 31, 44, 168
Palmerston North 76
Panekiri Bluff 61
Papa Aroha Scenic Reserve 75
Papanui Inlet 138
Paparoa National Park 117
Paradise Valley Springs 64–5
Parliament buildings,
Wellington 87
Parnell 37, 154
passports and visas 178–9
Penguin Place Yellow-eyed
Penguin Conservation
Reserve 139
pharmacies 186
Phelp's Gold Mine 115
Picton 90, 99
Picton Museum 99
Piha 40
places of worship 186
Pohutu 67
Point Kean 101
police 186
politics 18–19
Pollard Park 93
Polynesian Spa 62, 63
Pompallier House 45
population 6–7
Port Jackson 75
postal services 186
Poverty Bay 58
Premier House 88
Prince of Wales Feathers 67
public and school
holidays 186–7
public transport 24–5, 187–8
Puke Ariki 80
Pukeiti Rhododendron
Trust 80
Pukekura Park 79–80
Punakaiki 118
Pupu Springs 94, 95
Putiki 81
Puzzling World and
Great Maze 137

Q
Quarry Craft
Co-operative 49
Queen Charlotte Walkway 90
Queenstown 105, 126, 134–5,
140, 144, 155, 171, 172

R
rail travel 25, 124–5, 187–8
Rainbow Farm 64
Rainbow Springs 65, 154
Rakaia River 103
Rangitoto Island 41
Raukumara Range 58
retreats and sporting
lodges 172–3
Rewa's Maori Village 47
Riverland Family Park 81
Rocky's Goldmine Trail 57
Ross 118
Ross Historic Goldfields 118
Rotorua 62–3, 154, 168–9
Rotorua Art and History
Museum 62, 63
Routeburn Falls 145
Routeburn Track 142–5, 149
Royal Albatross Colony 139
Royal New Zealand Navy
Museum 42, 43
Ruakuri Cave 72–3
Ruapehu 72
rugby 160
Russell 44–5
Russell Museum 45

S
St Arnaud 99
St Faith's 63
St Heliers 40
sandflies 28–9
Sarjeant Art Gallery 81
Science Alive! 109
science centres 158–9
seal colonies 101, 119
senior citizens 188
Shantytown 113–14
sheep farming 110–11
Shipwrecks, Museum of 44
shopping 152–5, 185–6
skiing 116, 162
Skyline Gondola 63, 135
South Island
6, 90–145, 170–71
Southern Alps 103

Southern Scenic Route 131
Southland 126
Southland Museum and Art Gallery 131
Southlight Wildlife Reserve 139
Speights Brewery 129
Splash Planet 59
sport 20, 160–63
Springfield 124–5
Stables Complex 60
Staircase Viaduct 124
Stewart Island 136
Stoke 98
Stone Store 47
student and youth travel 188
Subritzky Homestead 46
Sugar Loaf Marine Park 80
sunburn 28–9
Suter Art Gallery 98
Sutherland Falls 148
swimming 159

T
Taiaroa Head 133
Taipa 46
Takaka 94
Takaka Museum 94, 95
Takapuna 40
Tane Mahuta 48
Taranaki 76–81
Tarlton, Kelly 34–5, 44
Tasman, Abel 50, 78, 92
Tasman Glacier 103, 116
Taupo 70–71
Taupo Bungy 70, 72
Taupo Hot Springs 70, 71
Tauranga 54
Tauranga Historic Village/Museum 54
Te Anau 126, 130
Te Mata Beach 74
Te Papa Tongarewa (Museum of New Zealand, Wellington) 83, 86
Te Puke 55
Te Wairoa Buried Village 66
Tekapo 118
telephone numbers, emergency 182
telephones 188–9
television and radio 185
Thames 56–7
thermal pools and springs 62, 66–7, 70, 114–15
Thorndon 88–9
Tiger Moth flights 137
Tikitere Springs Spa and Resort 62
Timaru 118
timber industry 10, 48
time 189
Time Tunnel 108, 158
tipping 189
toilets 189
Tongariro National Park 52, 72
Totaranui 92
tourism 7, 14
tourist offices 189
tracks, long-distance 148–9
TranzAlpine Express 105, 124–5
travel insurance 185–6
travel passes 187–8
travelling to New Zealand 178–9
Treaty of Waitangi 16, 17, 18–19, 32, 44
TSS *Earnslaw* 135
Tupare Gardens 80
Turangi 72
Twizel 118–19

U
Upper Hutt 77
Urewera National Park 61

V
Victoria Park Market 37, 154
Virginia Lake Scenic Reserve 81
volcanic activity 8–9, 24, 32, 52, 62, 66, 67, 72, 108

W
Wagener Museum 46
Waiheke Island 41
Waikato Museum of Art and History 59
Waima 48
Waimakariri River 103
Waimangu Volcanic Valley 66
Wainui Bay 92
Waiotapu Thermal Wonderland 66–7
Waipoua Kauri Forest 48–9
Wairakei Geothermal Power Station 70
Wairakei Prawn Farm 70, 71
Wairakei Steamfield 70, 71
Wairakei Thermal Valley 70, 71
Waitangi National Reserve 44
Waitangi Treaty House 44
Waitomo Caves 72–3
walking 144–5, 148–9
Walter Peak Farm 135
Wanaka 136–7
Wanganui 76, 80–81
Wanganui Regional Museum 81
Wanganui River 76
watersports 162–3
Wellington 76–7, 82–9, 155, 169
Wellington Zoo 87
West Arm Underground Powerhouse 130
West Coast Historical Museum 115
Westland National Park 112
Westport 119
Whakapapa Village 72
Whakarewarewa Thermal Village 67
Whakatane 55
Whakatane District Museum and Gallery 55
whale and dolphin watching 97
Whalers Bay 100
Whalers Cave 101
whaling 96, 97, 100
Whangarei 49
Whangarei Falls 49
Whatipu 40
White Island 55
white-water rafting 150–51
Whitianga 57
wildlife 159
Also see flora and fauna
Willowbank Wildlife Reserve 109
wines and winemaking 7, 166
wine trails 134, 166
woodcarving 22, 67
World Heritage Visitor Centre 114
World of Wearable Art and Collectable Car Complex 98–9

Y
yachting 163

ACKNOWLEDGEMENTS

Thomas Cook Publishing wishes to thank the following photographers, libraries and associations for their assistance in the preparation of this book.

ALEXANDER TURNBULL LIBRARY 18, 50
THE THOMAS COOK ARCHIVE 4
NEW ZEALAND PHOTOS 12, 20, 21, 32, 73, 76a, 79, 86, 90, 95, 101, 102, 116, 117, 123, 125, 129, 145, 146, 147, 149, 153a, 153b, 160a, 160b, 165, 167, 171, 177.

The remaining pictures (including spine and back cover) are held in the AA PHOTO LIBRARY and were taken by PAUL KENWARD.

FOR LABURNUM TECHNOLOGIES

Design Director Alpana Khare
Series Director Razia Grover
Editors Madhumadhavi Singh, Rajiv Jayaram
Designer Neeraj Aggarwal
Photo Editor Manju Singhal
DTP Designer Harish Aggarwal
CD Editor Arfin Zukof
CD Designer Sudhir Horo

Updating and additional research on this edition was done by Fran Robinson.
Thanks to Marie Lorimer for the Index.

Travellers

Feedback Form

Please help us improve future editions by taking part in our reader survey. Every returned form will be acknowledged. To show our appreciation we will send you a voucher entitling you to £1 off your next *Travellers* guide or any other Thomas Cook guidebook ordered direct from Thomas Cook Publishing. Just take a few minutes to complete and return this form to us.

We'd also be glad to hear of your comments, updates or recommendations on places we cover or you think that we ought to cover.

1. Which *Travellers* guide did you purchase?

____

2. Have you purchased other *Travellers* guides in the series?

   Yes ☐

   No ☐

   If Yes, please specify____________________

3. Which of the following tempted you into buying your *Travellers* guide: (Please tick as many as appropriate)

   The price ☐

   The FREE weblinks CD ☐

   The cover ☐

   The content ☐

   Other____________________

4. What do you think of :

   a) the cover design?____________________

   b) the design and layout styles within the book?____________________

   c) the FREE weblinks CD?____________________

5. Please tell us about any features that in your opinion could be changed, improved or added in future editions of the book or CD:

____

____

Your age category: ☐ under 21 ☐ 21-30 ☐ 31-40 ☐ 41-50 ☐ 51+

Mr/Mrs/Miss/Ms/Other

Surname____________________ Initials____________________

Full address: (Please include postal or zip code)____________________

____

Daytime telephone number:____________________

Email address:____________________

☐ Please tick here if you would be willing to participate in further customer surveys.

☐ Please tick here if you would like to receive information on new titles or special offers from Thomas Cook Publishing (please note we never give your details to third party companies).

Please detach this page and send it to: **The Editor, Travellers, Thomas Cook Publishing, PO Box 227, The Thomas Cook Business Park, Peterborough PE3 8XX, United Kingdom.**

tear along the perforation

The Editor, Travellers
Thomas Cook Publishing
PO Box 227
The Thomas Cook Business Park
Peterborough, PE3 8XX
United Kingdom

Thomas Cook
Publishing